LEARNING RESOURCES CTR/NEW ENGLAND TECH.
GEN   BT981.R867 1988
Russell, Jef   The Prince of Darkness :

3 0147 0001 3805 0

BT981 .R867

P9-ARM-846

Russell, Jeffrey Burton.

The prince of darkness

The Prince
of Darkness

OTHER BOOKS BY JEFFREY BURTON RUSSELL

Dissent and Reform in the Early Middle Ages (1965)
Medieval Civilization (1968)
A History of Medieval Christianity: Prophecy and Order (1968)
Religious Dissent in the Middle Ages (1971)
Witchcraft in the Middle Ages (1972)
The Devil: Perceptions of Evil from Antiquity to Primitive Christianity (1977)
A History of Witchcraft: Sorcerers, Heretics, Pagans (1980)
Medieval Heresies: A Bibliography (with C. T. Berkhout) (1981)
Satan: The Early Christian Tradition (1981)
Lucifer: The Devil in the Middle Ages (1984)
Mephistopheles: The Devil in the Modern World (1986)

The Prince of Darkness

*Radical Evil and the Power
of Good in History*

Jeffrey Burton Russell

Cornell University Press

Ithaca, New York

Copyright © 1988 by Cornell University

All rights reserved. Except for brief quotations in a review, this
book, or parts thereof, must not be reproduced in any form without
permission in writing from the publisher. For information, address
Cornell University Press, 124 Roberts Place, Ithaca, New York 14850.

First published 1988 by Cornell University Press.

Library of Congress Cataloging-in-Publication Data
Russell, Jeffrey Burton.
    The Prince of Darkness.

    Includes index.
        1. Devil—History of doctrines.   2. Good and evil—
History of doctrines.   I. Title.
BT981.R867   1988   235'.47   88-47744
ISBN 0-8014-2014-8 (alk. paper)

Printed in the United States of America

*The paper in this book is acid-free and meets the guidelines for
permanence and durability of the Committee on Production Guidelines
for Book Longevity of the Council on Library Resources.*

To Alberto, Cameron, Cheryl, Karen, Marylou, Miriam,
Pam, Rick, Tim, and the Good Old Days.

Contents

Illustrations

Preface

The attempt to comprehend the problem of evil has occupied me for twenty years. Through my four earlier volumes on the Devil I have tried to gain understanding of that problem by examining the history of evil's most powerful symbol.

This book, *The Prince of Darkness*, presents the main outlines of that history in a single volume. My intention here has been to write the story of the Devil in the Western world, from its beginnings down to our own times, for readers whose interest is immediate rather than academic. I have drawn on much of the material on which the four earlier books are based, but I have avoided their density of detail and their extensive footnotes in order to bring the most important questions into sharper focus and to make clearer the deep issues that underlie the story.

My quest for an understanding of evil has been personal search as well as scholarly research, and I invite the reader to join me on this difficult but rewarding journey. As I have grown in the course of the search, my view of the question continues to deepen. This book corrects some errors found in the four volumes and recasts some of their arguments in more mature form. Above all I have tried throughout to open myself and others to the understanding that knowledge without love, and scholarship without personal involvement and commitment, are dead. This book is for those who love to know and know how to love.

Readers who wish to follow up quotations, locate source materials, or be guided in further reading on particular topics can find that information by consulting the indexes and bibliographical sections of my earlier series on the Devil. The chapters in this book correspond to those volumes largely as follows: Chapters 2–4: *The Devil: Personifications of Evil from Antiquity to Primitive Christianity*; Chapters 5–7: *Satan: The Early Christian Tradition*; Chapters 8–10: *Lucifer: The Devil in the Middle Ages*; and Chapters 11–16: *Mephistopheles: The Devil in the Modern World*. All four were published by Cornell University Press. Readers may also wish to consult an excellent recent book by Neil Forsyth, *The Old Enemy: Satan and the Combat Myth* (Princeton: Princeton University Press, 1987).

Translations are my own except for those from the Hebrew and the Russian. For passages from the Hebrew Bible I have for the most part used the New International Version. In quoting from the two novels by Dostoevsky in Chapter 15, I have used the published translations of Constance Garnett.

My deep thanks are due again to all those who helped me with the first four volumes and also to J. Gordon Melton and Dennis Rohatyn.

JEFFREY BURTON RUSSELL

Santa Barbara, California

The Prince
of Darkness

I *Evil*

Evɪʟ is directly experienced and directly intuited. A young woman is beaten; an old man is mugged; a child is raped; a terrorist rips a plane apart in midair; a great nation bombs a civilian population. Those whose minds are not bent by personal or societal madness immediately respond to such actions with justifiable anger. You do not make abstract calculations in ethical philosophy when you see a baby being beaten. At the most fundamental level, evil is not abstract. It is real and tangible.

This direct perception of evil is the most important thing. But standing back to reflect on the general nature of evil is also valuable. What is evil? What do evil actions have in common? Philosophers have traditionally identified three kinds of evil. The first is *moral*, evil that occurs when an intelligent being knowingly and deliberately inflicts suffering upon another sentient being. This category excludes the surgeon's inflicting necessary pain on a patient. The issue is not physical pain, but suffering, which involves a conscious knowledge, anticipation, and dread of pain without an understanding of any good reason why one should be hurt. The second kind of evil is the *natural*, the suffering resulting from processes of nature such as cancers and tornadoes. Some argue abstractly that natural processes should not really be called evil, but this is an evasion, for we perceive them directly as such. Further, natural and moral evils overlap. A child may starve in a famine resulting from a drought, but if I could have saved him or her had I been more open with my bank account, is the evil natural or moral? Further, if any intelligent Being is responsible for the cosmos, then the suffering that occurs in the cosmos is that Being's responsibility, and again moral and natural ills converge. The third kind of evil is the *metaphysical*, an abstract concept that will not much occupy us in this book. Metaphysical evil is the necessary lack of perfection that exists in any created cosmos, since no cosmos can be perfect as God is perfect.

Evil also comes in different orders of magnitude. Some evil is personal, as when an individual murders a child. Some evil is transpersonal, as when a mob lynches a victim or a government bombs a city. There seem to be no limits to transpersonal evil, for we are now risking the entire human race and most of the life of this planet with our nuclear arsenals. Transgeneric evil may also exist. If intelligent and morally flawed beings exist on other planets, then evil extends beyond humanity. Finally, evil may also extend beyond the transgeneric to the cosmic. The human willingness to menace the entire planet with destruction in order to oppose whatever nation or group is currently defined as the enemy may reflect the will of the Devil himself, the Prince of Darkness who consciously chooses to destroy and ruin the cosmos to the extent he is able. Inflicting suffering for the sake of suffering, doing evil for evil's sake, the Devil is by definition the personification of cosmic evil.

Few educated people today take the concept of the Devil seriously. Some relativistically deny the existence of evil altogether. Others admit the existence of evil actions but not of evil individuals. Still others admit that persons can be evil but limit evil to human beings. Historians and anthropologists know, however, that the unexamined assumptions of a society tell us more about the society than they do about the truth of the assumptions.

Often people assume that in the modern world the idea of the Devil is old-fashioned and therefore false—an objection that assumes that "the modern world" (however defined) has discovered some metaphysical truth (however defined) that makes the existence of the Devil less likely now than it used to be. In fact, the Devil's existence is no less likely now than it ever was. Society's assumptions, styles, and prejudices have changed—and will change again—but the underlying problem of evil remains the same. Therefore the real question is whether the concept of the Devil makes any sense. Did it ever? Does it now? Will it in future?

Three general modes of thought exist in Western society at the end of the twentieth century. One is the traditional Judeo-Christian world view, which has been weakening steadily for the past two centuries but is now gaining renewed strength in some parts of the world. The second is the traditional scientific, materialist world view, increasingly dominant since the eighteenth century. This view is now undermined by twentieth-century physics, which suggests that "matter" is an intellectual

M. C. Escher, *The Scapegoat*, 1921. The Devil appears as the shadow side of God, the dark side of the divine nature. © M. C. Escher Heirs c/o Cordon Art—Baarn, Holland.

construct rather than ultimate reality. The third is New Age thought; hostile to both traditional views, it is characterized by a wide diversity of angles of vision and by a desire to explore reality beyond conventional lines. The constructive clash among these divergent views has produced signs that a new synthesis may be in gestation.

Where does the Devil fit in? Is the Evil One an outmoded superstition? The only universally valid definition of "superstition" is "a belief that is not coherent with one's overall world view." The idea of the Devil is indeed a superstition within the scientific world view, but it is not a superstition in the Christian and Muslim world views, because the concept is coherent within those views. New Age thinkers tend to be interested in the idea of the Devil but to reinterpret it from an inexhaustible variety of new points of view, which lack overall coherence.

Whether or not the Devil exists outside the human mind, the concept of the Devil has a long history and the most fruitful approach to it is historical.

The historical approach observes the origins of the concept, sketches its early lines, and shows its gradual development through the ages down to the present. The concept of the Devil is found in only a few religious traditions. There was no idea of a single personification of evil in ancient Greco-Roman religions, for example, and there was and is none in Hinduism or Buddhism. Most religions—from Buddhism to Marxism—have their demons, but only four major religions have had a real Devil. These are Mazdaism (Zoroastrianism), ancient Hebrew religion (but not modern Judaism), Christianity, and Islam. Through these four religions, the tradition of the Devil can be historically traced and defined.

By "tradition" I do not mean something that has been handed down unchanged. The idea that religious ideas have been passed down unaltered over the centuries from Moses, Jesus, or Muhammad is an illusion. Religious tradition is best understood as a continuity, but one that is dynamic, living, developing, and evolving. In Christianity, tradition is rooted in, and continuous with, the earliest Christian community and the person of Jesus. But the teachings of the Christian community (whether Catholic, Orthodox, or Protestant) today are not identical with those of the first century. They have developed substantially over the intervening centuries. Tradition connects modern Christianity with primitive Christianity, but the connection is dynamic, not static.

In this way, the Devil is defined by the historical tradition. Efforts to say that the Devil "really" is something different from the historical tradition are self-contradictory. Some modern Satanists, for example, enjoyed saying that the Devil is "really" a "good" being. But the very definition of the Devil is that he is evil. To call the Devil "good" is like calling a buzzing insect a horse. One is legally free, of course, to use words in whatever way one chooses, but if one wants to be understood one uses words in their normal sense. You would make a fool of yourself by trying to saddle up a horsefly. Phrases such as "the Devil is," "the Devil was," "the Devil became" appear in this book as shorthand for "the concept of the Devil is, was, or became." No one can say what the Devil is or is not in absolute reality, because we have no propositional access to realities beyond the human mind.

Historical theory provides a certain basis for limited human knowledge, but, like science, it has no room for statements about metaphysical reality. In fact, many historical theorists argued that humanity progresses by moving from the superstitious to the rational. In this view, old ideas such as the Devil and God are less likely to be true than new ones, and "old fashioned" replaces "untrue" as the criterion for rejection. This view makes sense neither to those believing in a rationally planned cosmos nor to those who believe that the cosmos is planless. In fact the progressive view is fundamentally incoherent, for it argues that there is no goal yet we are moving toward it. Only if one adopts this impossible, though enormously popular, view can one manage to dismiss ideas on the grounds that they are "outmoded." Notwithstanding, vague ideas of progress linked with vague ideas of relativism, despite the fact that the two are logically incompatible, to undermine the idea that theology was one road to truth.

A note on some words and names. No connection whatever exists between the word "Devil" and the word "evil," nor is there any between "Devil" and the Indo-European root *dev* found in the Indo-European *devas* and the English "divine." The English "Devil," like the German *Teufel* and the Spanish *diablo*, derives from the Greek *diabolos*. *Diabolos* means "slanderer" or a "perjuror" or an "adversary" in court. It was first applied to the Evil One in the translation of the Old Testament into Greek in the third and second centuries B.C.E. to render the Hebrew *satan*, "adversary," "obstacle," or "opponent." The Prince of Darkness has had many names, and I use the most common ones—Satan, Lucifer, and Mephistopheles—as synonyms for the Devil.

The basic reason for examining the Devil in the Judeo-Christian-Muslim traditions is that these traditions essentially created the concept. (I regret that this book is too short to provide an examination of the rich Islamic tradition. Readers interested in the Muslim Devil will find him discussed in my *Lucifer.*) There is also a second important reason for taking this approach. With their emphasis upon monotheism, these traditions had to cope with the responsibility of God for evil. How is the existence of evil reconcilable with that of a good and omnipotent God? The question has been answered along two radically different lines. One response is that God is fully responsible for the cosmos just as it is, and we live in a determined, "predestined" world. The alternative answer is that some restrictions or limitations exist on God's absolute power. A variety of such restrictions have been proposed by philosophers over the centuries: chaos, matter, free will, quantum randomness, and a principle of evil. This tension between determinism and freedom has always been a source of enormous intellectual and spiritual creativity and power. The tension setting the power of God against the existence of evil is the ultimate source of the concept of the Devil.

Discussing evil means using propositions: where it comes from, how it acts, what limits it, and so on. Discussions of evil are necessarily conceptual. But one must also keep the eye fixed upon the underlying reality of evil, which is the real experience of real suffering.

2　*The Devil around the World*

ALTHOUGH the concept of the Devil—a single personification of evil— does not exist in most religions and philosophies, the problem of evil exists in every world view except that of radical relativism. If the cosmos has any intrinsic meaning, if a moral intelligence of any kind exists, some effort needs to be made to reconcile that intelligence with the existence of evil. Most societies, observing both good and evil in the cosmos, perceive that moral intelligence as ambivalent. Their God has two faces, good and evil: he is a coincidence of opposites.

This ambivalence is expressed differently in different societies. Most polytheist views assume that the many gods are the manifestations of the one God, the one ambivalent principle. Hinduism offers a clear example of the ambiguity of the God. Brahma "creates the harmful and the helpful; the gentle and the cruel; truth and falsehood; life and death." This God manifests himself in a variety of forms. According to the *Brahmanas*, "the gods and demons both spoke truth, and they both spoke untruth. The gods relinquished untruth, and the demons relinquished truth." These demons can now be blamed for at least some of the evil in the world. But since all beings are aspects of the God, evil and good both ultimately stem from him and are integral parts of him.

Why does the God do evil, or cause it to be done, or permit it to be done? Theodicy is the attempt to understand the relationship of the God to a cosmos that suffers. Some theodicies are theological, rational, philo- sophical efforts to get at an answer; others are mythological, attempts to explain by telling stories.

Mythological theodicies often personify the malevolent aspects of the God and construct gods, demons, or other beings somewhat analogous to the Devil, but on the whole myth tends not to create wholly evil beings. Myth is close to the unconscious, and the unconscious is ambivalent. What comes from the unconscious is basically perception of self, and we sense ambivalence in ourselves. It is usually the conscious that rationalizes and distorts, splitting the natural ambivalence of good and evil into polarities, opposite absolutes. Religions such as Christianity and Islam that emphasize the rational over the mythological are thus more hospitable to the idea of the Devil. Still, myth is not an unformed outpouring of the unconscious; like poetry, art, or music, it arises from a creative tension between unconscious materials and conscious forms. Myth, like theology, often tries to separate the good from the evil in the God.

Good and evil alike come from the God. Because people feel a tension between good and evil in themselves, they feel a comparable tension within the God. Good and evil must be struggling within him. People also wish to feel that the God is good and benevolent, so they dislike attributing evil to him. For these reasons they tend to assume an opposition of forces within the godhead. Often they externalize this opposition, twinning the God into separate good and evil entities. In such divisions, the good side of the God is often identified with the "High God" and the bad side with the adversary of the High God. An additional tension arises: the tension between the unity and the diversity in the God. Since most religions have avoided assuming a plurality of ultimate principles, most have one ultimate God, and that one God remains a coincidence of opposites.

The coincidence of opposites is sometimes expressed as a war in heaven between good and evil gods. Historically, when a culture replaces one set of gods with another, it tends to relegate the losing set to the status of evil spirits. The Christians made demons out of the Olympian deities of Greece and Rome, just as the Olympian religion had earlier transformed the earthbound Titans into evil spirits. Early Indo-Iranian religion had two sets of gods, the asuras (ahuras) and the devas (daevas). In Iran, the ahuras defeated the daevas, and the leader of the ahuras became the High God Ahura Mazda, the god of light, while the defeated daevas were demoted to evil spirits under the rule of the lord of darkness. In India, the devas defeated the asuras. In one sense, the result in India was opposite to that in Iran, but in a deeper sense the process was the same, in that one group of deities was vanquished by another and relegated to the status of evil spirits.

Polytheists sometimes express the divine coincidence of opposites in individual deities who are ambivalent, with "two souls within their

Quetzalcoatl, 900–1250 C.E., limestone. The benevolent god of life and art is also god of death. The opposite sides of this freestanding sculpture show the two aspects of divinity. Courtesy the Brooklyn Museum, Henry L. Batterman and Frank Sherman Benson funds.

breasts." The great gods of India, including Kali, Shiva, and Durga, manifest opposite poles in a single being: benevolence and malevolence, creativity and destructiveness. Polytheists may also express the two faces of God in myths about closely related but adversary pairs of deities. The gods in each pair are seen as opposites, but always on a deeper level they are the same being. Among the Iroquois the earth's daughter bears twin sons, who quarrel within her womb. One twin is born in the normal way, but the second twin is born through his mother's armpit, killing her. The younger son, called Flint, strives unceasingly to undo the work of his constructive brother. The older son creates animals; Flint tries to imitate him, fails, and in his rage throws up rugged cliffs and mountains to divide tribe from tribe and so frustrate the unity his brother has planned for humanity. Like the yin and yang of Taoism, such twins or doublets are both opposite and united; beneath their conflict they seek integration and centering.

The evil aspects of the God are often associated with the underworld, but the underworld is itself ambivalent. It is good, for it is from beneath the earth that the crops spring forth and from the underground that rich metals can be mined. But it is also evil, for the dead are buried in the earth, and beneath the earth is a dark land where they wander in shadows. The gods of the underworld, such as the Greco-Roman Plouton or Pluto, are lords of both fertility and death. The Devil's association with hell comes from his identification with the malevolent aspects of the subterranean lord. The red glow of hellfire, together with the red tint of land scorched by fire and with the color of blood, led to the association of the Devil with the color red.

Blackness and darkness are almost always associated with evil, in opposition to the whiteness and light associated with good. This is true even in black Africa. Blackness has an immense range of negative and fearful associations: death, the underworld, the void, blindness, night stalked by robbers and ghosts. Psychologically it signifies the fearful, uncontrollable depths of the unconscious. It is also associated with depression, stupidity, sin, despair, dirt, poison, and plague.

The void, nothingness, chaos, is another symbol that myth links with the Devil. Chaos, yawning emptiness, is the formless, undifferentiated state that exists at or before the beginning of the world. "At first," says the Rig Veda, "there was only darkness wrapped in darkness." And Genesis 1.2 says, "The earth was without form, and void; and darkness moved over the face of the abyss." In one sense chaos is good, for it is the creative potency without which nothing could come into being. But in another sense it is evil, for it must be overcome, formed, and shaped if gods or humans are to exist. Chaos often appears in myth as a monster, such as the Hebrew Leviathan or the Babylonian Tiamat, who must be defeated by god or hero. The Mesoamericans said that primeval chaos was a thing with countless mouths swimming in the formless waters and devouring all that she could seize. She was vanquished by the gods Quetzalcoatl and Tezcatlipoca, who rent her body asunder to allow the universe to be formed. Chaos is a prerequisite for cosmos, but cosmos can be formed only by defeating chaos. At the end of time, cosmos may revert to chaos. This has the double effect of destroying the world but also returning to primeval creative power. The Tandava dance of Shiva expresses both joy and sorrow. It annihilates the illusory world (*maya*), but in so doing it integrates the world with Brahma. Many rites were aimed at the re-creation of chaos in order to regain and release creative force. Often connected with fertility, such rites sometimes became unbridled, uncontrolled license and could readily be perceived as threatening and destructive. Thus the Devil came to be linked with orgy, a symbol of the terrifying formlessness of chaos.

Chaos is often represented as a snake, serpent, or dragon. The Dayak of Borneo believed that the world is enclosed in a circle formed by the watersnake biting its tail. The primeval serpent pursuing itself in endless circles is another symbol of the coincidence of opposites, the union of beginning and end. Serpents help and heal; the symbol of the medical profession is the serpent of Aesculapius. Deities wearing snakes as their emblems often bear them in the shape of the crescent moon, symbol of growth and fertility. But through the moon the snake is also associated with night, death, and menstrual blood. Through the serpent the Devil is associated with these terrors and with the dragon of chaos that must be slain so that life and order may be released.

The crescent moon also suggests horns. Horns derived additional symbolic power from their connection with the phallus and with the procreative power of bull animals. Shiva may take the form of both bull and phallus; Vishnu and Krishna are also portrayed as bulls. Horns are also identified with the rays of the sun: horns or rays emanated from the brow of Moses coming down from his encounter with God. Hats in the shape of horns, such as medieval crowns or bishops' mitres, indicated the power of the wearer. The sign of horns (such as the upturned horseshoe) brings good luck, fertility, and power.

The Devil's horns therefore symbolize his princely power, but they also carry a powerful negative connotation. Horns bring to mind the danger of wild beasts and the bull that gores; they suggest the mysterious, frightening otherness of animals; and their association with the moon recalls not only fertility but also night, darkness, and death.

Legions of lesser spirits around the world manifest the terrors of nature. Wild and disruptive, they exhibit the strange, numinous quality that provokes the undirected terror that the Greeks named "panic" after the god Pan. They possess body or mind, causing disease or insanity. They appear as male incubi or female succubi, seducing sleepers. Their ugliness and deformity are outward and visible signs of their distorted natures. They may act as moral tempters, but more frequently they attack individuals directly and crudely. In traditional Japan, where the natural and supernatural worlds were closely intertwined, not only humans, but animals, plants, and even inanimate objects had ghosts. These ghosts were usually hostile, particularly the *oni*, whose horns and three hideous eyes signified both power and malevolence.

Demons both East and West frequently serve as executioners of the God's justice by tormenting the damned souls in hell. In Japan, twenty-four thousand demon servants worked unceasingly to drag the unfortunate souls before the divine tribunal of Emma-O. Grotesque and horrifying in appearance, the demons also use hideous tools of torture. In China and Japan as well as in the West, it is not always clear whether the demons are employees or inmates of hell—whether they suffer as well as meting out pain to others.

The evil spirit of temptation appears in some cultures. The nearest thing to the Devil in Buddhism is Mara, whose name means "death" or "thirst," and whose attributes are blindness, murkiness, death, and darkness. With his daughters Desire, Unrest, and Pleasure, he attempts to obstruct the lord Gautama's progress toward enlightenment, but the Buddha, knowing that the only true good lies in transcending the world, drives him away. The Mesoamericans believed that the man-god Quetzalcoatl was tempted by many demons who offered him wine and other enticements to lure him from the path of duty.

The similarities among the worldwide representations of evil are remarkable. Since many of these societies are not connected historically, the similarities suggest a common, inherent psychological response to common perceptions of evil. Certain civilizations, however, stood directly in the historical background of the Judeo-Christian concept of the Devil. Here the cultural connections are clear and pronounced. The most important of these civilizations were the cultures of Egypt, Mesopotamia, Canaan, and Greece.

The many gods of the Egyptians were manifestations of the one God. The God and the gods are ambivalent: they both help and hinder humanity. Since the God never changes, the cosmos never changes. The Egyptian cosmos is a stable coincidence of opposites, a manifestation of divine order and harmony. The universe is not a thing; it is alive; it pulses with godness. It is not merely the creation of the God; it is the God's outward and visible manifestation. In such a divine cosmos absolute evil cannot exist. Individual evil exists, but it is limited; it is an isolated act for which the individual is accountable and for which he will be punished in the afterlife. It produces a limited perturbation of *ma'at*, the ordered, harmonious justice of the cosmos, but *ma'at* quickly adjusts itself through the inevitable punishment of the wicked, and the serenity of the divine cosmos continues.

All Egyptian deities are manifestations of the whole cosmos and so reflect both the constructive and the destructive aspects of cosmic harmony. Even the merciful god Osiris is sometimes an adversary of the noble sun god Re, whereas a frequently destructive deity such as Seth is gracious to his own worshipers. The pharaoh, who is the human incarnation of the God on earth, shares the divine ambivalence: "that beneficent god, the fear of whom is throughout the countries like the fear of Sekhmet in a year of plague. . . . He fights without end, he spares not. . . . He is a master of graciousness, rich in sweetness, and he conquers by love."

No Egyptian deity ever became the principle of evil, but one god, Seth, displays the destructive element more than the others. From an early time in the development of Egyptian religion, Seth was an enemy of the sky god Horus. Horus was a god of northern Egypt, the low country where the Nile spread out in black, fertile, tillable plains. Seth was a god of the dry, arid south, where the red deserts stretched lifeless to the rocky, burning mountains on the horizon. Because of Seth's association with the desert, he was usually portrayed as a reddish animal of unknown identity, and redhaired people were considered in some special way his own. As Egyptian religion developed, Seth came to be identified more and more with the power of death and locked in endless struggle with Horus or Osiris, gods of goodness and life.

Still, the Egyptians did not lose the sense that the gods represented one divine principle. The deadly enemies Seth and Horus were also perceived as brothers, twins, doublets, sometimes even as one god with two heads. The conflict between them was a violation of *ma'at* and had to be resolved. The Egyptians were torn between two solutions. In one, they

The Horus-Seth god, Egypt. Horus and Seth are a doublet, representing two sides of the divine principle. The followers of the two gods were often antagonistic, but in some places Seth, who looks here toward our left, was worshiped together with Horus as one god.

united Seth and Horus as one god, but this answer left the persistence of dissension in the cosmos unexplained. So they also considered another solution, one in which Seth seeks to restore the cosmic unity, but in all the wrong ways. Here Seth's role approaches that of Satan.

Seth seeks to resolve the conflict by destroying his adversary, whether Horus or Osiris. He tricks Osiris into getting into a large chest, locks it up, and sinks it into the Nile. Isis bears her dead husband a son, Horus the Younger, who takes his father's place as Seth's adversary. Seth tries unsuccessfully to murder the baby Horus, and when Horus grows up Seth marshals a huge army to crush his ancient enemy. Always thinking wrong, Seth tries to restore the divine union by an act of grotesque force: he attempts to sodomize the divine Horus. Horus, resisting, castrates Seth and so deprives him of his power, but Seth in turn tears out one of Horus' eyes and buries it. The struggle between desert and fertility, death and life, south and north, the underworld and the earth, had begun to prefigure the Judeo-Christian struggle of good against evil. From the Egyptian point of view, the cosmos could not be resolved by bloody conflicts but only by peaceful centering and integration. True to the actual state of the world, the myth relates no such reconciliation.

The civilizations that arose in Mesopotamia, where both human conflicts and natural disasters were far more frequent than in Egypt, saw the cosmos as far more fundamentally unsettled. The Egyptians had to explain a world in which evil intruded into divine harmony, the Sumerians and Babylonians one in which harmony was barely visible at all. The world had been fundamentally alienated from the divine plan, and the inscrutable gods might help, abandon, or simply ignore a nation, a city, or an individual. A Babylonian poem similar to the Book of Job presents a dialogue between a just man who is suffering and his friend. The sufferer inquires why those who worship the gods suffer and those who ignore them prosper. His friend entreats him to submit to his lot with good grace, but the sufferer complains that nowhere do the gods seem to block evil men or evil spirits. "How have I profited," he inquires, "that I have bowed down to my God?" He receives no satisfactory reply. The cosmos of the Mesopotamians was sorely out of joint, and they were deeply troubled that neither they nor the gods could set it right.

In consequence, the Mesopotamian world was filled with hostile demons. These were generally spirits of lesser dignity and power than gods. The terrible *annunaki* were the jailers of the dead in hell. The *etimmu* were the ghosts of the many who had died unhappy. The *utukku* lived in desert places or graveyards. There were demons of plagues, nightmares, windstorms, drought, warfare, and every human ill. One of the most frightful was Pazuzu, god of the howling north winds that leached the soil of moisture and withered the crops. Another was Lilitu, the ancestral prototype of the Lilith of Isaiah 34. Lilitu was a frigid, barren "maid of desolation," part human and part bird of prey, who roamed the night draining men of their bodily fluids. Such demons were everywhere, and people had to protect themselves by enlisting the aid of a more powerful spirit. "The man who has no god as he walks in the street, the demon covers him as a garment."

Canaanite or Phoenician religion influenced Hebrew thought even more directly. The high God of Canaan was El, the god of sky and sun, often portrayed as a bull. His son was Baal, whose name means "the lord." Baal was god of vegetation and fertility; his symbols were the bull and the crescent horns. The central Canaanite myth was the conflict of Baal, aided by his sister Anath, against the god Mot, prince of sterility and death.

The lord Baal goes out to do battle with Mot, but after a long struggle the prince of death defeats him, and the lord is forced to humiliate himself before his fierce foe, promising to be his slave. Mot kills him, sending him to the underworld. Baal is gone from the face of the earth for seven years, during which the crops wither and the world is barren. Death would have ruled forever, but Baal's sister Anath, the terrible maiden goddess of love and war, wanders the world, seeks out Mot, and, "Death, thou shalt die." She seizes Mot, and "with sword she cleaves him. With fan she winnows him—with fire she burns him. With hand-mill she grinds him—in the field she sows him." In one and the same deed, Anath kills Mot and refertilizes the earth, and indeed Death's death revives her brother Baal, who returns triumphant from the under-world while the earth bursts into bloom. Mot too revives, however, and Baal and Mot are locked in eternal combat. This eternal warfare is the struggle of a doublet—Baal and Mot, life and death—both the God, both representing the cosmos, a universe in which good and evil are forever entwined.

The apparently contradictory ethical qualities of the Greek gods, which the Christians so disdained, derived in part from the fact that each god of the classical period is a synthesis of diverse elements from ancient local cults. More important, the ambiguities display the coincidence of opposites. Both good and evil proceed from the God, of whom the individual gods are manifestations. Ethical ambivalence was expressed either within the personality of a single deity or in twin or doublet deities.

A few Greco-Roman deities had direct influence on the Devil. The Christians associated all the pagan deities with demons, but Pan more than others. Pan was feared for his association with the wilderness, the favorite haunt of hostile spirits, and for his sexuality. Sexual passion, which suspends reason, was suspect to both Greek rationalism and Christian asceticism; a god of sexuality could easily be identified as evil, especially since sexuality was linked through fertility to the underworld and to death. Pan, hairy and goatlike, with horns and cloven hooves, was the son of Hermes. A phallic deity like his father, he represented sexual desire in both its creative and its threatening aspects. Pan's horns, hooves, shaggy fur, and outsized phallus became part of the Christian image of Satan.

The curious, deep association between fertility and death marked Hades, the ruler of the underworld, who presided over the dark and dreadful kingdom of dead souls and who brought death to crops, animals, and humans. Hades' other name was Pluto, god of wealth, for the underworld yields the tender crops and offers hope of renewed life. The ambivalence of Hades was reflected in that of his spouse, the gentle Persephone, lady of springtime, whose cruel husband ravished her from the face of the earth every autumn. Emerging from her underground prison every year, Persephone caused the earth to green. But it was also she who led the Erinyes, the spirits of vengeance, in their pitiless search for revenge.

Charun, the Etruscan god of death, made his own contribution to the shape of the Evil One. Charun derived his name from the Greek Charon, boatman of the dead, but the Etruscan god was far more horrible than the grizzled old ferryman. Charun had a huge, hooked nose similar to a bird's beak, a shaggy beard and hair, long, pointed, bestial ears, grinding teeth, and grimacing lips. Sometimes he is shown with wings or with serpents growing from his blue-colored body. He commonly wielded a huge mallet with which he struck the head of a person about to die. Most of these characteristics, except the mallet, appeared in medieval and modern pictures of the Devil.

Each of the religions so far discussed has been monist, assuming a single divine principle underlying the diversity of the cosmos. About 1200 B.C. the Iranian prophet Zarathushtra laid the basis for the first

Pan, sixth century Coptic ivory preserved in the ambo of Henry II at Aachen. Here the iconography of Pan coalesces with that of the Devil: cloven hooves, goat's legs, horns, beast's ears, saturnine face, and goatee. The context and the pan pipes identify the figure as Pan rather than Satan. Courtesy Schwann Pädagogischer Verlag, Dusseldorf.

thoroughly dualist religion, Zoroastrianism or Mazdaism. Zarathush-tra's revelation was that evil is not an aspect of the good God but a completely separate principle.

Monism and dualism are not separated by an unbridgeable gap. Rather, religions form a spectrum between extreme dualism and absolute monism; almost all lie somewhere between the poles. Extreme monism, which asserts the absolute unity and absolute power of the one divine principle, is represented most strongly by prophetic and rabbinic Judaism and by Islam. The monist polytheisms of Egypt, Greece, and India are in their own way near the same pole. To the extent that religions limit the power of God—by randomness, chaos, matter, free will, or evil—they move away from this pole. The opposite pole, extreme dualism, represented by Zoroastrianism, posits two absolutely independent principles. Christian theologies lie between the two extremes, their positions on the spectrum varying according to the degree to which they allow limitations to God's sovereignty, from Luther and Calvin near one pole through Augustine and Aquinas to the Manicheans and Process theology nearer to the other.

The dualism found in Christianity differs from the extreme dualism of Iran, however, not only in degree but also in kind. Iranian dualism is a division between a good principle and an evil principle, both of them spiritual in nature. Christian dualism draws on Greek Orphism as well as on Mazdaist dualism. Orphism supposed an opposition, not between two principles, but between spirit (which is basically good) and matter (which is basically evil). The Christian Devil was an evil spirit, but he was also linked to matter in opposition to spirit.

Zarathushtra's dualism was a radical innovation in the history of religion. It denied the unity and omnipotence of God in order to preserve his perfect goodness. Zarathushtra was the first person to put forward the idea of an absolute principle of evil, whose personification, Angra Mainyu or Ahriman, is the first real Devil in world religion. Although the two principles are entirely independent, they clash, and in the fullness of time the good spirit will inevitably prevail over the evil one.

Zarathushtra's original ideas were modified and transformed over the centuries. In the third century of the Christian era the Pahlavi books provided a full account of the cosmic struggle. In the beginning there were two spirits, Ohrmazd and Ahriman, and they were separated by the void. Ohrmazd is goodness and light. He is eternal, unlimited in time. In space, however, he is limited by the void, and also by Ahriman, who lies on the other side of the void. Only by engaging and defeating

Ahriman can Ohrmazd overcome these limitations and become infinite as well as eternal. But since Ohrmazd is free of both ambition and hostility, he provokes no struggle with his opposite.

Ahriman is darkness and evil. He is limited in space by the void and by Ohrmazd. His existence is precarious: Ahriman "is not," or "he once was not and again will not be," or "he was and is, yet will not be." The texts are thus ambiguous about Ahriman's origin: he is from the beginning, like Ohrmazd, yet essentially he does not exist, and he will certainly perish. On the one hand, Mazdaism asserted that the two principles are both absolute, yet on the other hand it implied the inferiority of the darkness to the light. This ambiguity in Mazdaism was never resolved; some theologians stressed the equality of the principles, others the contingency of Ahriman's existence. The latter view fitted both Greek philosophy and Hebrew-Christian revelation better, and influence between these and Mazdaism was mutual. Though Zarathushtra lived long before Christianity, the Pahlavi books are post-Christian and may show Christian influence.

Ahriman is the essence of destruction. He is "the Destroyer. . . , the accursed destructive Spirit who is all wickedness and full of death." Ahriman is evil both by nature and by choice. In the eternal beginning, Ohrmazd knows of the existence of Ahriman on the other side of the void, but Ahriman is ignorant of the light. He is bound by darkness, ignorance, and hatred. In the course of the first three thousand years, Ahriman gradually discerns a point of light across the gulf and, seeing that light, covets it, longs for it, lusts for it, and determines to possess it. Ohrmazd, ever loving and peaceful, tries to avert a struggle by offering Ahriman peace. Ahriman, blinded by his evil nature, takes Ohrmazd's loving offer as a sign of weakness and refuses it, preferring to press his advantage. Ohrmazd reveals to him the terrible fate that awaits him in eternity, and Ahriman, stunned, falls into the void, where he remains imprisoned for another three thousand years.

Having bound Ahriman in the darkness, Ohrmazd now creates the cosmos by thinking it. All things bright and beautiful come from Ohrmazd. He creates matter, and it is good. He then goes on to place in the cosmos four manifestations of life: vegetation, fire, the primal bull (or ox), and the ideal man. The man, Gayomart, is shining, complete, and in all ways a perfect microcosm. Ohrmazd looks on what he has made, and sees that it is good.

But Ahriman, who has lain bound in the outer darkness for three thousand years, is revived by the ministrations of Jeh, the Liar Whore,

Birth of Ohrmazd and Ahriman, silver plaque, eighth century B.C. The large central figure is Zurvan; emerging from him are his twin sons, the doublet Ohrmazd and Ahriman, the light and dark sides of the divine principle. Courtesy of the Cincinnati Art Museum and Photographie Giraudon, Paris.

and he renews his assault upon Ohrmazd and the world Ohrmazd has created. In his envy and lust, Ahriman determines to lay hold of the beautiful cosmos and shape it to his own ends, using his weapons of darkness, lust, and disorder. For yet another three thousand years the warfare rages with the forces almost evenly matched. Almost, but not quite, for the defeat of evil, though postponed, is inevitable. Despairing, yet still enormously powerful, Ahriman bursts forth from the outer darkness and attacks the sky, rending it apart, and plunges down through the atmosphere toward the earth. Reaching the earth in his plummeting descent, he tunnels a vast hole through it and, emerging on the other side, enters the primal waters beneath. Violence and disorder have entered the created cosmos for the first time. Ahriman causes darkness to cover the earth; he creates ugly and loathsome creatures such as vipers and scorpions, and he unleashes the destructive powers of drought, disease, and death. He creates a whole host of demons and, turning the fury of his destructive force against the jewel of Ohrmazd's creation, he destroys life, killing the fire, the plants, the primal ox, and Gayomart, the perfect man. Of the orderly and benevolent cosmos Ahriman has made a disorderly, noxious ruin.

He prepares to return to the outer darkness to celebrate his revenge. But Ohrmazd will not allow his creation to perish. He creates the *fravashis*, the souls of men yet to be born. These freely enlist in Ohrmazd's service against the ancient foe, and they prevent Ahriman from making his escape into the void. They bind him within the cosmos and within time, so that Ohrmazd may repair his ruined world and resurrect his beloved creation. The corpse of the great ox fertilizes the sterile land, and a gentle rain wets the dry earth, so that plants again may green the world. The fire is rekindled. The seed of the dead Gayomart enters the womb of the earth, and from that union spring the ancestors of all humankind, Mashye and Mashyane.

The first human couple have free will, and initially they choose to love and serve Ohrmazd. But Ahriman tempts them to sin by using against them the essence of sin itself: the lie. The lie is that Ahriman, not Ohrmazd, has created the world, and Mashye and Mashyane believe it. Beguiled by falsehood, they sin again, offering an ox in sacrifice. To the Mazdaists cattle were holy manifestations of the primal ox. The result of the first couple's sin is ambivalent. On the one hand, they gain knowledge and the arts of civilization. But at the same time, strife, hatred, disease, poverty, and death intrude into a world hitherto perfect. The human couple's behavior becomes bent. Though Ohrmazd wishes them to produce children, they refrain from intercourse for fifty years, and when at last they come together and engender twins, their alienation from the original cosmic harmony has become so great that they devour their own children.

Later children survive to become the ancestors of the human race, but the effects of the original alienation remain with us, and we live in a world distorted by Ahriman and by the defection of the first parents. Humanity incorporates three natures: the divine, derived from Ohrmazd, the brutal and sinful, derived from Mashye and Mashyane, and the demonic, derived from Ahriman. Our hope lies in suppressing the evil and bringing the divine elements forward.

Ahriman meanwhile continues his efforts to disfigure the world by tempting us to embrace disharmony. Prince of evil, he commands a vast host of demons led by seven archfiends who aid him in his struggle against the light. The demons can change their forms and attributes unceasingly. Ahriman himself can adopt any form he wishes, often appearing as a lion, a snake, a lizard, or even a handsome youth. His countless disguises are a sign of his inner nature, that of liar and deceiver.

The end of the cosmos occurs after eons of warfare in which Ahriman seeks to distort creation and Ohrmazd to protect it. Ohrmazd presses the forces of evil on every side. Sensing their imminent defeat, they turn their destructive powers against one another, causing disruption in their own ranks. All the more frenzied by the impending doom, they rack the world in one last spasm of hatred. The sun and moon pale in the heavens, and the stars are shaken from the sky. At last the prince of darkness and his minions are exhausted, and Ahriman falls, this time utterly and finally. Opinion was divided as to whether he was annihilated or forever imprisoned, but in both versions evil is forever removed from the cosmos, and Ohrmazd reigns, infinite, eternal, and omnipotent.

The victory of Ohrmazd brings about the *frashkart*, the end of the corrupted world and the restoration of the cosmos to its primal perfection, or better, for there is no longer any potential for spoiling the shining world. A savior named Soshyans, the last of three beneficent beings born in the endtimes to virgins, appears and resurrects the dead, and all are eventually admitted to eternal bliss. Thus evil, though it may have no origin, does have an end.

This powerful spiritual dualism left a number of difficulties unresolved. If the two spirits are equal, why should the good one necessarily prevail? If they are not equal, what limits the initial power of the evil spirit? And why does it take so long for the good spirit to overwhelm the evil one? If in eternity the power of one spirit wills the destruction of the other and is capable of destroying it, why does it not win its battle in that eternal, timeless moment?

Quite a different kind of dualism arose in Greece under the name of Orphism. A tradition originating about the sixth century B.C., it posited a cosmic struggle not between two spirits, but between spirit and matter. The myth of Dionysos and the Titans lies at the center of Orphism. At the beginning of the world was Phanes, a being combining both sexes. Phanes produces Ouranos, who sires Kronos, the father of Zeus. Kronos castrates Ouranos, from whose blood the evil Titans arise. The Titans plot to take control of the cosmos, and Zeus, leader of the heavenly gods, struggles to prevent them. After defeating the Titans, Zeus swallows Phanes, thus taking the original principle into himself, becoming a creator god, and producing all things anew, including even the Titans. He also fathers a son, Dionysos. Hating Zeus and envious of the happiness of the infant Dionysos, the Titans approach the child, distract him with a glittering mirror, and seize him. They tear him apart and devour him. But Athene, heavenly goddess of wisdom, rescues the boy's heart and brings it to Zeus, who consumes it himself. Zeus now has intercourse with the mortal girl Semele, who gives birth anew to Dionysos. Pleased with the resurrection of his son, Zeus proceeds to punish his murderers by blasting them to ashes with thunderbolts. From the ashes of the Titans springs the human race.

This myth proposes a dual nature for humanity, both material and spiritual. The material part of our nature derives from the evil Titans, the spiritual part from the god Dionysos whom they devoured. The divine soul is in eternal conflict with the evil, Titanic body that imprisons it. The soul is immortal, but it is trapped like a prisoner in the mortal body: our task on earth is to escape this bodily prison by means of ritual purification. The view that the soul is good and the body evil encountered the Mazdaist idea of the warfare between two spirits sometime around the fourth century B.C. Gradually the two beliefs combined, with matter and the body placed under the power of the evil spirit and soul under the jurisdiction of the good spirit. The new idea that the body was a product of cosmic evil spread widely and came to influence Jewish, Gnostic, and Christian beliefs.

The pagan Greeks believed in a number of malicious spirits, though none that approached the status of a principle of evil. Still, Greek views on spirits produced a linguistic complication. Our word "demon," which is sometimes (imprecisely) used synonymously with "devil," derives from the Greek *daimon*, which did not necessarily connote an evil being. Homer frequently used *daimon* as the equivalent of *theos*, "god." In the centuries following Homer's time, a *daimon* (or *daimonion*) was generally held to be a spiritual being inferior to a god. The word was still ambiguous at the time of Socrates, whose guiding spirit was a "demon," but Plato's pupil Xenocrates established the negativity of the term by dividing the good gods from the evil demons and shifting the destructive qualities of the gods onto the demons. The Stoics and Plutarch followed suit. Plutarch argued that if tradition says that Apollo destroyed a city, it must really have been a demon taking the shape of Apollo. The negative meaning was further set in the second century B.C.E. by the Septuagint translation of the Hebrew Bible into Greek, which used *daimonion* to denote the evil spirits of the Hebrews.

The Greeks were the first to explore the question of evil rationally as well as mythologically. Plato and his followers wavered between dualism and monism. They were monist in their belief that everything that exists is a product of, or emanation from, one principle. But their monism was limited by their view that there is an element in the cosmos that resists the one principle. Sometimes they saw this element as the lowest emanation of the one principle, sometimes as something entirely independent of the one. This lowest (or independent) element was usually considered to be matter. The more material a thing is, the more removed it is from the one principle, which is ultimate reality.

In such a world what are the sources of evil? The Platonists offered a number of suggestions. One was that evil was metaphysically necessary. Since the phenomenal world can never adequately reflect the real world of ideas, it inevitably falls short and is less perfect, real, and good. Metaphysical evil was closely linked in Platonic thought to the idea that evil has no real being at all and consists merely of lack or privation of goodness. A withered cow that gives no milk is an evil, but the evil lies not in the being of the cow but in its *lack* of vitality and health. It is the nonbeing in the cow, not its being, that is at fault. Further, if evil had no real being it could have no principle. On this ground, later philosophers and theologians argued either that the Devil could not exist or that if he did exist he was not a true principle of evil but rather a subordinate spirit or angel whose evil lay not in his angelic being but in his lack of perfection. His enormous power magnified this lack, like a hugely powerful vacuum. The absolute coldness of the Devil is really his complete *lack* of heat.

But the Platonists never argued that evil's lack of ultimate reality

Pan and Olympus, Pompeii, first century C.E. Pan teaches the young god Olympus to play the syrinx. Courtesy Mansell Collection, London.

meant that there was no moral evil in the world. Plato was well aware of wars, murders, and lies. Evil exists, but it exists as a lack of good, just as holes in a Swiss cheese exist only as lack of cheese. The evil of a lie is the absence of truth. Plato did not think that the nonbeing of evil removed evil from the world, only that it removed responsibility for evil from the creator. Evil arose not from the God, but from matter.

The invention of philosophy as an alternative to myth as a means of describing and explaining the world was the most influential contribution of Greek and Hellenistic civilization. The Greeks for the first time conducted a rational investigation of the universe—philosophy—and, by applying philosophy to the divine principle, invented theology. Philosophy made theodicy, the effort to reconcile the existence of evil with the existence of the God, a problem for rational analysis. Through philosophical and literary reflection, the Greeks obtained generalized and moralized standards of behavior to which men, gods, and even the divine principle must conform. A thing is not good or evil because the God so names it arbitrarily. Rather, if the God disapproves of something, it is because the thing is intrinsically evil. The divine principle is perfect both morally and ontologically (in its being). Greek philosophy had no room for imperfection in the God, who was an abstract perfection beyond fault, beyond personality.

In Hebrew religion, where the God was truly a person, with intelligence and will, who intervened repeatedly and directly in human affairs, the question of God's responsibility for evil was more than an intellectual question. It was an anguished need to understand a personality with whom one is involved at the deepest levels of one's being.

3　The Good Lord and the Devil

THE word "Devil" comes indirectly from the Hebrew *satan*, "one who obstructs," and the Devil and Satan are one in origin and concept. Hebrew religion originally attributed all that is in heaven and earth, whether constructive or destructive, to the one God. But the Hebrews' intense desire to understand the meaning of evil in a world ruled by God led them to develop the concept of the Evil One over a long period of time. The evolution of the idea can be traced from the Old Testament period through the era of Apocalyptic Judaism to the first century of the Christian era.

Although some traces of an earlier polytheism seem to appear in the Old Testament, the biblical writers came gradually to identify the God of Israel with the one God of the cosmos, turning monism into monotheism. The Old Testament was compiled over a long period from about 1000 B.C.E. to nearly 100 B.C.E. Most of its books were written down during or after the period of the Exile in Babylonia (586–538). When in the third and second centuries B.C.E. the Hebrew Scriptures were translated into Greek (the Septuagint translation), this translation reflected a canon of Scripture (a standard as to which books were to be included) accepted among educated Jews at the time. Some of these books were rejected from the canon by the rabbis from the time of the Council of Jamnia (90 C.E.) and are now known as the Apocrypha ("hidden books").

The Old Testament God was responsible for the entire cosmos and so was easily perceived as a coincidence of inner opposites reflecting the ambivalence of the cosmos. He was both light and darkness, construction and destruction, good and evil. Genesis 1 may designate the cosmos that God creates as "good," but Jeremiah 45.5 has God saying, "Behold, I will

bring evil upon all flesh," and Isaiah 45.7 says, "I make light and darkness, good and evil; I the Lord do these things." (See Appendix One for a
list of Old Testament passages reflecting the ambivalence of God.) The
Old Testament God is powerfully benevolent, but he had a shadow side,
and that shadow is part of the background of the Hebrew Satan.

In the first place, God's benevolence was usually limited to the Hebrews and did not extend to the Gentiles. God enjoined the Hebrews to
be just, but primarily to other Israelites. When the Israelites invaded
Canaan, Joshua "captured the city [of Hazor] and put its king to death
with the sword. [The Israelites] killed every living thing in it, and wiped
them all out; they spared nothing that drew breath, and Hazor itself they
destroyed by fire. . . . The Israelites plundered all these cities and kept
for themselves the cattle and any other spoil they took; but they put every
living soul to the sword until they had destroyed every one; they did not
leave alive any that drew breath." The Israelites attributed this policy to
the will of God. If the Canaanites perished offering resistance to the
conquering Israelites, it was their own fault. More, their fault was part of
God's plan. "It was the Lord's purpose that they should offer an obsti-
nate resistance to the Israelites in battle, and that thus they should be
annihilated without mercy and utterly destroyed" (Josh. 11).

To the Israelites themselves God was scarcely milder. When one
among them had kept some of the spoil from a captured city for himself
rather than giving it to God in the care of his priests, God punished all
the children of Israel, causing them to suffer serious defeats at the hands
of the Canaanites. When Joshua asked God what was to be done, God
replied that Joshua was to discover the culprit by casting lots. The lot fell
upon Achan. Achan confessed, and the Israelites took him up to the Vale
of Achor and stoned him to death, whereupon God's "anger was abated."
In reward, God delivered the city of Ai to the Israelites, and they "cut
down to the last man all the citizens of Ai who were in the open country
or in the wilderness to which they had pursued them," and then returned
"to Ai and put it to the sword. The number who were killed that day,
men and women, was twelve thousand, the whole population of Ai"
(Josh. 7–8). The logic was pitiless: God had made a covenant with his
people Israel: any Gentile who stood in Israel's path was to be destroyed,
as well as any Israelite who violated the covenant.

Since the God of Israel was the only God, the supreme power in the
cosmos, and since, unlike the abstract God of the Greeks, he had personality and will, no deed could be done unless he willed it. Consequently,
when anyone transgressed morality, God was responsible for the trans-

gression as well as for its punishment. So, in Genesis 12.17, God causes Abraham to pretend that Sarah is his sister rather than his wife while they are in the land of Egypt. When Pharaoh, innocently believing Abraham's lie that she was not his wife, takes her for his own, God punishes Pharaoh, striking him and his entire household with grave diseases. In Exodus, God repeatedly hardens Pharaoh's heart, causing him to deny the Hebrews' request to leave Egypt. God visits the unfortunate Egyptians with plague after plague. Each time Pharaoh begins to yield, God hardens his heart to resist further and to bring further disasters upon himself and his people. At last God punishes him by slaying all the firstborn children of Egypt, passing over the children of Israel and sparing them alone. In Deuteronomy 32.41–42, God sounds not unlike the destroying deities of the pagans. He says:

> When I have whetted my flashing sword,
> when I have set my hand to judgement,
> then will I punish my adversaries
> and take vengeance upon my enemies.
> I will make my arrows drunk with blood,
> my soul shall devour flesh,
> blood of slain and captives,
> the heads of the enemy princes.

The harsh nature of God in preprophetic Hebrew religion reflects the savage mores of the wandering, conquering Israelites. As the Hebrews became more settled, the teaching of the prophets emphasized mercy and care for the poor, widowed, and homeless and insisted upon the responsibility of the individual for avoiding promiscuity, drunkenness, bribery, and lying. The Hebrew sense of good and evil shifted from its previous emphasis upon ritual and taboo in the direction of a humane ethic of mutual and communal responsibility. As this occurred, the Hebrew concept of God changed. No longer easy about ascribing rapine and destruction to God's will, the Hebrews gradually turned from belief in an ambivalent God to belief in a God who is wholly good. They came to perceive evil as alien to God's nature. Yet they remained the most ardent monotheists and thus were forced to face the dilemma of evil in its most poignant form: the reconciliation of the existence of evil with the existence of an all-powerful and all-good God.

Where could evil come from? One answer was that it was the result of the sin of humanity. God had made the human race happy in the Garden of Eden, but the first couple disobeyed him and in consequence were expelled from Paradise. The Old Testament writers did not make this story the basis for a doctrine of original sin, as rabbinic and Christian writers would do later, but the theme of human perversity continued through Cain, the flood at the time of Noah, Sodom and Gomorrah, and the repeated failures of the Israelites to obey their covenant with God. The idea that humanity was alienated from God was already firm in Genesis 6.5–6: "When the Lord saw that man had done much evil on earth and that his thoughts and inclinations were always evil, he regretted having made man on earth." Still, the alienation of humanity in itself seemed insufficient to explain the vast and terrifying quantity of evil in the world.

Another answer was to posit as the source of evil a spiritual being opposed to the Lord God. To the extent that one faced the enormous power of evil in the world, one ascribed enormous power to this spiritual prince of evil. Hebrew monotheism was here in a difficult position. The Hebrews' insistence upon God's omnipotence and sovereignty did not allow them to believe that this opposing principle was independent of God, yet their insistence on God's goodness no longer permitted it to be part of God. It had therefore to be a spirit that was both opposed and subject to God. God must remain omnipotent and somehow responsible for this evil spirit. In effect the old, ambivalent God was divided into two parts, a good Lord and an evil devil. The more one faced the power of evil, the more one tended in the direction of dualism, seeing the cosmos as a battleground between good and evil. The result was a tension between monotheism and a kind of practical, implicit dualism, a tension that became typical of late Hebrew religion and of Christianity.

The gradual division in Hebrew thought of the concept of the God into the two aspects of good Lord and evil Devil proceeded along two faultlines in the original idea of God. The first faultline was the "sons of God," the *bene ha-elohim*; the second was the "messenger of God," the *mal'ak Yahweh*.

In the Old Testament, the Lord God of Hosts is sometimes surrounded by a heavenly council. The members of this council are the bene ha-elohim, the "sons of God." The very early Hebrews may have perceived their God as surrounded by a pantheon of lesser gods. As the Hebrews developed strict monotheism, the idea of a pantheon faded, and the bene ha-elohim became shadowy, undefined figures. Yet they played an essential part in separating the evil aspect of the divine nature off from the good.

The Book of Genesis relates that early in the history of the human race, the bene ha-elohim looked upon the daughters of men and found them beautiful. They had intercourse with these women, begetting a race of giants. Following these events, the Lord sent the deluge upon the earth, although this punishment was ascribed not to the sins of the "sons of God" but to those of humans, who "had done much evil on the earth" (Gen. 6.5). The Book of Psalms says that "God takes his stand in the court of heaven to deliver judgement among the gods themselves" and concludes "Gods you may be, sons you all of the Most High, yet you shall die as men die; princes fall, every one of them, and so shall you" (Ps. 82.1–7). The Lord judges the members of his heavenly court (for an unspecified sin) and punishes them. Explaining the nature of this sin and this fall was left to the writers of the Apocalyptic period, much later.

During the Apocalyptic period (200 B.C.E. to 100 C.E.) appeared a number of Jewish books known as pseudepigrapha ("false writings"). Unlike the Apocrypha, the pseudepigrapha were never included in any canon of the Old Testament, but they nonetheless enjoyed wide influence. Since many of them reported visions or revelations of the end of the world, they were called Apocalyptic, "books of revelation." Written during centuries when the Jews were suffering from Syrian and Roman oppression, they are deeply concerned with the problem of evil and the power of Satan. The wretched condition of the Jews under foreign occupation suggested that Satan had established his reign where kings and prophets once had ruled. This reign of Satan was sometimes called the "old age." Soon the Messiah, God's "anointed one," a king of Israel descended from David's royal line, would come, break the Devil's power, reestablish the kingdom of Israel, and usher in a new age of justice and freedom.

The Jews of the Apocalyptic period could not understand why God had abandoned Israel and allowed evil to rule the world in their time. Such a degree of evil was more than God would ordain and greater than mere humans could cause. It must therefore be the work of a powerful spiritual force. The Apocalyptic writers studied the Old Testament and found a hint of such a force in the sinful bene ha-elohim. They proceeded to develop these hints into full, colorful accounts, as in the Book of Enoch. Enoch is taken on an inspection tour of Sheol, the shadowy underworld place of the dead, "the land of destruction, forgetfulness, and silence." During the journey he sees the sons of God in their fallen state and learns that these "angels, the children of heaven, saw and lusted after" the daughters of men. The author is here affirming the original closeness of the bene ha-elohim to the Lord, for "children of heaven" was a common Jewish metonymy for God. Yet, by demoting them to the status of angels, the author removed them safely beyond the limits of the divine nature itself, giving himself a free hand in declaring such beings completely evil.

To these Watcher angels—as they were now called because of their prurient interest in mortal women—the Book of Enoch ascribed a leader named Semyaza. A wealth of names of different origins—Belial, Mastema, Azazel, Satanail, Sammael, Semyaza, and Satan—congealed during the Apocalyptic period around one figure, that of the Evil One, a being who personified the single origin and essence of evil. The Devil— the personification of evil itself—is to be distinguished from the demons, the evil spirits who serve as his henchmen. What is most important is the development of the concept of a single principle—or, better, principal— of evil.

With this principal the name of Satan was most closely linked. The Hebrew word *satan* derives from a root meaning "oppose," "obstruct," or "accuse." The basic denotation of the word is "opponent." In this simple sense the word *satan* appears as a common noun several times in the Old Testament in reference to a human opponent, as when David says to the sons of Zeruiah, "What right have you to . . . play the satan against me today?" (2 Sam. 19.22). In another Old Testament passage, the angel of the Lord blocks the road on which Balaam seeks to travel. Here for the first time a supernatural being is called a satan, but again simply as a common noun. The angel is not a being called a satan; he is a satan only while he blocks the road (Num. 22.22–35).

Zechariah 3.1–2, however, reveals a striking development: "Then he showed me Joshua the high priest standing before the angel of the Lord, with the Adversary standing at his right hand to accuse him. The Lord said to the Adversary, 'The Lord rebuke you, Satan, the Lord rebuke you who are venting your spite on Jerusalem.'" The idea of a personality is beginning to emerge, a supernatural being whose nature is to obstruct and to accuse. Satan as accuser would become a common theme in Apocalyptic and Christian literature, helping to confirm the Septuagint translation of *satan* as *diabolos*, "slanderer" or "opposing witness." Finally, the Zechariah passage offers a hint of Satan's opposition to God as well as to humans, for the Lord reproaches him for his activities. Still, Satan's role here is essentially as God's tool for the punishment of sinners, a tool that simply went too far in its duties and failed to understand that God limits justice with mercy. That God permits Satan to stand and speak before him in the heavenly court indicates the origin of

Christ exorcising a demon. Armenian gospels, A.D. 1202. Christ's powers of exorcism were a sign that he could overcome the kingdom of Satan and replace it with the kingdom of God. Courtesy Walters Art Gallery, Baltimore.

Satan as one of the bene ha-elohim. And this in turn linked Satan with the fall of the Watcher Angels.

In the Book of Enoch, the sin of the Watcher angels is lust: they descend from heaven to earth in order to seduce human women. But in punishment they are thrust down from earth into underworld pits of darkness by the avenging angels Michael, Gabriel, Raphael, and Uriel. The Apocalyptic Book of Jubilees specified that nine parts of the angels fell while one part remained sinless and loyal to God. (Medieval writers later reversed these proportions.) The Book of the Secrets of Enoch (2 Enoch) added to the myth the significant new element that the angels rebelled on account of pride. The key passage is: "And one from out the order of angels, having turned away with the order that was under him, conceived of an impossible thought, to place his throne higher than the clouds above the earth, that he might become equal in rank to any power. And I threw him out from the height with his angels, and he was flying in the air continuously above the bottomless." It may be that this passage is of later, Christian origin; at any rate, the combination of the motifs of rebellion and lust melded two originally different sins on the part of the angels.

In yet another way the idea of a prideful fall was associated with the Devil. Isaiah 14.12–15 had said:

> How did you come to fall from heaven, bright son of the morning,
> how thrown to the earth, you who enslaved the nations?
> You thought to yourself,
> I will scale the heavens;
> I will set my throne above the stars of God,
> I will sit on the mountain where the gods meet
> in the deep recesses of the north.
> I will rise above the thunder clouds
> and make myself like the Most High.
> Now are you fallen into Sheol,
> into the depths of the abyss.

Isaiah's specific reference was to a king of Babylonia or Assyria, metaphorically likened to the morning star whose rays are erased by the rising of the sun. Scholars have found traces of Canaanite mythology in the passage as well, but nothing indicates that Isaiah was even vaguely thinking of the Devil. By the Apocalyptic period, however, Isaiah's fallen king or fallen star was being linked with the fallen angel. In addition to 2 Enoch, other passages in the Qumran texts, in the Apocalyptic Life of Adam (14.16), and in the New Testament (Luke 10.18) indicate that the connection between the bright son of the morning and the Devil was being made at the time.

Yet another view of Satan's fall appears in the Books of Adam and Eve, where out of envy of humanity he refuses God's command to bow down to Adam. Thus Apocalyptic literature united five hitherto separate ideas: (1) the sin of the Devil as pride; (2) the ruin of the angels through lust; (3) the fall of the "bright son of the morning;" (4) Satan's envy of humanity; (5) Satan's role as prince of demons.

The second great faultline upon which the concept of the God divided was the mal'ak Yahweh. The mal'ak is the emissary or messenger of God. Like the bene ha-elohim, the mal'ak is an aspect of the divine nature. He differs from the "children of God" in one important respect: they remain in heaven, but the mal'ak roams the world in God's service. In the early Old Testament literature, the mal'ak is the voice of God, the spirit of God, the God himself. When Moses is addressed from the burning thornbush in Exodus 3.2 by the mal'ak and in Exodus 3.4 by God himself, the identity of the mal'ak and God is clear. The concept of the mal'ak was meant to represent the side of God that is turned toward humans, or the aspect of God that humans perceive, or the manifestation of God in his relationship with humans. The Septuagint translated mal'ak as *angelos*, "messenger," from which the word "angel" derives. The mal'ak, like God himself, was originally morally ambivalent. In Exodus 12.23, God—and the mal'ak—slaughter the firstborn of Egypt.

The elision of the mal'ak with the bene ha-elohim and the tendency of both to become identified with evil are clearest in the Book of Job. The more the bene ha-elohim and the mal'ak were seen as distinct from God, the easier it was to thrust upon them the evil elements of the divine character, leaving the Lord only with the good. In Job, that process is still incomplete, for God and Satan are still working closely together:

The day came when the members of the court of heaven took their places in the presence of the Lord, and Satan was there among them. The Lord asked him where he had been. "Ranging over the earth," he said, "from end to end." Then the Lord asked Satan. "Have you considered my servant Job? You will find no one like him on earth, a man of blameless and upright life, who fears God and sets his face against wrongdoing." Satan answered the Lord, "Has not Job good reason to be God-fearing? Have you not hedged him round on every side with your protection, him and his family and all his possessions? Whatever he does you have blessed, and his herds have increased beyond measure. But stretch out your hand and touch all that he has, and then he will curse you to your face."

Then the Lord said to Satan, "So be it. All that he has is in your hands; only Job himself you must not touch." And Satan left the Lord's presence. [Job 1.6–12]

Job's family and possessions are destroyed, and

Once again the day came when the members of the court of heaven took their places in the presence of the Lord, and Satan was there among them. The Lord asked him where he had been. "Ranging over the earth," he said, "from end to end." Then the Lord asked Satan, "Have you considered my servant Job? You will find no one like him on earth, a man of blameless and upright life, who fears God and sets his face against wrongdoing. You excited me to ruin him without a cause, but his integrity is still unshaken." Satan answered the Lord, "Skin for skin! There is nothing the man will grudge to save himself. But stretch out your hand and touch his bone and his flesh, and see if he will not curse you to your face."

Then the Lord said to Satan, "So be it. He is in your hands; but spare his life." And Satan left the Lord's presence, and he smote Job with running sores from head to foot, so that he took a piece of a broken pot to scratch himself as he sat among the ashes. [Job 2.1–8]

In Job, Satan is already a personality with the function of accusing, opposing, and harming human beings. He is not yet the principle of evil, for he is still one of the heavenly court and does nothing without God's consent and command. Still, Job already hints of an opposition between Satan and the Lord. Rather than simply acting as an instrument of the Lord's will, Satan persuades God to work evil upon his faithful servant Job. God agrees only with reservations, later reproaching Satan for having tempted him. Satan works as the shadow, the dark side of God, the destructive power wielded by God only reluctantly. Further, it is Satan himself who as mal'ak goes down to the earth and torments Job.

A spirit behaving like the mal'ak appears in Judges 9.22–23: "After Abimelech had been prince over Israel for three years, God sent an evil spirit to make a breach between Abimelech and the citizens of Shechem." In 1 Samuel 16–19, an evil spirit from the Lord deranges Saul, causing him to prophesy against his will and inciting him to hurl a javelin at David. The murderous mal'ak's function as the shadow of God is even clearer in 2 Samuel 24.13–16. "Is it to be three years of famine in your land," God asks David through the mouth of the prophet, "or three months of flight with the enemy at your heels, or three days of pestilence in your land?" David in desperation chooses plague as the least evil, "so the Lord sent a pestilence throughout Israel . . . [and] seventy thousand of the people died. Then the angel (mal'ak) stretched out his arm towards Jerusalem to destroy it, but the Lord repented of the evil and said to the

angel who was destroying the people, 'Enough, stay your hand.' " Here
the destroying mal'ak almost gets out of control, and the Lord restrains
him at the last moment. On one level, the Hebrews knew that the mal'ak
was God, but on another they began to imagine him as a separate entity.
On that level they could begin to excuse God for the existence of evil by
blaming it upon the mal'ak.

The separation of the mal'ak from the godhead is sharper in the
dialogue of 1 Kings 22.19–23. Michaiah says, "I saw the Lord seated on
his throne, with all the host of heaven in attendance on his right and on
his left. The Lord said, 'Who will entice Ahab to attack and fall on
Ramothgilead?' One said one thing and one said another; then a spirit
came forward and stood before the Lord and said, 'I will entice him.'
'How?' said the Lord. 'I will go out,' he replied, 'and be a lying spirit in
the mouth of all his prophets.' 'You shall entice him,' said the Lord, 'and
you shall succeed; go and do it.' " The evil spirit here appears first in the
company of the bene ha-elohim and then goes out over the earth as a
mal'ak. The mal'ak does not have to persuade God to destroy Ahab, for
that is already the Lord's intent. But if in this way he is less independent
than the Satan in Job, in another way his independence of Yahweh is
even more distinct: "I will go out and be a lying spirit in the mouth of all
his prophets." The evil mal'ak is not only an opponent of the human race;
he is prince of lies and lord of deceit.

The Hebrews were at least unconsciously aware of the gradual distinction that they were making between God and the mal'ak. In 2 Samuel
David sins in taking a census of the Israelites: "Once again the Israelites
felt the Lord's anger, when he incited David against them and gave him
orders that Israel and Judah should be counted" (24.1). God had declared
such a census a sin, but now he commanded David to take one in order
that he might have reason to punish the people of Israel. The text is
understandable in terms of God's original ambivalence. But the writer of
Chronicles, a later work derived from Samuel and Kings, could no longer
in his time understand the ambiguity. The Lord, he reasoned, could not
have willed David to sin. It could not have been the Lord; it must have
been the evil mal'ak. So the writer revised the passage to read: "Now
Satan, setting himself against Israel, incited David to count the people"
(1 Chron. 21.1).

Gradually the mal'ak obtained its independence from God; gradually
its destructive aspect was emphasized; finally it became the personification of the dark side of the divine nature. The mal'ak was now the evil
angel, Satan, the obstructor, the liar, the destroying spirit.

The crucial development was further advanced in the Apocalyptic period. In the Book of Jubilees the evil mal'ak has become Mastema, prince of evil spirits and virtually independent of the Lord. He tempts, accuses, destroys, and punishes humans, taking onto himself all the evil characteristics once ascribed to God. He and his followers lead astray "the children of the sons of Noah . . . to make them err and destroy them." Where the mal'ak of God or God himself had in the Old Testament slain the firstborn of Egypt, that carnage was now Mastema's work. Where God's power had mysteriously worked against his own followers, that power was now ascribed to Mastema. One of the strangest passages of the Bible is Exodus 4.24–25, where God lurks in the desert waiting for Moses, in order to kill him. In Jubilees it is Mastema, rather than God, who thus lies murderously in wait. In Genesis, God puts Abraham to the test, asking him to sacrifice his son. In Jubilees, it is Mastema who is responsible: "And the prince Mastema came and said before God, 'Behold, Abraham loves Isaac his son, and he delights in him above all things else; bid him offer him as a burnt offering on the altar, and Thou wilt see if he will do this command."

Evil is now done by the mal'ak rather than by God. Yet God has created Satan and even specifically grants him the power to tempt and destroy. Why? Did it really solve the problem of God's responsibility for evil to shunt that evil onto a personality that God has created and maintains? Apocalyptic literature answered that the Lord permits evil only for a while, and after eons of struggle he will finally destroy the evil angels. At the end of the world the Messiah will come and judge Mastema. The power of the evil angels will be annihilated, and they will be bound and imprisoned forever. Still, the Apocalyptic writings leave an unresolved paradox: evil is done by the mal'ak; the mal'ak is created by and subject to God; God must therefore will the existence of evil, even if indirectly. One approach to this dilemma was to emphasize the mal'ak's or angel's freedom of will. God wills the creation of the angel, but the angel's evil is a free choice of the angel rather than God's choice. The problem with such a solution was that God is still responsible for creating a cosmos in which such an evil force is allowed to roam. Another approach was to widen the distance between the Lord and the Devil to the point that the Devil became almost a separate principle of evil. The problem with this dualistic solution was that it contradicted the fundamental monotheistic premise of Hebrew religion.

The most dualistic of the Apocalyptic groups were the Essenes of Qumran, whose ideas the discovery of the Dead Sea Scrolls brought into full view. The Essenes believed that the psychological conflict within the human individual between the good inclination and the evil inclination reflects a struggle between good and evil groups of humans, which in turn reflects the cosmic warfare between two opposing spirits, one goodness and light, the other evil and darkness. "From the God of knowledge comes all that is and shall be. . . . He has created man to govern the world and has appointed for him two spirits in which to walk until the time of his visitation: the spirits of truth and falsehood. Those born of truth spring from a fountain of light, but those born of falsehood spring from a source of darkness. All the children of righteousness are ruled by the Prince of Light and walk in the ways of light, but those born of falsehood are ruled by the Angel of Darkness and walk in the ways of darkness." Here the solution is to posit two opposing spirits, both subject to God.

These spirits are not abstractions, but persons of terrible power: on the one hand the Prince of Light; on the other the Prince of Darkness, the Destroying Angel. Those who follow the Lord of Light are the children of light; those who follow the Angel of Darkness are the children of darkness. The merciless war between the two spirits is in deadly and ageless earnest. Yet, terrible though the conflict is, it is not absolute, for the two spirits are not wholly independent as in Iran. Since all ultimately comes from God, the Lord "establishes all things by his design, and without him nothing is done." The Lord of Light, who is assimilated to the ultimate God, the God of Israel, creates and directs all things. Ultimately even the Prince of Darkness is subject to him. The sovereignty of God is preserved, though barely.

The conflict between the armies of darkness and light has raged since the foundation of the earth, but as the world nears its end the legions of darkness are active as never before. The endtime is at hand, and Satan is even now expending his utmost energies to destroy the universe before the inevitable triumph of the Lord of Light. "During all those years Satan shall be unleashed against Israel. . . . As long as the dominion of Satan endures . . . the Angel of Darkness leads all the children of righteousness astray." All the sins of Israel are the result of this dominion of Satan, who manifests himself in each of us as the *yetser ha-ra*, the evil inclination within human beings.

Still, the underlying message of Qumran is hopeful. If this is the worst of ages, if Satan now walks the earth in brazen triumph, these are signs that the Lord will soon arise and smite him and open a new age of goodness and light. For the Lord of Light never takes his hands off the

Christ separating the sheep from the goats. This is the earliest known portrayal of the Devil, who sits at Christ's left hand with the goats, while the good angel sits at the Lord's right hand with the sheep. The Devil is blue, the color of the lower air into which he has been thrust down; the good angel is red, the color of fire and the realm of the ether in which the angels dwell. Sixth-century mosaic in San Apollinare Nuovo, Ravenna. Courtesy of Hirmer Verlag, Munich.

evil mal'ak, whose "dominion [is] in accordance with the mysteries of God. . . . [God], Thou hast created Satan, the Angel of Malevolence, for the Pit; his [reign] is in Darkness and his purpose is to bring about wickedness and iniquity." Having created Satan and used him as an instrument of vengeance against sinners, the Lord will soon bring him down. The Messiah will save the righteous elect, the children of light, and will lead them into an earthly kingdom of peace, happiness, and prosperity. But the Gentiles and those Jews who are faithless to the covenant will be punished with Satan and his angels forever. So the old age of Satan comes to an end, the wickedness of the world passes, and the new age of the Lord dawns.

Though monotheists, the Essenes had much in common with dualists. In Apocalyptic, Qumran, and Mazdaist sources alike, the Devil is the head of a host of evil spirits who, like good spirits, are arranged in orders and ranks. The chief functions of the Apocalyptic Devil, to seduce, accuse, and destroy, are also those of Ahriman. In both Apocalyptic Judaism and Mazdaism the cosmos is divided into two forces of light and darkness locked in deadly combat: the children of light war against the children of darkness. Toward the end of the world, the Prince of Darkness seems for a while to increase his power in a dark and miserable age, but that age is followed by the triumph of the Prince of Light and the perpetual imprisonment or destruction of the Prince of Darkness. Two fundamental differences remained. Jewish dualism was more ethical, Iranian more cosmological; the Jewish writers always affirmed the subordination of the evil spirit to God. Still, the Apocalyptic Devil often acts *as if* he were a principle independent of God. Apocalyptic Judaism remained monotheistic, but because of the problem of evil it was drawn in the direction of radical dualism.

Having come to discard the idea that evil as well as good proceeds from the divine nature and to insist that God fiercely rejects evil, the Jews were drawn to personify evil as a dark Prince in opposition to God. But as monotheists they also declined to sever the two, insisting that only one principle can exist, one God alone. Neither pure dualism nor pure monism, the Hebrew position was ambiguous. Far from being a defect, this ambiguity was a great virtue: it was founded in a creative tension, and it did not permit an evasion of the problem of evil. God is good; evil exists. There is no easy resolution to the dilemma, and the difficulty of the Hebrew view testifies to its deepness. It was the Hebrews, loving God with such intensity, who first faced the problem of evil with such poignancy.

4 *Christ and the Power of Evil*

NEW Testament ideas of the Devil derived primarily from Hebrew thought, especially the Apocalyptic tradition. Greek influence was secondary. Since the New Testament was composed by a number of writers over a period of half a century, differences in point of view exist; still, the variations are not great, and consistent generalizations can be made. The New Testament inherited several ideas about the Devil. The Devil is a fallen angel. He is the head of a demonic host. He is the principle of evil. Evil is nonbeing. The New Testament absorbed, refined, and transformed these elements.

The names that the New Testament gives the Prince of Darkness reflect the double background of Hellenism and Apocalyptic Judaism. Most often he is "Satan" or "the Devil," but he is also "Beelzeboul," a name derived from the king of Ekron in 2 Kings 1.2–3. He is also called "the Enemy," "Belial," "the Tempter," "the Accuser," "the Evil One," "the Prince of This World," and "the Prince of Demons" (See Appendix 2). The term "prince" (*archon*) for the Devil is always contrasted with the term "lord" (*kyrios*) for Christ.

The equation of Lucifer, "the lightbearer," with Satan is not clear in the New Testament. Although the Septuagint had translated the "bright morning star" that fell in Isaiah 14 as *heosphoros* ("dawn-bringer"), which also became *phosphoros* ("light-bearer"), or *lucifer* in Latin, and although the fallen angels are likened to fallen stars in Revelation 12.4, the term "bearer of light" in the New Testament is reserved to Christ. The earliest Christian text making the equation of Lucifer with Satan is *Against Marcion* (2.10) by Tertullian (c. 170–220). Nonetheless, the assumption was common in the Apocalyptic writings, and Jesus' statement in Luke

10.18—"I saw Satan falling like lightning from heaven"—indicates that the earliest Christians shared it.

The struggle between God and the Evil One is at the heart of the New Testament. In the New Testament world view, either you follow God or you are subject to Satan. Because of sin, the world lies under the Devil's power; Christ comes to break that power and to heal the alienation between humanity and God. Satan extends his hatred of God to Christ and to humanity. The Devil is a liar and a sinner from the beginning (1 John 3–8) and has death at his command (Heb. 2.14). He is the adversary of Christ (Mark 8.33, 22.3; John 13.2, 13.27), a function clearest in the temptations he offers the Savior to induce him to abandon his redemptive mission (Matt. 4.1–11; Mark 1.13; Luke 4.1–13). In this Satan continues his Old Testament role of thwarter and obstructor, as he does later against Paul (1 Thess. 2.18).

The Devil is associated with flesh, the death, and this world, all of which obstruct the kingdom of God. Two Greek words have been translated as "world" in English Bibles: one is *aion*, used by Paul; the other is *kosmos*, used by John. They have similar meanings, and the Devil is called both lord of the aion and lord of the kosmos (Matt. 9.34, 12.24–28; Mark 3.22–26; John 12.31, 14.30, 16.11; 2 Cor. 4.4; Eph. 2.2; 1 John 4.3–4). The kingdom of the Devil, which is this world, is contrasted to the kingdom of the Lord, which is not of this world. Since the moment of original sin; the Devil has been increasing his power over this world, until now, at this latter day, his sway has become nearly complete. But now God sends Christ to break the power of the old age and to replace it with the new age, the kingdom of God.

Although the meaning of "the kingdom of God" is unclear, what is meant by "this age" or "this world" is clearer. *Kosmos* can mean the natural world; it can mean human society; or it can mean those people who are sinners. *Aion* can mean the time allotted to the material world; the material world itself; or the present, sin-ridden time as opposed to the kingdom of God to come. The Devil is lord of the natural world in his power to cause death, disease, and natural disasters; he is lord of human society because of its tendency to sin. It is in the sense of sinful human society that the terms *kosmos* and *aion* were most often used, for the New Testament emphasizes the problem of moral evil more than that of natural evil.

The world of nature is created by the good Lord for good purposes. Yet the Lord has allowed Satan temporary power over the world. As a result, "the whole world lies in the Evil One" (1 John 5.19). The struggle between the old age of the world ruled by Satan and the new age of the kindgom of God is sometimes expressed as the opposition between spirit and body, sometimes as that between light and darkness.

The Devil is prince of a host of evil spirits. The origins of the Devil and of the demons are quite distinct. The demons derived from the minor evil spirits of the Near East, whereas the Devil derives from the Hebrew mal'ak, the shadow of the Lord, and the Mazdaist principle of evil. The demons are lesser spirits, the Devil the personification of evil itself. The New Testament maintained the distinction by differentiating between the terms *diabolos* and *daimonion*, but it was a distinction that was often blurred, and many English translations muddle it further by translating *daimonion* as "devil."

A blurring of conceptions lay behind this blurring of vocabulary. The tendency to blend the Devil with the demons had two sources. One was the late Hellenistic philosophical tradition that a level of spirits existed between God and humankind. Some of these spirits were good, others evil. By the first century of the Christian era the evil spirits usually went by the name of *daimonia*, "demons." This Hellenistic classification would lump Satan with the other evil spirits in the category of *daimonia*.

The second source of blending was the late Hebrew tradition of the fallen angels. The Hebrew malakim or angels occupied a space in the chain between God and humanity, just as the Greek daimonia did. The blending of malakim with daimonia was encouraged by the Septuagint's translation of a wide variety of Old Testament words for evil spirits into the Greek *daimonia*. Finally, Apocalyptic literature was beginning to perceive the Devil as the head of the host of evil angels. Christianity adopted that tradition for itself and made the Devil the prince of the fallen angels in their struggle against God (Matt. 9.34, 12.24–28, 25.41; Mark 3.22–26; Luke 11.14–15, 13.16; Acts 10.38; 2 Cor. 5.5, 11.4, 12.7; Eph. 2.2, 6.12; Col. 1.13).

Christianity, like Apocalyptic Judaism, had to maintain a careful balance: it could not make the Devil a principle of evil independent of God, yet he had to be more than simply one of a multitude of demons. He had to be the prince (or principal) of evil without being the principle of evil.

The essential function of Satan in the New Testament is to obstruct the kingdom of God as long and as thoroughly as he can. One of his favorite weapons is possession. Ordinarily the demons, Satan's servants, do the actual possessing, though in the Johannine literature Satan does it himself. By exorcising the demons and by curing diseases sent by them,

Christ heals a demoniac while Satan, with black wings on his head, looks on in horrified astonishment. Stuttgart Gospels, ninth century. Courtesy Bildarchiv Foto Marburg.

Jesus makes war upon Satan's kingdom and thereby makes known to the people that the new age is come. "If I drive out demons by the power of God it is because the kingdom of God is come among you" (Matt. 12.28). The exorcism of demons represents no quirk here, no irrelevant accretion of superstition, but rather is central to the war against Satan and therefore to the meaning of the gospels. Each act of exorcism represented one installment of the destruction of the old age, one step closer to the time when Satan will no longer control the world.

The Devil is the prince of evil humans as well as of demons. Evildoers are called followers or sons of the Devil (Matt. 5.37, 16.23; Mark 8.33; Luke 22.3; John 8.44, 13.2, 13.27; Acts 13.10; 1 Cor. 5.5; 1 Tim. 1.20, 3.6–7, 8.15; 1 John 3.8–12). Christ calls Judas the Devil for acting to bring about the crucifixion, and that is clearly Satan's work. Christ also calls Peter the Devil for tempting Jesus to shirk the cross; trying to *avert* the crucifixion is also Satan's work, for Christ needs to die in order to reconcile humanity to God.

Temptation is Satan's most effective weapon (Matt. 6.13; Mark 4.15; Luke 8.12; 1 Cor. 7.5; 2 Cor. 2.11; Eph. 4.27, 6.11; 2 Tim. 2.26; 1 Pet. 5.8). But the idea that the Devil is the serpent that tempted Adam and Eve is not apparent in the New Testament. The Evil One is connected with a serpent only in John 8.44, 1 John 3.10, and Revelation 12–13, and the identification seems to be more with Leviathan (Ps. 74.13) and Rahab (Job 26.12) than with the serpent of Eden. The idea that the Devil was the original tempter of humanity may be implied in the New Testament, but it only later became a firm part of Christian belief.

The Devil also retained some of his old characteristics as agent of God in his role of tempter and as accuser and punisher of sinners (Luke 22.31; 1 Cor. 5.5; 1 Tim. 1.20; James 4.7). The Devil can also harm people physically (Luke 13.11–16; 2 Cor. 12.7). In later Christian tradition Satan ruled hell and suffered there himself, but neither point is clear in the New Testament. The two common New Testament words for hell are *hades* and *geenna*. In the Septuagint, *hades* usually translated the Hebrew *Sheol*, and the New Testament understanding of this place is similar to the Hebrew: beneath the earth, it is the abode of souls temporarily separated from their bodies until the time of resurrection. Geenna is a much more terrible place of eternal fire and punishment for the wicked. Sheol and Geenna, originally distinct, merged in early Christian thought as hell.

Hell is related to eschatology—the end of the world. The Book of Revelation says that the Devil is bound in chains as a result of Christ's redeeming act, but that he will be loosed upon the world again as the endtime approaches. But here things were muddled until Dante and Milton centuries later tried to straighten them out. Several different interpretations of the ruin of Satan and his fellow angels have been put forward at one time or another. The first set of differences has to do with the nature of his fall: it has been viewed as (1) a moral lapse; (2) a loss of dignity; (3) a literal ejection from heaven; (4) a voluntary departure from heaven. The second set of differences has to do with the geography of the fall: (1) from heaven to earth; (2) from heaven into the underworld; (3) from earth (or air) into the underworld. The third set is chronological: Satan fell (1) at the beginning of the world before the fall of Adam: (2) from envy of Adam; (3) with the Watcher angels at the time of Noah; (4) at the advent of Christ; (5) at the Passion of Christ; (6) at the second coming of Christ; (7) a thousand years after the second coming.

The New Testament itself admits a wide range of interpretations on these questions. (1) At the beginning of the world there was war in heaven, and Michael cast out the Devil and his angels. They were plunged into the underworld, from which, however, they issued forth to tempt humankind. (2) The angels fell long after Adam, when they lusted after the daughters of men; they were cast down from heaven into the underworld but issued forth again to do us harm. (3) The kingdom of God arrived on earth with the advent of Christ, and his exorcism of demons is proof of his power over Satan. (4) Christ's Passion itself hurled Satan down. (5) The kingdom of Satan has been weakened but not finally toppled by the coming of Christ. Christ will come again, and at the last judgment Satan will be destroyed, or at least cast forever into hell. This last chronology, found in Revelation, indicates the shifting faith of the Christian community after the first century, when it had become clear that Christ's first coming had not removed evil from the world. As his reappearance delayed, the ruin of Satan was further postponed. (6) At the second coming, Christ will bind Satan for a thousand years, and at the end of the thousand years he will issue forth once more and then finally be destroyed.

The inconsistency of these accounts is inherited from Apocalyptic Judaism. It permitted wide scope in subsequent Christian views, particularly among those involved in millenarian speculations on the basis of the Book of Revelation. Still, there is complete consistency on the essential point, which is that the new age brought by Christ is at war with the old age ruled by Satan.

Other eschatological adversaries of the kingdom of God were linked with the Devil: the Antichrist, the beasts, and the dragon (Rev. 11–19). The iconography of the beasts had only a limited influence on the iconography of Satan. Both the dragon and the beast from the sea have ten horns and seven heads; these do not match the appearance of the Devil in later tradition. Revelation 13.11 assigns the beast from the land two horns. The later Devil seldom has more than one head, though he often has a face on belly or buttocks, and he never has more than two horns. The two-horned image prevailed because the beast from the land fitted Satan's associations with horned wild animals, with Pan and the satyrs, and with the crescent moon. Further, two horns of power are traditionally assigned to Moses and other numinous figures. Demons in the New Testament are associated with a number of animals: locusts, scorpions, leopards, lions, and bears. The Devil himself has direct associations only with the serpent, the dragon, and the lion. The lion did not become a lasting symbol of the Devil because it was used for Mark the Evangelist and for Christ himself.

Despite its inconsistencies, the New Testament fixed the overall concept of the Devil into a more coherent pattern than Apocalyptic literature had done. The Devil is a creature of God, a fallen angel, but as chief of fallen angels and of all evil powers he often acts almost as an opposite principle to God. He is lord of this world, chief of a vast multitude of powers spiritual and physical, angelic and human, that are arrayed against the coming of the kingdom of God. Satan is not only the Lord's chief opponent; he is the prince of all opposition to the Lord. Anyone who does not follow the Lord is under Satan's power. As Satan was the opponent of the good Lord of the Hebrews, so he is now the opponent of Christ, the Son of the good Lord. As Christ commands the armies of light, Satan commands those of darkness. The cosmos is torn between light and darkness, good and evil, spirit and matter, soul and body, the new age and the old age, the Lord and Satan. The Lord is the creator of all things and the guarantor of their goodness, but Satan and his kingdom have twisted and corrupted this world. Christ comes to destroy the old, evil eon and to establish the kingdom of God in its place. In the end, Satan and his powers will be defeated and Christ's kingdom established forever.

There is a touch of dualism here, first in the extent of Satan's power as lord of this world and second in the intense opposition between spirit and flesh. But these dualistic tendencies were subject to the fundamental belief that the good God created the world, which, though corrupted, remains essentially good. Satan himself is a creature of God. At the end

Demons lead a damned soul toward the gates of hell; inside the prisoners are being tortured. Stuttgart Gospels, ninth century. Courtesy Bildarchiv Foto Marburg.

of time all evil is banished and ambiguities and dualities are resolved in Christ's final victory.

Meanwhile, natural ills such as disease and storms could be attributed to the Devil, whether they are sent upon us as diabolical afflictions or whether they are meant as punishment for our sins. God made the cosmos good; its failings are the fault of the Evil One. Moral evil would doubtless exist in humankind without Satan, but he constantly abets it through temptation, and all who sin fall under his power. Every day, in every place, and in every individual, Satan and his forces are striving to block the kingdom of God. The Devil of the New Testament is not tangential to the fundamental message, not a mere symbol. The saving mission of Christ can be fully understood only in terms of opposition to the Devil. That is the whole point of the New Testament: the world is full of grief and suffering, but beyond the power of Satan is a greater power that gives meanings to that suffering.

While primitive Christianity was giving the Devil considerable attention, Jewish thought was moving in the other direction. After the fall of Jerusalem to the Romans in 70 C.E. the Temple was pulled down, and the Jews were exiled from Palestine. In the diaspora, the "scattering," they settled throughout the Mediterranean and Europe. With the cultic center gone, Jewish religion entered a new stage. The center of Jewish religious life was now the synagogue rather than the Temple; its leaders were the rabbis or "teachers" rather than the old priests and prophets. Rabbinic Judaism rejected the dualistic tendencies of the Apocalyptic writers and insisted upon the unity of the one, benevolent Lord. Evil results, the rabbis argued, from the imperfect state of the created world (metaphysical evil) and from human misuse of free will (moral evil), not from the machinations of a cosmic enemy. Most of the rabbis rejected the concept of a personified being leading the forces of evil and preferred to speak of the Devil only as a symbol of the tendency to evil within humans.

According to rabbinic teaching, two antagonistic spirits inhabit each individual: one a tendency to good (*yetser ha-tob*) and the other a tendency to evil (*yetser ha-ra*). The rabbis argued that the Lord had created both tendencies, but he gave humanity the Law so that we might overcome the evil yetser by following Torah. The Devil was perceived as a personification of the yetser ha-ra: Rabbi Simon ben Lakish wrote that "Satan and the angel of death are one." The rabbis discarded the tradition of the rebellion of the angels, since the angels have no evil yetser and cannot sin. Still, some of the old traditions persisted in the aggadah—moral stories, legends, and sermons—where the Devil, called Sammael more often than Satan, is a high angel who falls from grace, uses the serpent to tempt Adam and Eve, and acts as tempter, accuser, destroyer, and angel of death. Many Christian legends about demons have their origins in the aggadah. But even in the aggadah, Satan has no existence independent of the Lord, who uses him as a tester of hearts, an agent to report our sins on high, and an official in charge of punishing them.

The kabbalah, the literature of the Jewish magical and mystical movement that reached its height in the thirteenth century of the Christian era and remained popular into the eighteenth, paid the Devil much more attention than the rabbis did. Influenced by Greek philosophy, Gnosticism, and Christianity, the kabbalah taught that all things come forth from the divine being in a series of emanations, each inferior to the one preceding. Originally God was both good and evil: his right hand was love and mercy and his left hand wrath and destruction. The destructive aspect of the God's personality broke away from the good aspect and henceforth was known as Satan. Rabbi Isaac Luria offered the argument that God contracted into himself in order to make room for the Creation; therefore the created world suffers from incompleteness, absence of God, evil. A later interpretation of Luria's ideas says that God contains within himself a minute grain of evil called the "root of strict judgment." Jewish legends report details about Satan or Sammael: he has twelve wings; he is covered with eyes; he is hairy like a goat; he can shift his shape at will; he is a rebel angel whom humanity can defeat only by following Torah.

On the whole, the place of the Devil in Jewish thought after the Apocalyptic period was slight and, such as it was, largely derived from Christianity, whose concern with the Evil One was great from the outset.

Before A.D. 150 Christians were a small minority in the Mediterranean world, an environment still mostly pagan, although the Jews were a strong element in many Mediterranean cities. But hostility between Christians and Jews mounted after the fall of Jerusalem in 70, when the Sadducees, Zealots, and Essenes were defeated and the Pharisees emerged as the dominant faction among the Jews. The Pharisees, struggling to achieve Jewish unity and resentful of the Christians' failure to support the revolt against the Romans, excluded Christians from the synagogues.

As yet, Christianity possessed no body of defined doctrine. In the early years of the second century there was no canon of the New Testament, and a number of the books circulated as inspired were eventually excluded from Scripture when the canon was finally set at the end of the fourth century. Still, a set of attitudes and beliefs was being formed among the Christian writers who followed the apostles. The works of these writers, who are known as "the apostolic fathers," include "the Epistle of Barnabas" and the works of Clement of Rome, Ignatius of Antioch, Polycarp, and Papias. Clement, bishop of Rome, writing about 95, perceived the Devil as a distinct personality trying to split the Christian community by sowing temptation and dissension. Saint Ignatius, bishop of Antioch, who was to be martyred in 107, saw the Devil as "ruler of this age," whose power has recently been shaken by the Incarnation and will finally be shattered by the second coming of Christ. The new age will be characterized by a radical transformation of the very nature of the world and its inhabitants. In this new kingdom evil will have no place.

In the meantime, said Ignatius, the world is ruled by the evil archon, whose design is to thwart Christ's work of salvation by diverting the Christian people from pursuing the goal of the kingdom of God. The Devil pits himself personally against each Christian. Ignatius felt the evil prince working within him to lure him away from his steadfast faith and to persuade him to shirk martyrdom. "I long to suffer," he wrote, "but I do not know whether I am worthy. . . . I need the meekness in which the prince of this world is undone."

The image of martyrdom was never far from Ignatius' mind, and he viewed the world as a bloody arena in which Christ and his followers are locked in deadly combat with the Devil and his. The human race is divided between the children of light and the children of darkness. Those who are not members of Christ's body are limbs of the Devil's. In this war martyrdom, the witness a Christian bears to Jesus under persecution, is the most important weapon of the athletes of Christ against the servants of Satan. Persecution comes from the Devil, who is responsible for the hostility of both the Roman government and the Roman mob, but martyrdom itself is a gift of God, a sign of God's providence turning evil into good. As an ordinary athlete strives in the arena for a material victory, the athlete of Christ strives for a spiritual victory over Satan by preserving his faith to the death.

The Roman persecution of the Christians is a sign that the empire is the visible manifestation of the old age, the kingdom of Satan on earth. But the Devil's most dangerous followers are not the pagans, but Christians who disrupt the Christian community. The Devil encourages schismatics, who divide the community with their factionalism, and heretics, who divide it with false doctrines. A bishop himself, Ignatius argued that the bishops as successors of the apostles alone had the authority that could guarantee organizational stability and doctrinal orthodoxy. When the bishop is obeyed, tranquility reigns, and Satan is weakened, but anyone who disobeys the bishop is guilty of adoring the Devil.

The "Epistle of Barnabas," the work of an unknown author, was written about 118 in the Jewish-Christian community of Egypt. "Barnabas" wrote from the perspective of the Hellenistic, allegorized Jewish thought that the rabbis tended to reject. He was deeply infused with ethical dualism, particularly by the image of the "two roads," the road of light and the road of darkness. In the Old Testament, the Lord elected Israel from among the nations and elected from among the Israelites those who are faithful to Torah. Christianity broadened the saving choice of God from Israel to the human race as a whole, but Christianity continued to insist that God elected only those who were faithful to him. Since the center of salvation has shifted from Torah to Christ, Barnabas argued, the church, the community of people faithful to Jesus, replaces the saving remnant of Israel faithful to Torah.

For Barnabas, the kingdom of this world under Satan's rule is at war with the kingdom of heaven. Though weakened by the Incarnation, Satan retains his grip on the present age until the impending return of Christ. Until that moment, the angels and humans on the side of light are locked in a terrible struggle against the angels and humans on the side of darkness. The powers of darkness could attack an individual's body from without ("obsession") or from within ("possession"). But though obsession and possession might cause disease or madness, they could not corrupt the soul, because they occurred against the victims' free will. A more effective weapon of the Evil One was "oppression" or temptation, which assaults the will. Satan cannot force the will or compel anyone to sin, for the Holy Spirit is at work in our hearts protecting us. Anyone who yields to the temptations that "the Black One" introduces into the soul is cut off from Christ and places himself on the side of darkness. Barnabas made the explicit symbolic connection between evil, darkness, and blackness, symbolism that was to have a long and sinister history in Christian civilization.

Polycarp, who died at the hands of the pagans about 156, warned of the many plots that Satan hatches against the martyrs. The Devil incites the pagans to torture the Christians and at the same time creeps into the Christians' souls to tempt them to deny their faith. Heretics as well as apostates were linked with Satan. "Anyone who does not believe that

Jesus Christ is come in the flesh is an antichrist, and anyone who does not believe in the cross's testimony that Jesus really suffered and died is of the Devil." Polycarp distinguished sharply between the orthodox Christians, who were "the community of the first born of God," and the heretics, "the first born children of Satan." The opposition between the orthodox and the heretics—those who believed differently from the Christian community—was not a simple difference of opinion but part of the cosmic struggle between good and evil. Polycarp's two deepest fears were that the church would be undermined by persecution from without and that it would be torn apart by heresy from within. Heresy was the greater danger, for in these early stages Christianity had as yet no established creed or doctrine and the danger that the community would be fragmented and dissipated was real.

The unknown author of "The Shepherd of Hermas," the earliest Christian book of pastoral care, added to the image of the two roads that of the two cities, one the community of those serving the Lord, the other the community of those serving Satan. Corresponding to the two ways, the two kingdoms, the two cities, are two angels that struggle against each other in the human heart. Papias conflated the ancient story of the Watcher angels with another Jewish Apocalyptic tradition that held that God had appointed angels to govern the earth and its nations. Each nation had its ruling angel, but these angels had abused their power and fallen under the sway of the evil prince of this world, a circumstance that explains the warfare and persecutions of the nations. As yet, Christian thought remained largely figurative and mythical and deeply influenced by Apocalyptic speculation.

5   *Satan and Heresy*

In the mid-second century Christianity underwent a significant change. The mythical and intuitive thought that had prevailed among the apostolic fathers began to be accompanied by theology—analytical and logical reflection on revelation. The new writers, known as "apologetes," recognized that Christianity, which had to compete intellectually with both rabbinic thought and Greek philosophy, needed an intellectually coherent foundation. This meant that the borders between orthodoxy and heresy (and between good and evil) had to be more clearly drawn. Dissension within the Christian community was an increasing problem. Radical differences of opinion arose on a number of issues. When each issue was resolved, the winning side was considered orthodox and the losers heretics.

The most significant opposition to the emerging consensus of the fathers was Gnosticism. Modern scholars use the term "gnostic" in a variety of senses. "Gnosis" is usually defined as a general attitude appearing in late Hebrew thought and Christianity and deriving from Mazdaism, Platonism, and Mithraism. This general attitude gradually found expression in a movement, first among the Jews and Jewish Christians and later among the Greek Christians. This movement, in contrast to the general attitude called Gnosis, is generally known as Gnosticism. Gnostic thought among the early Jewish Christians was not far removed from the ethical dualism of the early fathers. Then, after about A.D. 150, Gnosticism became more mythologized, more Hellenized, and more radically dualistic. Some Christian writers had already perceived Gnosticism as a threat to Christian unity; now the fathers began to think of Gnosticism as a dangerous heresy, the work of the Evil One.

The conflict between the Gnostics and the fathers helped define the boundaries of the Christian tradition. Like any movement, Christianity was threatened by two opposite difficulties. If its boundaries were too narrowly defined, it risked becoming too rigid, too exclusive, so small and uninviting that it courted destruction. But if it defined its boundaries too widely, so that anyone might call himself a Christian while believing anything at all, it could face endless divisions and subdivisions or else eventually evaporate into meaningless platitudes. Instinctively, the community sought a middle road, opening itself to every nation and class, yet at the same time excluding those whose views were too different to be reconciled or accommodated within the growing consensus. Gradually the consensus excluded Gnosticism.

The orthodox tendency to draw boundaries worked against the Gnostics, but the weaknesses inherent in Gnosticism itself were the essential reason for its exclusion. The mythologies of Gnosticism became overburdened, complicated, unbelievable; its appeal was elitist, its organization incoherent; it split into a wide variety of sects with a fantastic diversity of myths and theologies. Though its influence continued to reappear sporadically for centuries, Gnosticism had become an intellectual dead end by the fourth century.

The central themes of Gnosticism nonetheless produced views on evil that are important both in themselves and in the responses they evoked from the orthodox. Gnosticism's appeal lay in its championship of radical dualist theodicy: God is not responsible for evil because evil arises from a malevolent principle independent of God. The Gnostics argued that each individual experiences a world that is alien, terrifying, filled with death, disease, wars, and enemies. This world is so riddled with evil that it must be only a shadow of something better and beyond. The Gnostics melded the Mazdaist view of a cosmic battle between spirits with the Orphic view of a struggle between the goodness of spirit and the evil of matter. The human body, material flesh, is a wretched prison constructed by Satan to incarcerate the soul. The good God would never have created such a gross world, so it must instead be the artifact of one or more blind and inferior spirits. The Gnostics called these evil spirits archons or eons, recalling the apostolic doctrine of the evil archon of this world, but with the great difference that the apostolics never even hinted that the cosmos could have been created by any spirit lesser than God.

Orthodox Christianity and Gnosticism both absorbed some elements of dualism, but Gnosticism was much closer to the dualist end of the spectrum than was Christianity. For Christians, the Devil had great power to obstruct the work of Christ, but he was always limited and held in check by God. God's providence turned every evil to good, for the cosmos he created is essentially good. The Gnostics too believed in the ultimate victory of good over evil, but their belief that the created cosmos is essentially evil gave the Devil far greater scope and power.

The Gnostics disagreed among themselves as to the nature of the evil creator of the cosmos. The most extreme claimed that two independent spiritual principles existed; the more moderate that the creator of this world was a subsidiary power, a creature whom God had created good but who had fallen into evil. This ignorant, blind, corrupt spirit was identified with the Devil. Because the Old Testament ascribed the creation of the material universe to God, and because the creator of the cosmos was actually Satan, it followed that the being that the Old Testament called God was really Satan. Accordingly the Gnostics rejected the Old Testament (or most of it) and condemned the Jews—and the Christians who believed in the Old Testament—for worshiping the Devil.

The Gnostic view of the human condition was dark: a human being is a spirit trapped in a gross body like a pearl buried in mud. Humankind is the microcosm: both the small world of humanity and the great world of the cosmos are battlegrounds in the war between the good spirit of light and the evil spirit of matter. Originally humans were created pure spirit by God, but the Evil One entrapped us in matter. It is our duty to liberate our spirits from this prison of flesh. We have no way of doing this by ourselves, but God empowers us to do so by sending us a savior, Christ, to teach us our true being, origin, and destiny. God salvages the sparks of light imprisoned in the flesh by teaching us to overcome the forces that pull us down toward sensuality and sin. Satan constantly struggles in each individual for the opposite purpose, tempting us to pursue gross material pleasures instead of our true spiritual heritage.

One of the leading Gnostics of the second century, Marcion, put forward a typical Gnostic theodicy. Marcion perceived a shocking contrast between the harsh God of the Old Testament and the loving God of the New. They could not, he thought, be one and the same deity. The God who tempted people to sin and then punished them for what he tempted them to do, the God who hardened hearts and laid waste to lands, could not be the merciful Lord revealed by Christ. Deeply disturbed by this discrepancy, Marcion inquired how God can be all-good and all-powerful in a world in which evil is manifest. His answer was that God is all-good but not all-powerful. The good God of the Gospel is

Satan, at Christ's left, tries to persuade Jesus to hurl himself down from the pinnacle of the Temple, while angels hover above and a multitude watch. Illumination, Book of Kells, c. A.D. 790. Courtesy Board of Trinity College, Dublin.

limited in his power by the existence and activities of the God of Law, who is the Prince of Darkness.

The God of Law is just, but he is also harsh and warlike, coldly hewing to the letter of a stern law. This is the God of the Old Testament, the creator of the corrupt, material world, the "author of evils." On the other side, the good God is kind and warmly merciful. Before the mission of Christ this God was wholly unknown to us and even now remains hidden from our understanding. The wonder of Christ is that for the first time he gave us a glimpse of this true, hidden God. The true God is the father of Jesus, whom he sent to us for the purpose of revealing the hidden truth about the cosmos as opposed to the lies spread by the Evil One. Though each of the two gods is an independent principle, the evil god is (for unexplained reasons) weaker and will eventually perish. His days have been numbered by Christ, and in the end he will be defeated by the good God and will disappear along with the material world he has created. Only spirit will remain, and with it love and mercy.

In the meantime, the material world and the human body in particular imprison, defile, and corrupt our spirits. The true God shuns and despises matter, so it is inconceivable that his Son would have taken on this gross flesh. Christ's body was an illusion, a mere appearance that he adopted so as to be able to communicate with us in a way that we could understand. Since Christ had no body, he did not die on the cross and did not redeem us by his Passion. Rather, his mission was to reveal the gnosis, the saving knowledge that teaches us to liberate our spirits from our bodies.

It is unclear whether Marcion regarded Satan as the evil god himself or merely as a creature of the evil god, a position that some other Gnostics took. Here lies one of the numerous muddles of Gnostic mythology, for if the Devil has a superior in evil, then that superior must be the real Devil. The only useful definition of the Devil is "chief of the forces of evil." Marcion's evil creator god, whatever Marcion chose to call him, is the true Devil.

The unnecessary complications of Gnosticism multiplied with Valentine, a second-century Egyptian Gnostic. Valentine and his disciple Ptolemy constructed a cluttered mythology in which the God, the "primal being," emanates eight "higher eons" who in turn emanate twenty-two lower eons, all the eons together forming the "pleroma," the fullness of the divine nature. The Valentinians thus explained evil by positing not two separate principles but rather a gradual degradation of the one principle down through the series of emanations. Although each of the thirty emanations of the pleroma is part of the divine, each successive one is farther removed from its source and therefore less perfect. Such imperfection produces ignorance, error, and fear. The lowest of the thirty emanations, Sophia, is most deficient because farthest from perfect Being, and the void of her deficiency engenders pride (hubris). The pleroma rejects her pride, thrusting it out into the void, where it becomes a being called Achamoth, who wanders miserably in the emptiness. Evil thus has two sources: a metaphysical evil built into the degradation of the emanations, and a moral evil resulting from the sinful choice made by the lowest emanation.

Achamoth now produces the Old Testament God, who creates the cosmos out of soul, mind, and matter. Humans are a mixture of these elements. Three classes of people exist, each dominated by one of the three elements: those dominated by flesh and incapable of being saved; those dominated by mind, who can be saved only with difficulty; and those in whom soul dominates and who attain salvation by responding to the true knowledge (gnosis) given them by Christ.

Because the creator God is not the true God at all, but a subsidiary and corrupt being, in the Valentinian view the revolt of Adam and Eve takes on a reverse moral meaning. Rebellion against the Creator was a virtue, and the serpent was a benefactor teaching humanity a certain degree of gnosis: the principles of good and evil that the evil creator had been trying to keep hidden. The work of the serpent, therefore, was expanded and fulfilled later by Christ. In most Gnostic mythologies, however, the serpent of Eden remained negative and was identified with the Devil. The Valentinians and other Gnostics introduced all these complexities in order to preserve the goodness of God by buffering him from this gross world by a thick cloud of emanations. But emanationism fails to relieve God of responsibility for evil, for God's choice to emanate and dissipate himself entails the choice to permit the ignorance and evil that inevitably result from the emanations.

Before the canon of the New Testament was finally set in the fourth century, a number of books with a claim to inspiration enjoyed wide circulation. Those that were eventually excluded from the canon are known as the Christian Apocrypha. Many of these books were Gnostic; others occupied the broad borderland between orthodoxy and heresy. Many legends and popular traditions of Christianity had their origins in such Apocryphal books as *The Ascension of Isaiah* and *The Acts of Peter*. *The Ascension of Isaiah*, for example, recounts a story, popular for centuries, in which the Israelite king Manasseh abandoned God and worshiped Beliar, the prince of unrighteousness who rules this world. Beliar urges Manasseh to witchcraft, magic, divination, adultery, and persecution of the just, as well as to the fundamental sin of forsaking the true God. Beliar is furious at the prophet Isaiah for having foretold the coming of the Messiah, but the Devil cannot prevent the triumph of the Lord, who "will come with his angels . . . and will drag Beliar with his hosts into Gehenna."

Against heretical books and heretical ideas the Christian community gradually constructed an intellectual defense, drawing ever clearer borders beyond which ideas could no longer be considered Christian. Justin Martyr (c. 100–165), one of the first Christian theologians, was the first to discuss the problem of evil in rational, theological terms. For Justin, Christ and the Christian community were at war with the evil angels led by Satan. Angels live in heaven or in the air. The "geographical" or cosmographical location of the angels was an important part of the fathers' view of the world, a view they shared with other Hellenistic philosophers.

First of all, theirs was a true and complete cosmology, embracing in one unified system a physical, moral, and spiritual cosmos. Second, it was both physically and spiritually hierarchical. At the center of the cosmos is the heavy, material earth, farthest removed from God (and sometimes, though by no means certainly at this period, thought to enclose hell). As we look up from the earth we look up toward heaven, which is both physically and spiritually the loftiest and farthest removed from earth. Between earth and heaven are a number of spheres (see Figure 1). Just above the earth is the air. Here dwell the more material angels, whom most of the fathers identified with the fallen angels. Above the air is the sphere of the moon. Beyond the sphere of the moon, space is penetrated by a finer medium, the ether. Here dwell the good angels, finer, higher, more ethereal. Past the sphere of the moon are the spheres of the planets—Mercury, Venus, the Sun, Mars, Jupiter, and Saturn—and past the planets the sphere of the fixed stars. Each sphere is higher, closer to God, less material, more spiritual, good, and beautiful. The glory of the fixed stars reflects that of heaven. Beyond the stars is the primum mobile, the sphere that moves the entire universe, and beyond that final sphere, beyond all, is the unimaginable purity, beauty, and light of God's heaven. In such a world, the force of evil weighs us down, like gravitation, toward the heavy center and away from that lightness and light that opens up into heavenly glory.

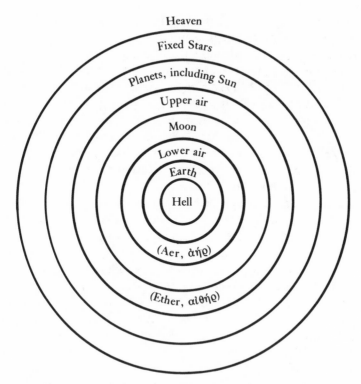

Figure 1. Cosmological conceptions of the early fathers

    Justin organized evil spiritual powers into three categories. First was the Devil, an angel of great power created by God. He fell from grace by sinning, either at the creation of the cosmos or at the moment he determined to corrupt Adam and Eve. Taking the Book of Revelation's identification of Satan with a serpent or dragon to refer to the serpent of Genesis rather than to the monsters Leviathan and Rahab, Justin established the connection between the Devil and the serpent of Eden forever after. The second category consisted of the other fallen angels, who did not sin until the time of Noah, when they lustfully fathered children on human women. The third consisted of the demons, the children of this illicit union. Justin's threefold division between Devil, fallen angels, and demons was later abandoned by tradition, along with the whole story of the Watcher angels. After the fifth century, the fallen angels and demons were united in one and the same category. Satan, a fallen angel himself, was only partly absorbed into that category, for his intrinsic function kept him aloof. It was he, not the lesser angels who followed him, who was solely responsible for introducing evil into the cosmos.

Justin believed that God punished humanity for the original sin of Adam and Eve by giving the Devil temporary power over the cosmos. The primary function of Christ is to destroy Satan's power over us. This view, adopted by most of the fathers, posed a perennial problem for Christians. Suppose that original sin plunged us into Satan's power and that Christ's sacrifice saved us from that power. How is it that we do not observe the collapse of that power at the time of the Incarnation or at least immediately afterward? The earliest Christians presumed that Christ would come again soon, but as the second coming delayed, the question became more acute. Justin groped toward an answer. The Devil held full power over the world from the time of Adam to the time of Christ. Christ undermined the old age, the kingdom of Satan, through his Incarnation and Passion, but he will not complete its destruction until the second coming. The new age, the kingdom of God, likewise began to emerge with the Incarnation but would not be complete until the second coming. Justin did not know why God allowed the process to take so long, but he suggested that the final destruction of Satan's kingdom is being postponed until enough Christians die in the faith to fill up the heavenly ranks left vacant by the fallen angels.

It is also postponed by Satan's determination to preserve his own power as long as possible. From the moment of Christ's Passion Satan knew that his doom was sure, but he continues to strive viciously and vainly against his fate by undermining the Christian community. His efforts are unremitting, for he is incapable of repentance. His ultimate punishment is as certain as his ultimate defeat. He and his angels have already been cast down from heaven, but at present they still roam the world and will do so until their final fall at the end of time. Then they will be consumed by fire and will perish forever. Justin's view that the Devil's punishment was reserved till the end of time was followed by some of the fathers, but the opposing view that the evil angels were punished from the moment of their sin eventually prevailed. The prevailing doctrine left an odd contradiction, for it implied that the Devil was at the same time being punished in hell *and* roaming the world seeking the ruin and destruction of souls. Later efforts to resolve the contradiction produced some colorful passages in literature.

At the time of the Incarnation, Justin said, the Devil tempted Christ but failed to corrupt him, so the Evil One's attentions are now focused on the Christian community. The Devil plays upon our weaknesses, our irrationality, and our attachments to worldly pleasures and comforts. One of his favorite ploys is to deter the Gentiles from accepting salvation by persuading them that demons are gods. The demons dwelt in the pagan idols and consumed the sacrifices offered in temples. The pagan gods were not illusions but actual demons, a fact that explains the gods' notorious cruel, fickle, and adulterous behavior. Sacrifice to an idol was not silly but sinful, an act of worship of the Devil, a blasphemy against Christ, a deed worthy of damnation.

The Devil stimulates dreams and visions to confuse and corrupt us. Demons promote magic, false doctrines, unjust laws, and above all persecution. Still, Christians are to take no violent action in defending themselves against the Romans, for violence is moral capitulation to the Devil. Satan loves war and violence, and even violence against persecutors, even warfare against the kingdom of Satan, is Satan's own work. Justin proved true to his ideals by dying a martyr himself.

Toward the end of the second century, two theologians brought concern for morality, sin, and atonement to the forefront of discussions about evil: Irenaeus and Tertullian. Irenaeus (c. 140–202) firmly rejected the Gnostic contention that the world was the product of an evil creator. Rather, the creator was the Logos, the "Word" of the good God. The angels are a part of the cosmos that God has created; all that God creates is good; the Devil was therefore created good. The Devil sinned of his own free will out of envy of God, wishing to be adored like his maker, and out of envy of the happiness of humanity. This scenario points up the early Christian difficulty with the chronology of Satan's fall. Did he sin through envy of God and enter Eden with his heart already corrupted, or did he sin at the moment he tempted Adam and Eve? Irenaeus blurred the two, as did many of the other early fathers. The question was not resolved until the time of John Cassian (360–435), who wrote that all Christians now agreed that Satan had fallen from pride and envy of God and that when Adam was created the Devil merely extended his earlier hatred of God to hatred of humanity as well, thus compounding his sin.

Irenaeus, always more interested in human responsibility than in demons, dwelt upon the story of Eden. God created Adam and Eve good and placed them in Paradise to live happily in close relationship with him. But Satan, envious of God's favors to them and knowing their weakness, entered the Garden. Using the serpent as his tool, he tempted them to sin, approaching Eve first as the weaker of the two (Gen. 3.1–6). God had created the first parents with complete free will; they were not forced to obey him; neither could they be compelled to sin. Had the

In *The Temptation of Christ*, the artist revived the early medieval tradition of portraying the Devil in semihuman rather than bestial form. Meister of Schloss Lichtenstein, oil on canvas, fifteenth century. Courtesy Oesterreichische Galerie, Vienna.

Devil not existed, they would still have had the freedom to choose evil. The Devil is thus not necessary to explain the origins of human sin. Humanity is responsible for its own predicament. Irenaeus went further and said that if one looks to place responsibility on someone other than humanity, God must himself bear some of the blame, for God permitted the Devil to tempt Adam and Eve, and he could have made the first parents stronger against temptation.

The free choice of Adam and Eve to sin erased the freedom of humanity and delivered it into bondage to Satan and to death. Since we freely delivered ourselves into Satan's power, God justly and rightly allows the Prince of Darkness to hold us until we are redeemed. In strict justice, God could have left us in Satan's grasp forever, but in his mercy he sent his Son to save us. It was Christ's suffering, his Passion, that broke our chains. The Passion began with Satan's temptation of Christ, the second Adam, in the desert. This temptation was a recapitulation of that of the first Adam, except that this time the Devil failed. The Passion culminated in the trial, condemnation, and crucifixion of Jesus.

Christian tradition has interpreted the saving work of the Passion in four different ways. According to the first interpretation, human nature is sanctified, dignified, transformed, and saved by the very act of Christ's becoming man. According to the second, "sacrifice theory," Jesus, both man and God, offered himself as a sacrifice to his Father on behalf of humanity. The third interpretation, put forward later, was that the Passion was a sheer act of love, God's choice to share human suffering and to take all the pain of the world onto himself. The fourth interpretation, "ransom theory," emphasized the role of the Devil. Its first strong proponent was Irenaeus. According to ransom theory, Satan legally and justly held us in his grip. In order to liberate us, God needed to pay him a ransom. Only God could pay the price, because only God could freely choose to pay it. Under the Devil's power, humans had neither the freedom to choose nor the means to pay. Thus God handed Jesus over to the Evil One in order to obtain the release of imprisoned humanity. The Devil eagerly accepted the ransom, but when he did so he overstepped the boundaries of justice, for Jesus, being sinless, could not justly be held. By breaking the rules of justice, the Devil lost his rights and could no longer hold either Jesus or the human race.

Ultimately ransom theory had its roots in the apostolic emphasis upon the cosmic battle between God and Satan. Whereas sacrifice theory places the emphasis upon humanity's relationship with God, ransom theory removes humanity from center stage and sets the warfare between the two great supernatural powers in its place. Some fathers preferred sacrifice theory; others followed Irenaeus in preferring ransom. Their choice depended upon whether they emphasized theodicy or atonement in dealing with the problem of evil.

Rational theodicy is a philosophical effort to reconcile the existence of God with that of evil. The theology of atonement, on the other hand, emphasizing God's destruction of evil through the triumph of Christ, depended on faith and could convince only believers. The fathers often combined the approaches, but essentially they do not fit together. Theodicy is monistic in tendency, explaining evil as a necessary part of God's overall cosmic plan; atonement tends toward dualism, recognizing the existence of an irreconcilable evil so radical that God himself must die in order to draw its sting. Theodicy emphasized God's sovereignty, atonement God's struggle against evil. The tension between theodicy and atonement is reflected in the tension between sacrifice and ransom. Those fathers more inclined to theodicy tended toward sacrifice theory because it emphasizes the basic goodness of God's cosmos. The cosmos has been distorted by sin, but it can be straightened out by reconciliation between God and the human race. Evil in this view is less radical, less an ultimate force in opposition to God, so the Devil plays little role in this scheme. On the other hand, those fathers inclined to atonement tended toward ransom theory and saw the power of God pitted against the power of Satan in a cosmic battle so dire that God triumphed only at the cost of offering his only Son to the Prince of Darkness.

Irenaeus observed that even after the Incarnation the Devil is still exerting himself vigorously to thwart salvation by encouraging paganism, idolatry, sorcery, blasphemy, apostasy, and heresy. Heretics and other unbelievers are soldiers of Satan's army in his war against Christ. This doctrine had a baleful effect, for it suggested that Christians have not only the right but the duty to fight against unbelievers, and the basis was laid for future holy wars and persecutions. The armies of Satan continue their vain warfare against the Christian community, and as the endtime approaches they will make one last concerted attack led by the Antichrist, an apostate, murderer, and robber who will have "all the Devil's power" behind him. Sinners and unbelievers will flock to Antichrist's banner, but he will be defeated, and the world will come to an end. The Antichrist is a human being, not a fallen angel, but his function at the end of the world is the same as Satan's: both represent the last, desperate effort of the powers of evil to block God's saving plan.

The diabology of Tertullian was as influential as that of Irenaeus.

Born about 170 into a wealthy literary family, Tertullian converted to Christianity in his twenties, joined the ascetic Montanist sect, and died about 220. The first great Latin theologian, Tertullian helped establish Latin theological vocabulary. The old strain of Jewish ethical dualism was strong in his thought, and he insisted that a disciplined moral life was part of the campaign against the Devil, whereas an immoral, worldly life was service to Satan. This emphasis on morality led Tertullian to argue that evil is not the work of God or of an evil principle, but of sin and sin alone. His refutation of Gnostic dualism was direct and compelling. An evil principle separate from God is impossible, for its existence would be tantamount to that of two gods. God is by definition an all-powerful being. Two all-powerful gods cannot exist. The principle that the simplest explanation fitting the facts is the best one also excludes dualism, for one should never assume two entities when one will do. Further, if the cosmos were in strict balance between two equal and opposite forces we would observe no change, but we observe that change occurs. On the other hand, if the slightest imbalance existed between the two forces they would not be equal; one would have superiority, however slight. But any superiority in a struggle between two cosmic principles would bring immediate victory to one, for if in eternity a scale is tipped to one side it is tipped forever. The victory of the one force over the other would be eternal, and we would observe no struggle between good and evil in the world. The two opposing forces could not wax and wane with time, for time does not exist in eternity. In this material world, where time does exist, whichever principle was victorious in eternity would not allow the other principle even a moment to work its schemes. Finally, if absolute Being exists, it must be one; the alternative to Being is not another being, but only nonbeing. Dualism is a logically impossible response to the problem of evil.

Having knocked down the dualists' house, Tertullian was then obliged to defend his own. If evil comes neither from God nor from an independent principle, where does it come from? From two sources, Tertullian replied, the sin of angels and the sin of humans. God grants both angels and humans freedom, because freedom is the greatest good. But we use this freedom to bring about evil. The essence of sin is concern with the limited goods of this world rather than the infinite good of God. The world in itself is created good, but inherent in it is the danger of worldliness, the tendency to prefer its limited pleasures to infinite joy. "The world comes from God, but worldliness comes from the Devil." Creation is good, but our attachment to worldly goods is sinful.

The existence of evil in the world is so obvious, Tertullian said, that people can grasp the existence of the Devil by direct experience. The mind intuits the Devil's existence from its experience of evil, just as it intuits the existence of God directly by virtue of its experience of beauty and goodness. "We learn and understand the Lord and his rival, the Creator and the Destroyer, at one and the same time."

Tertullian helped form the Christian view that the reason God gave angels and humans freedom to sin was that a world without free will would be a world of mere puppets. God created the world in order to extend or expand the total sum of goodness, and goodness could be increased only by his making creatures free to choose the good freely. God could not provide thus for good without allowing also for evil, since true free will entails the real possibility of choosing evil.

Before his fall, Satan had been the foremost angel. Tertullian's view on this subject was generally but not universally accepted, since some fathers argued (illogically) that only the lower angels were subject to sin. Tertullian differed from most of the fathers in considering angels inferior to humans on the grounds that the Bible specifies humans, not angels, as being made in God's image; most of the fathers deemed angels ontologically superior to humans. Tertullian believed that angels had bodies, albeit of a substance so marvelously tenuous and refined as to be imperceptible to our senses. They had the power, however, to assume any form they chose and to shift their shapes at will. Satan's ability to transform himself into an apparent angel of light accounts for his persuasiveness in swaying people to idolatry and heresy.

The essence of the evil of idolatry and heresy is that they are lies. Whatever God creates good, the Devil seeks to pervert, thus distorting God's beautiful creation. As the lie is the worst of sins, so the Devil is the incarnation of the Lie itself, the mocking ape of God. The lie creeps into ordinary life every day and everywhere, Tertullian warned. Satan rules astrology, magic, horseraces, bath houses, taverns, and theaters. The theater is Satan's special place of congregation. "Whoever enters into communion with the Devil by going to shows separates himself from the Lord." Shows are idolatrous; they provoke passions that overwhelm our reason; worst of all, they are empty lies, for an actor pretends to be something he is not. The same applied to women's makeup: it is a lie for a woman to make herself up to look different from what she is, a blasphemy to try to improve on God's handiwork.

Satan, Tertullian believed, uses a lethal combination of lies and fear to urge us to such sins, as well as to anger, lust, avarice, and all the other

Demons torment sinners according to their vices, here adultery and lust. Fresco by Taddeo di Bartolo (1362–1422) at San Gimignano, Italy. Courtesy Soprintendenza alle Gallerie e Opere d'Arte, Siena.

vices. He is also the cause, with God's permission, of natural ills such as disease, drought, famine, evil dreams, and death itself. Some of these disasters are sent by Satan under God's command to punish us for our sins. Thus God permits Satan two functions: he allows him to tempt us and then uses him as a tool to punish us. Satan has his own motives in doing us harm, but he does not seem to grasp that his every act is turned to good by Providence.

Against the constant assaults of the Evil One the Christian has only one protection: Jesus Christ. As God had cast the Devil down from heaven at the time of his first rebellion, so Christ's Passion sends Satan sprawling a second time. A third, final punishment awaits him at the end of time.

Christians can use the name of the Christ and the sign of the cross to drive demons away, but it is baptism that assures us Christ's protection, Tertullian emphasized, for baptism makes us members of Christ's body. "If the Son of God has appeared . . . to destroy the works if the Devil, he has destroyed them by delivering the soul through baptism." Baptism recapitulates God's miracle for Moses at the parting of the Red Sea. Believers pass through the dangerous waters of this world by means of the grace of baptism while the Devil drowns like Pharaoh in the flood. "When we have entered the water" of baptism, "we confess our faith according to the words of divine law, and we declare that we have renounced the Devil, his pomps, and his angels." A "pomp" was originally a pagan procession in honor of a deity. "Here is what the pomps of the Devil are," Tertullian explained: "worldly dignities, honors, solemnities, and, at the heart of them all, idolatry. Shows, luxuries, and all the vanities of this world are rooted in idolatry, the veneration of the works of Satan instead of the works of the Lord." If one's ultimate concern is wealth or some other worldly value, one is an idolater, worshiping a worldly thing in the place of the Lord.

Tertullian helped to standardize baptismal procedures. Until about 200, baptism was often preceded by a separate rite of exorcism, but beginning about that time, the exorcism and formal renunciation of Satan were incorporated into the baptismal rite. The Christian's confrontation with the Devil at baptism had three elements: (1) the expulsion of demons from the candidate by exorcism; (2) the candidate's voluntary renunciation of the Devil; (3) measures against future demonic assaults on the new Christian. The exorcism itself had two dimensions: the exorcism of the water and oil used at baptism, and the exorcism of the candidate himself. The exorcism of the candidate became standard practice, although it carried the dubious theological implication that the candidate was not only subject to Satan through original sin but was also actually possessed by him. The voluntary renunciation of Satan became the core of the baptismal rite, symbolizing the candidate's transition from the army of Satan to that of Christ. The oldest known formula is: "I renounce you, Satan, and your angels, and your vanities ["pomps"]. In most rites, the renunciation was followed by the recitation of a statement of faith, making the conversion from Satan to Christ sharp and clear.

The Alexandrian fathers Clement and Origen constructed a sophisticated and detailed Christian diabology with the help of ideas drawn from Stoicism and Platonism. So open were they to Platonic thought in particular that third-century Christian diabology cannot be understood without reference to Neoplatonist philosophy.

For the Neoplatonists, whose views were soon to be clearly formulated by Plotinus (205–270), the principle of the cosmos was the One. The One is perfect, and it comprises all that is. Yet we perceive multiplicity in the universe. How is this? The One, desiring a cosmos full of forms, emanates Being. Being in turn emanates *nous*, "mind," which contains all the ideas that are the forms, the patterns, on the model of which the universe will be constructed. These emanations are good, because the One produced them, and because they complete the world of forms that the One desired. In no sense are these emanations evil; yet of logical necessity nous is less perfect than the Being that emanates it. Nous produces *psyche*, the world soul, which is nous thinking itself (like the Christian Trinity in which the Son is the Father's thought of himself). Psyche emanates the physical universe by impressing the ideas and forms upon prime matter. The material world is an emanation ultimately proceeding from the One and therefore ultimately good.

But here Neoplatonism found itself in a contradiction, for matter is also evil. Only the One is infinitely perfect and good, and each succeeding emanation declines a degree further from that good. The last and least emanation is matter, which is farthest from the One and least like the One. Since matter is at the farthest possible remove from the good, it may be said that matter lacks all goodness. Sense objects are at least remotely related to the higher world because they at least possess forms, but unformed matter is total deficiency, total privation, total nonbeing, total nongood. The word for total lack of good is evil. And Plotinus goes further. Not only is matter evil because it is totally devoid of good; it acts positively for evil in that it impedes the design of the One and lures the individual soul into error.

Thus the Neoplatonist view of matter is like one of those optical illusions that shifts its shape as you look at it. On the one hand Plotinus is a monist, insisting that even the lowest emanation of the One, no matter how deprived of Being, still retained at least an infinitesimal element of being and goodness. On the other hand he is close to being a dualist in perceiving in matter something opposed to the One and therefore evil.

A human being, like every other object, is an emanation of psyche. But there are two elements in each individual: the soul, which is spirit and relatively close to psyche, and the body, which is matter, remote from psyche and tending to evil. The body acts as a drag upon the soul, weighing it down and holding it back from its search for union with the spiritual realm. Two chief sources of evil thus exist in the world. One is matter itself, whose evil lies in its lack of good. The other is the wrong choice of the human soul, benighted and corrupted by its union with the body. The privation inherent in matter explains natural ills such as earthquakes and diseases; human blindness explains moral evils such as murder and war.

The Neoplatonist cosmology is hierarchical, with a spectrum stretching down from the greatest to the least, with individual beings in the universe fitting into the scale at different points. This pattern of a great chain of being dominated Western thought through Clement and Origen and Augustine and Aquinas down to Charles Darwin. Its hierarchical assumptions penetrated every aspect of thought from religion through law and politics to economics. But in the great chain described by Plotinus lurked a contradiction that haunted Christian theology for centuries. The contradiction arose from the effort to combine two incompatible scales of value: the ontological and the moral.

The first scale is ontological, based on degrees of being or reality. Here the One is most real and matter least real:

The One = Perfection = Most Ideal or Spiritual = Infinite Reality
Being
Nous
Psyche
The Material Universe
    Humans
    Animals
    Plants
    Inanimate Objects
Unformed Matter = Nonbeing = Least Real = Infinite Privation

The higher a being, the more it partakes of spirit and the closer to perfection it is. The lower a being, the more it is material, deprived of spirit, and closer to nonbeing. Beings higher on the scale are more real, beings lower on the scale less real. Matter, at the very bottom, is so unreal that it totters on the verge of complete nothingness. In the ontological scale, evil is privation, lack of good, and it "exists" only in the sense of lacking true existence, like holes in a Swiss cheese. The scale proceeds downward from an infinite score at the top to a score of zero at the bottom.

The second scale is calibrated not by ontology but by moral value:

> The One = Perfection = Infinite Good
> Being
> Nous
> Psyche
> The material Universe
> > Humans
> > Animals
> > Plants
> > Inanimate Objects
> Unformed Matter = Total Imperfection = Infinite Evil

Here the value assigned at the top of the scale is infinite good rather than infinite reality. Each descending step is more evil, until the bottom of the scale is totally evil. In this scale it is possible to conceive of a principle of evil, the utter negative of unformed matter resisting the formative power of the good. The two scales, though similar, are logically distinct, but the distinction was unclear to the Neoplatonists. For them, Being = Good and Nonbeing = Evil.

Clement of Alexandria (c. 150–210) attempted a Christian explanation of evil incorporating both scales. God exists absolutely; his being is total and perfect, and it is totally and perfectly good. Though complete in himself, God wishes to share his goodness and extend it to other beings, so he creates the cosmos. Since God alone is perfect, whatever he creates must necessarily be less real and less good than himself. The created world is real, but not wholly real; it is good, but not wholly good. The cosmos is only a deficient copy of true reality.

Not everything is equally deficient. A vast variety of forms compose the cosmos, and the differences among these forms make it inevitable that some are more deficient than others. Below God at the top of the scale are the angels, in turn divided hierarchically among themselves, the greatest angels being the most real, the most good, the closest to God. Below angels come humans, then animals, plants, stones, and so on down to primal, unformed matter, which is least real, least good, least spiritual, most deprived of being, and hence most evil. This is a form of the metaphysical theory that any created cosmos is necessarily less perfect than its creator.

This theory combined the two incompatible scales of reality and goodness, confusing ontological and moral terms. A man is ontologically higher than a cow. Then which is "better," a healthy, productive cow, or a degenerate human sadist? A genius is ontologically higher than a retarded person. Then which is "better," a kind retarded person or a cruel genius? The questions appear absurd because they *are* absurd: the ontological and the moral cannot fit into the same scale. The confusion touches diabology directly. The Devil, being one of the angels, is ontologically very high on the scale, yet morally he is the lowest and most debased of all beings. Ontologically, unformed matter is farthest from God; morally the Devil is farthest; yet any identification between the Devil and unformed matter is both tenuous and illogical.

An even more basic confusion relates to the nature of being and nonbeing. By equating evil with nonbeing, Clement seemed to be saying that evil does not exist. But he was aware of rape, murder, torture, and war. What he meant was that evil does not share in God's being, which is absolute reality and absolute good. Thus evil cannot be said to *be*. It is merely *absence* of good, just as the holes in the cheese are mere absence of cheese. Yet at the same time evil exercises real power, just as cold, which is merely absence of heat, can kill.

The Devil ruled the world unchecked until the Incarnation, when Christ broke the bonds that held us in slavery. Clement integrated Christ's descent into hell into the act of atonement. The Passion consisted of the whole course of Christ's agony from the Garden of Gethsemani to the moment of resurrection. Hints of the descent into hell appear in the New Testament, but its meaning was left ill defined. By the second century, the belief had become widely accepted as the explanation of what Christ was doing between his crucifixion on Friday afternoon and his resurrection on Sunday morning. By dying, Christ meant death to die, and he went to seek out his enemies Death and the Devil in the underworld where they dwelt.

The descent into hell became a vehicle for a theology that embraced both justice and mercy. Since God had delayed the Incarnation for centuries after the original sin, millions of humans might have been deprived of the opportunity for salvation solely because they happened to have lived and died before Christ came: The idea of such injustice seemed scandalous, and the Christian community sought a way to extend salvation to the dead. If during his descent to the prison house of death Christ preached to those who had died previously, then the effects of atonement could be felt by all.

The point of discussion in Clement's time was the question of whom Christ favored with this preaching and whom he released from hell. Three general answers were possible: (1) he preached to the people of the Old Testament, the prophets, the patriarchs, and all the Jews who had been faithful to the covenant; (2) he preached to all the righteous dead, both Jews and Gentiles; (3) he preached to all the dead without exception. Tradition never resolved the question, but Clement, with his cosmopolitan understanding of Greek culture, opted for the salvation of all the just, Gentile as well as Jew.

As legend began to diverge from theology, Hell and Death were often personified. Tertullian himself introduced the vivid image of Christ breaking the bolts and smashing down the doors of hell. In the early third century, the anonymous author of the visionary book called "The Teachings of Silvanus" described an elaborate story: Christ descends to the underworld, but Hell, fearing the loss of his prisoners, bars his way. Christ smashes the bronze bars and iron bolts of Hell's gate, and when Hell attempts to bind him in chains, the Savior bursts his bonds. Finding Hell and Death arrayed with the Devil against him, he "breaks Hell's bow" to show that the three evil powers are forever vanquished. By the fourth century the myth was frequently expressed in a dramatic dialogue between Christ and the powers of darkness, and in the sixth-century apocryphal "Gospel of Nicodemus" that form was firmly established.

In "Nicodemus," Satan or Beelzebub informs Hell that he has instigated the Savior's crucifixion, that Christ is now Death's prisoner, and that the evil powers need to keep watch to ensure that he does not escape. Hell is skeptical of their ability to hold the divine Lord in their grasp, but Satan sneers at his cowardice. Hell whines that if Christ could free Lazarus from Death's shadow he might be able to rob him of all his precious prey. Satan demands that Hell help him resist Jesus, but Hell sulkily tells him to go stop the Savior if he can. Hell bars his massive doors, but in one shattering moment of triumphant glory Christ speaks but a word and they crumble, letting light pierce the ancient dark. Christ orders angels to bind Satan and turns him over to Hell to hold until the second coming. Hell, Satan's erstwhile ally, has now become his warden.

Clement suspected that in time even Satan might be saved. He admitted that the Evil One had persisted in his sin from the beginning, but a number of considerations urged Clement toward universalism—the idea that the fullness of time would bring salvation to all without exception. First, the limitless nature of God's mercy seemed to call for the ultimate salvation of all free and intelligent beings. Second, the indelibility of free will suggested that the Devil might retain the capacity to repent at any time. Third, Clement's theory of being called for the ultimate fulfillment of potential goodness on the part of every creature. Fourth, Christ at his second coming would wish to extend the good news of his salvation to all. Clement left the development of this universalist thesis to his fellow Alexandrian, Origen.

Origen (c. 185–254), the most inventive diabologist in the whole Christian tradition, declared that "no one will be able to know the origin of evils who has not grasped the truth about the so-called Devil and his angels, and who he was [before] he became the Devil, and how he became" the Devil. The Devil is the source of all evil, yet all things come from God. How can these statements be reconciled? God created the cosmos, said Origen, in order to add to the sum total of goodness. Since moral goodness requires freedom of choice, God created beings with true freedom. Without them the world would be incapable of good and therefore pointless. Such freedom entails the ability to do evil. If any free being were consistently compelled to do good rather than evil, its free-dom—the purpose of its existence—would be negated. Truly free crea-tures will naturally choose evil on some occasions. Therefore moral evil is entailed in creation. Origen's argument was the first explicit statement of what is known as the "free-will defense" of God's goodness. God could not, so the argument goes, create a world in which real good exists without creating one in which real evil also exists.

According to Origen, God first created a number of intelligent beings, a number that remains forever fixed. These intelligences were all created both equal and free. Using the freedom that God willed for them, they all chose to depart from the divine unity. The intelligences thus departed from perfection, but in different degrees, so that each sank as far away from God as it chose. Those who sank least remained in the ethereal realms near heaven and possessed purely ethereal bodies; those who sank further fell into the lower air and acquired thicker material bodies of air. These ethereal and aerial beings, called angels, remained fine intel-ligences.

Other intelligences sank as far down as the earth, where they acquired gross material bodies and became human. Still others fell all the way to the underworld and became demons. Thus for Origen the fall was not a fall of angels who were plunged into hell but rather a fall of pristine intelligences into three categories: angels, humans, and demons. Further, the fall was a diversification of being rather than a moral lapse.

Serious difficulties mar this theory. Scripture and tradition caused Origen to supplement the diversification of being with a moral choice of evil by which some of the intelligences who became angels later sinned and were demoted, some to the status of humans, others to that of demons. This confusion of the ontological and moral scales hopelessly undermined the coherence of Origen's scheme. And the confusion got worse. Not all humans were sinners, Origen stumbled on to explain. Elijah, John the Baptist, and of course Christ himself all took on human bodies to accomplish good. But most of the intelligences that became human were sinners. As humans they confirmed their fleshly grossness with more sin, some even sinking into the status of demons.

Because all the intelligences were originally equal, all have the potential for both falling and rising. One's position in the cosmos is one's own choice, and one can choose to mount upward or to sink further. All who respond to Christ and accept his grace will rise in the chain of being. Humans can become angels. Angels too may change: an archangel may become a demon, and Satan may rise again to regain his place in heaven. This line of thought increases the muddle, for it provides for ontological rising and falling on the basis of moral choice. On the whole the Christian tradition preferred to maintain that ontological status does not change: angels remain angels, and humans remain humans.

Satan's moral choice, Origen said, was to prefer nonbeing and purposelessness to real being and true purpose. He was the first intelligence to fall by moral fault, "the first of all beings that were in peace and lived in blessedness who lost his wings and fell from the blessed state." The great angel who had sung among the seraphim chose to debase himself. Since the fall of the intelligences occurred before the creation of the material world, envy of humanity played no part in it. The motive of the intelligences was sheer pride: they preferred their own will to God's.

This ordering of events permitted Origen to confirm the identity of Satan with Lucifer. Bringing together diverse Old Testament passages from Job, Ezechiel, and Isaiah, he argued that the King of Babylon, the Prince of Tyre, and the Dragon were all the Devil. He used these scriptures to underline Satan's pride and his headlong fall from grace. The King of Babylon, Isaiah's bright son of the morning, is Lucifer, and Lucifer is Satan. The Prince of Tyre also is Satan:

Thou sealest up the sum, full of wisdom, and perfect in beauty. Thou hast been in Eden the garden of God. . . . Thou art the anointed cherub and I have set thee so. . . . Thou wast perfect in thy ways from the day that thou wast created, till iniquity was found in thee. . . . Thine heart was lifted up because of thy beauty, thou hast corrupted thy wisdom by reason of thy brightness; I will cast thee to the ground. . . . I will bring forth a fire from the midst of thee, [and] it shall devour thee. [Ezech. 28.12–19]

The Dragon Leviathan is the same as the Dragon of Revelation, which had long been equated with Satan:

Canst thou draw out Leviathan with an hook? . . . Canst thou put a hook into his nose? [Job 41.1–2]

Origen's use of these colorful passages firmly established the tradition that the Devil had been among the greatest of the angels, beautiful and wise, that his pride had at the beginning of the world led him to rebel against God, and that he had been expelled from heaven and awaited punishment in fire. Many of the later elaborations of legend and literature derive from Origen's conflation of these texts.

Origen attempted to reconcile the sacrifice and ransom theories of the atonement through allegory, explaining that the sacrifice was a means of overthrowing the powers of evil, but it was ransom that he emphasized. He dwelt upon the divine trick that God had played upon Satan by offering him a prize that he had no right to hold so that when he attempted to lay hands on the Savior he violated justice and lost both the Savior and the human race. Origen admitted that this divine duping of the Devil seemed undignified, but he noted that it is analogous to God's hardening Pharaoh's heart so that he might punish him. The crucifixion had a double meaning. In the eyes of the world it meant the defeat of Jesus, but in the real world of God it meant the Devil's destruction.

Although the Passion battered Satan's proud tower, it did not immediately pull it down; rather, it set in motion a process that would culminate in the second coming. Meanwhile, Satan is allowed to continue to assault us. Such a view, common among the fathers, ran the risk of representing the Passion as a stage in the process of salvation rather than as the very act of salvation itself, but it did face the demonstrable fact that sin and evil did not cease at the time of Christ. If the Devil's kingdom will not be finally overthrown before the second coming, what is its current condition? Various accounts were current in Origen's time. (1) Satan and the demons were imprisoned in hell at the time of the Passion and will be confined there until allowed to emerge and aid the Antichrist in the last battle. (2) Some demons are even now in hell, while others are allowed under God's permission to roam the world seeking the ruin and destruction of souls. (3) The demons work in shifts, periodically changing places between hell and earth. (4) The demons are jailers of the damned as well as prisoners themselves. Origen inclined to the view that their punishment was reserved till the end of the world and that until then the evil spirits are allowed to wander the earth oppressing humanity.

Influenced by Clement, Origen argued for the salvation of Satan, basing his belief on the idea that all things will eventually return to the God who has made them. In the fullness of time, God will be all in all. "The destruction of the last enemy may be understood in this way," Origen wrote, "not that its substance, which was made by God, shall perish, but that the hostile purpose and will that proceeded not from God but from itself will come to an end. It will be destroyed, therefore, not in the sense of ceasing to be, but of being no longer an enemy and no longer death." Everything that God creates will in the end be reunited with him. The Devil will perish in that he will cease to be the Devil, for the evil in him will be burnt away, and his angelic nature will be restored and reunited with the Lord.

Origen's view of the return of all things to God had two not entirely compatible bases, and this produced a confusion as to whether Satan's salvation was a necessity or only a possibility. One basis was ontological. The essential being of all that exists proceeds from God; evil is merely nonbeing. The Devil's being, however eroded by sin, must derive from God and so must eventually be drawn back to God. In this argument, the salvation of Satan is a necessity. The other basis is God's mercy. Since God's mercy is limitless, it allows every intelligence to repent, so long as the cosmos shall endure. In this argument the salvation of Satan is a possibility. The fact that he has not repented so far is no proof that he may not do so in future. Only when the cosmos ceases to exist and time is at an end can the hope of repentance be removed.

The idea of the universal return did not win wide favor. In addition to its underlying inconsistencies, its assertion that the entire cosmos would be reunited with God seemed to fit poorly with the New Testament idea of the ultimate union of believers with Christ. Still, Origen's idea of universal reunion has repeatedly surfaced in different forms among Christian mystics, and universalism—the appeal to God's mercy for the salvation of all—has frequently been revived in the subsequent history of theology. Overall, Origen's diabology was the most complete and influential of those of the early fathers.

6 Dualism and the Desert

As the security of life in the Roman Empire waned in the third and fourth centuries, the power of the Devil seemed to increase. Insecurity and fear abetted a resurgence of dualism, which found new expressions in the theology of Lactantius (c. 245–325), in a new heresy, Manicheism, and in the penetrating psychology of monasticism.

Lactantius demanded to understand why the just suffered as much in life as the unjust. The cosmos seemed to be full of perplexing polarities: earth vs. heaven, hell vs. heaven, darkness vs. light, death vs. life, night vs. day, cold vs. warm. Why would God, whose mind and purpose are unity, construct the cosmos with these oppositions? The duality of good and evil was especially puzzling: "Why does the true God permit these things to exist instead of removing or deleting the evil? Why did he in the very beginning make a prince of demons who would corrupt and destroy everything? . . . What is the cause and principle of evils?" Lactantius' answers were startlingly original.

First, evil is logically necessary. This argument went past the metaphysical view that any created world is imperfect. Evil is an absolute necessity, Lactantius argued, for "good cannot be understood without evil, nor evil without good." Good and evil are defined only by opposition to each other, so that good could not exist if evil did not.

Second and even more startling, it is positively desirable that evil should exist: "I tell you in short that God wishes it to be so." God wishes it because we could not comprehend virtue unless we comprehended the alternative of vice. If God had created a world without evil, he would have created a world without the alternatives that make freedom possible. "We could not perceive virtue unless the opposite vice also existed, nor could we accomplish virtue unless we were tempted to its opposite; God willed this distinction and distance between good and evil so that we might be able to grasp the nature of good by contrasting it with the nature of evil. . . . To exclude evil is to eliminate virtue."

These are attractive arguments. It is logically impossible for good alone to exist, and even if it were, that would be undesirable, for it would eliminate true freedom of choice. Further, Lactantius argued, evil must exist powerfully and compellingly. If we were allured only by petty vices, we would exercise only petty virtues. If no vast and terrifying power of evil loomed in our minds, we would have no idea of the vast and glorious power of the Lord. The greatness of the contrast reveals the greatness of our opportunity to humble evil by joining ourselves to Christ. "God willed this opposition because he wanted us to take on the responsibility for combat and to stand prepared in the line of battle." Only our experience of the power of temptation and of the glamour of evil can make us realize our need for the grace of Christ.

Up to this point, Lactantius remained monistic, courageously attributing evil to God's plan. But now, shrinking from the idea that evil proceeds from the Lord himself, he took refuge in cosmic ethical dualism. At the very beginning, "before he made anything else, God made two sources of things, each source opposed to the other and each struggling against the other. These two sources are the two spirits, the just spirit and the corrupt spirit, and one of them is like the right hand of God while the other is like his left." God knowingly created the Devil, knowing that he is corrupt and unjust. All good proceeds from the Lord, all evil from the Devil.

On one level, this shift of evil from God to the Devil does not work, for Lactantius admits that God remains ultimately responsible. Further, the idea of a warfare between a good and an evil spirit from the beginning of time edges toward dualism in a way that not only contradicts Christian tradition but also undermines Lactantius' initial courageous monism. On another level, Lactantius' theodicy is a sketchy predecessor of the idea of the two wills of God put forward by the late medieval nominalists and by Luther: evil must exist in God's overall plan, but God also hates it and wishes us to fight with him against it.

Unfortunately Lactantius' efforts to clarify his views only muddled them further. If the "Good Spirit" is not God himself, is it God's Son? Lactantius was inconsistent, but he sometimes thought of Christ and Satan as twin angels, one beloved and the other rejected, heavenly counterparts of Cain and Abel. Although Lactantius meant this twinship of Christ and Satan metaphorically, it went further in the direction of dualism than Christian tradition could countenance.

Lactantius argued that experience teaches us that the evil principle is active in the world as an "anti-God, [the] enemy of good and the foe of justice, who wills the opposite of what God wills." This perverted power envies God and directs its malevolence against Christ and against humanity, whom he urges to give up hope of heaven and serve him instead. All his efforts are vain, for God's Providence turns Satan's every evil action to ultimate good. In the end, Satan and his followers, the evil angels, will be defeated. They have already endured a "first death" when they fell from heaven, losing their pure forms and sinking down with gross bodies into the lower air. In this first death they lost their purely spiritual being and their immortality, a loss that prepared them for the "second death" to come.

The "second death" of the evil angels, eternal punishment in hell, will not occur before the end of the world. Though broken by Christ's Passion, the Evil One is meanwhile regathering his forces. God allows time to elapse between the first and second coming of Christ in order to groom humans for heaven, but Satan uses that time for his own evil purposes. As the endtime approaches, Antichrist will appear, and all evil spirits and humans will rise up in a final assault upon the Christian community. For a short while the Evil One will prevail, but then Christ will return to earth and plunge him into eternal fire, bringing the remainder of the cosmos back into eternal harmony with God. Lactantius' use of the Book of Revelation contrasted sharply with Origen's allegorical reading. Allegory permitted Origen to argue for a return of all to God; but Lactantius, in common with most of the church, insisted upon the eternal punishment of the damned.

The dualism of Mani and his followers went much further beyond the limits of Christianity than Lactantius did. Mani, born into a princely family near Babylon in 216 and executed by the Mazdaists in Iran in 277, was the founder of Manicheism, an eclectic doctrine influenced by Judaism, Mazdaism, and Buddhism. Its closest affinities were with Gnosticism, and it became one of the most influential and long-lived of Christian heresies. Mani taught the existence of two eternal principles, that of spirit, light, and truth, and that of matter, darkness, and falsehood. These two principles are personified as God and the Prince of Darkness, and although they are both eternal, only the principle of light is divine. The kingdom of God consists of light, force, and wisdom working together in serene harmony; the kingdom of darkness is chaotic, noisy, and confused. God creates the Mother of Life, who in turn creates Primeval Man; the three exist in a Father/Mother/Son Trinity. The Prince of Darkness attacks and defeats Primeval Man, who in his fear prays to his Father and Mother for help. The Father sends a divine Messenger, the Spirit of Light, to rescue Primeval Man, but his soul still remains trapped in the commotion of darkness, and the Father sends down a new Messenger, the Living Spirit, to defeat the demons or archons. The Living Spirit rescues the soul of Primeval Man and cleanses and purifies the light, making the sun and the moon. Some particles of light remain trapped in darkness, however, so the Father sends a Third Messenger. The Third Messenger presents himself as a beautiful virgin to the male archons who, lusting for her, ejaculate the light that they had been holding captive as sperm, and this sperm/light falls upon the earth, causing vegetables to grow.

Meanwhile the female demons perceive the Third Messenger as a handsome youth who impregnates them. Their children come to life as monsters and devour the young plants, thus imprisoning the light again. The archons also produce Adam and Eve, an evil act trapping yet more spirit inside gross material bodies. The act is itself repulsive: the Prince of Darkness produces one male and one female demon, and the male demon consumes the monsters who have eaten the lightbearing plants and afterward mates with the female demon. Adam and Eve are the offspring of this filthy union, the nauseating product of a diabolical combination of cannibalism and lust. The Father of Light, appalled but undeterred, sends the Third Messenger down yet again, this time under the appearance (though not the reality) of flesh and in the person of "Jesus the Shiner."

Jesus goes to Adam and tells him the truth: Adam's body is an evil imposture invented by demons, so he must try to rescue his soul for the world of light. Adam, Eve, and their descendants can be saved only by grasping this message and liberating our souls from their disgusting prisons. At the endtime, after a great final war, spirit will be liberated from matter, Jesus will rule the cosmos for a while, and then all matter will finally be destroyed. While those who have freed their spirits mount to heaven, those who have dwelt in darkness will be rolled together in a dense, dark mass and buried in the eternal pit.

The mythological complexities of Manicheism, which far exceed this outline, were designed to remove responsibility for evil from God by interposing an intricate series of mythological figures between him and the world of experience. Like the Gnostic myths, they failed to do so.

Still, Manichean ideas influenced orthodox thinkers—Augustine himself was a Manichean for a while—and reappeared throughout the centuries among such heretical groups as the Bogomils and Cathars. The presence of this extreme dualism beyond the edge of Christianity exerted a gravitational attraction within Christianity itself, sharpening the tension between soul and body and enhancing the role of the Devil as lord of matter and the flesh.

The struggle between soul and body was prominent in early monastic thought. The purpose of Christian monasticism was to provide a life of solitude and reflection in which an individual could devote his or her entire time to the contemplation of God undisturbed by the distractions of life in the world. Monasticism began with Saint Anthony (251–356), the first hermit, and Saint Pachomius (286–346), who founded community monasticism.

Hermits and monks withdrew into remote, unpeopled places in order to escape the temptations of society. In Egypt and Syria, where monasticism began and flourished, they usually sought out the dry mountains of the deserts. There the monks met the power of the Devil head on. The desert was a familiar haunt of Satan, for it was there that he had tempted Christ and there that he later regrouped his demonic forces after having been driven out of the cities of the Roman Empire by the spread of Christian churches. The Evil One was particularly hostile to the monks because they went out into the desert to challenge him deliberately and because their faith seemed to be putting them beyond his reach. The tales told of the monks' battles with the Devil added a rich layer of experience, detail, and color to Satan's personality.

One of the most influential works of monastic diabology was the *Life of Anthony*, composed by Athanasius, the bishop of Alexandria, about 360. Athanasius paints the great hermit's life as a constant struggle against the Devil and his demons. In their fall from heaven, Satan and his followers had separated themselves from the rest of the cosmos, condemning themselves to a life of nothingness, darkness, and nonbeing. The demons, who inherently lack form, can take visible shapes and create images and fantasies in the minds of their victims. The Devil might appear as a huge giant living in the air, or as a black boy, a sign of his empty darkness and of his puerile impotence against the power of Christ. He and his demons often take the form of beasts as sign of their brutish stupidity or of monsters as sign that they have no true place in the cosmos. Athanasius' description became a pattern for iconography: the Devil's "eyes are like the morning star. In his mouth gape burning lamps,

Cernunnos, the Celtic horned god of the wilderness, was incorporated into the iconography and folklore of the Devil. Detail from the Gundestrup cauldron, second or first century B.C., excavated in Denmark. Courtesy Nationalmuseet, Copenhagen.

and hearthfuls of fire are cast forth. The smoke of a furnace blazing with the fire of coals flares from his nostrils. His breath is of coals, and from his mouth issues flame."

Athanasius had to face the fact that in spite of Christ's sacrifice demons still ranged the world. He explained that Christ had shattered the demons' power except insofar as he gave them permission to act as tempters or accusers. Christ has put the hook into Leviathan's nose and leads him about, tamed. By associating ourselves with Christ's sacrifice and by relying with faith upon his grace we hasten the Devil's final ruin. Athanasius puts this story into Anthony's mouth:

Someone knocked at the door of my cell, and opening it I saw a person of great size and tallness. I enquired, "Who are you?," and he replied, "Satan." When I asked, "Why are you here?" he answered, "Why do the monks and other Christians blame me undeservedly? Why do they curse me every hour?" I answered, "Why do you trouble them?" He replied, "I don't trouble them, for I am become weak: they trouble themselves. Haven't they read that 'the swords of the Enemy are finished and the cities destroyed for him'? I no longer have a weapon or a city. The Christians are spread everywhere, and even the desert is now filled with monks. Let them take care of themselves and cease cursing me." I marveled at God's grace and said to Satan, "Although you are a liar and never speak the truth, you have spoken the truth here, albeit against your will. For the coming of Christ has weakened you, and He has cast you down and stripped you." But when he heard the Savior's name, he was unable to bear its burning, and he vanished.

The Devil has the power to take on the shape of an angel of light, as Saint Paul has said. He can sing beautifully, quote the Bible, echo prayers, or assume the appearance of a monk. Still, feigning good is so great an effort for demons that they usually slip back to ugly shapes emitting repulsive stenches. In their innermost reality they are heavy, invisible substances sinking toward darkness and ruin.

The closer Anthony's life came to the imitation of Christ, the more the Devil hated him. At each crucial decision in his life, Satan attacked him vehemently: first when he withdrew to a tomb near his village, then when he went off to live in a ruined fort in the desert near the river, and finally when he went deep into the deadly desert near the Red Sea. Demonic assaults are usually managed by subsidiary demons, but the Devil himself takes over if the monk's resistance is great enough. When Anthony decided to go out to the abandoned tomb, the Devil, hating his youthful goodness and fearing his spiritual potential, whispered into his mind temptations to acts that were good in themselves. The Devil suggested all the benevolent donations Anthony could make if he kept his money and reminded him of the responsibility he had for the care of his young sister. Later, when Anthony was more advanced in the spiritual life, Satan tempted him to measures of asceticism that would make his monastic vocation an intolerable burden.

Seeing that such subtle temptations were failing, the Devil became cruder. When the young Anthony failed to yield to thoughts about his estate and his sister, the Prince of Darkness instilled in his mind images of wealth, banquets, and glory. He raised a cloud of doubt about the monastic vocation by introducing images of the dangers and discomforts of life in the desert. He suggested lewd thoughts and took on the tempting form of a sensuous young woman. The demons always fitted their temptations to the age and circumstances of their victims. To older monks they proposed quiet comforts; to younger ones sexual luxuries:

One evening a demon took the shape of a pretty woman traveling in the desert. She came to the door of a monk's cave, pretending to be tired and exhausted from her journey. She fell at the monk's knees to plead with him. "Night overtook me while I was wandering in the desert, and now I am frightened. Just let me rest in a corner of your cell so that I don't fall prey to the wild animals." The monk, feeling pity, received her inside the cave, asking her why she was traveling alone in the desert. She began to converse normally enough but bit by bit sweetened her words and played upon his sympathies. The sweetness of her speech gradually took possession of his mind until she had turned it entirely to thoughts of lust. She began to mix jokes and laughter in her speech, reaching up to touch his chin and beard as if in reverence and then stroking his throat and neck. The monk began to burn with desire, but just as he was about to consummate his passion, the demon let out a terrible shriek in a hoarse voice, slipped away from his embrace, and departed, laughing filthily at his shame.

If blandishments do not succeed, Satan uses demonic assaults (obsessions) to terrify the monk into abandoning his vocation. Sometimes the Devil sends dreams and hallucinations to frighten monks in their sleep, and sometimes the demons present themselves externally to the senses, exuding disgusting odors and setting up a nerve-shattering din. Anthony was once awakened by horrible shrieking noises and the walls of his hut shaking; then the demons irrupted in terrifying shapes as lions, bears, leopards, bulls, serpents, asps, scorpions, and wolves, uttering grating, guttural noises. Saint Hilarion heard babies crying, cattle lowing, women weeping, lions roaring, and the muffled sounds of ignorant armies clashing by night; he witnessed a terrible struggle of gladiators before his very eyes, one falling dead at his feet before he realized that it was all a dumb-show of demons. The demons descend from the horrible to the silly in order to distract the monk from contemplation. They dance, sing, whistle, fart, caper, and prance. Sometimes they stage comedies: Pachomius watched tiny demons carefully attach a rope to a leaf and then pretend to strain in a vain effort to budge it. Ordinarily it was assumed that such manifestations had no power to harm the monk bodily, but physical assaults were occasionally recorded. Satan once leaped on Hilarion's back and whipped him; a pack of demons waylaid Anthony, beating him and leaving him unconscious on the ground. In his old age Anthony used to relate to his young brothers how he had often repelled the Evil One with physical blows. It is idle to speculate what "really" happened on such occasions; what matters is that these stories were widely perceived as literal accounts of demonic behavior.

To combat such assaults, the monks used the sign of the cross and the name of Jesus. To these ordinary defenses they added their special spiritual acumen and experience. Anthony's ascetic life, fasting, and vigils blunted the Enemy's attacks. Other weapons were exorcism, contempt shown by ignoring the demons or blowing or hissing at them, and simple courage. When a spirit approaches, one should boldly confront it and ask it what it is. If an angel, it will reveal itself; if a demon, it will flee such courage in gibbering fear.

The monks were not always confident that they could tell a demon from an angel, and the ability to discern the action of a good spirit from that of an evil one became the basis of a sophisticated psychology. We all have shifting moods and urges, and we know that what seems right one day can seem wrong the next. We can make serious mistakes because we are misled by passing impulses. By exercising discernment, monks could tell whether a given impulse came ultimately from God or from the Devil. They learned to do this both for themselves and for others, so that they were frequently visited by ordinary people seeking advice. The discernment of spirits gave the monks skill in interpreting dreams and what Freud would call, centuries later, the psychopathology of everyday life.

The greatest of the monastic psychologists was Evagrius of Pontus (born 345). He led an ascetic life in the desert, going so far as to pass a winter night standing in the water of a well. Influenced by the *Life of Anthony*, Evagrius gave demons an important role in the world. Out of the hundred chapters of his *Practical Advice*, demons play an important part in sixty-seven. Also influenced by Origen, Evagrius imagined ranks of demons, the lower ones having fallen further from grace than the higher ones. As angels dwelling close to God, the demons had possessed great knowledge and power, but they had lost these qualities when they fell. They have no true knowledge, only superficial cleverness, and they lack all understanding that truth proceeds from God and points toward him. Unable to see God or the good angels anymore, they are still capable of discerning the material world. They scrutinize the daily lives of men and women for opportunities to attack us. Unable to penetrate our souls, which are protected by God's presence within, the demons are forced to rely upon their observation of our actions, our words, and even our body language. They never understand truth or love and constantly misinterpret them, but they are immensely cunning in their grasp of human weakness and sin. They have mastered human languages and sciences, and they constantly use their skills to trick and delude us.

The demons dwell in the air, where they travel on wings. They can make themselves tiny enough to enter our bodies by the air that we draw through the nose (one explanation of the superstition of saying "bless you" to someone who sneezes). They have thin, whistling, reedy voices. Their size, color, and form are appropriate to their low status in the chain of being, but although they can see us, we can never see them unless they take on false shapes to delude us.

As each demon occupies a different place in the evil hierarchy, each has its own personality. Some are more vicious, some more persistent, some quicker, some more cowardly than others. The monk used his discernment both to distinguish a good spirit from an evil one and to determine what sort of evil spirit he was confronted with. Since the demons' purpose is to destroy God's image and likeness in our souls, Evagrius said, they attempt to abort every virtue and besiege us most determinedly when they suspect us of contemplating any good action. Martyrs, monks, saints, and hermits constitute a kind of holy lightning rod attracting the hostile attention of the Prince of Darkness away from the rest of the community, an elite armed by God with a special fortitude.

The demons attack both mind and body. Though they cannot enter our souls, they suggest fears and temptations to our minds by manipulating our senses. They tempt most people with sex, wealth, and power. With monks, Evagrius noted, they have a subtler chore: "The greater the progress the soul makes, the more fearful the adversaries that take over the war against him." Sophisticated demons subtly divert sophisticated monks from their contemplation of God with illusions and obsessions of such delicacy that only the discerning monk specially protected by God's grace can readily find the means to resist. Less advanced monks had to face the cruder assaults of demons who tickled their noses, made them drowsy during prayer, swelled their bellies with flatulence, or even caused serious disease or injury.

Evagrius' psychology of temptation derived its initial assumptions from Origen. Our souls, having fallen from heaven and now being embedded in the body, are bent, their vision of God blurred. They are dominated by emotional turmoils they cannot shake off. It is this turmoil, this absorption in self, that we must transcend through the grace of Christ if we are again to ascend to heaven. From turmoil arise worldly desires, which open gates for the demons lurking to attack us. Watching us carefully, Satan sees when we are weakened by a particular desire and then sends into the breach demonic troops suited and trained to exploit that particular temptation. Alert to each tiny breach, the demons pour through the hole and enlarge the beachhead. A desire for a woman may quicken in a man's heart, for example; the demons will rush in, flooding the mind with lewd images until his soul is a boiling cauldron. A woman may begin to dwell too much upon the investments she plans for her financial security; the demons will obsess her with money, turning need into greed and enslaving her to avarice.

Our only protection against demonic assaults is to respond to divine grace with faith. If we do, Christ helps us to discern between good and evil spirits and among the varieties of evil spirits, so that we may know what weapons are most appropriate to turn against our spiritual enemies. Evagrius prescribed a morally good life, prayer, asceticism, and frequent recourse to the name of Jesus. He also urged active and assertive resistance to evil spirits. One should not be passive when tempted by demons but rather thrust them angrily out of the mind and then go on to take diversionary counteractions. A monk tossing awake at night with lustful thoughts, for example, should quickly rise and go to the infirmary to do an act of kindness, thus flouting Satan by turning a temptation into an occasion for virtue.

The monastic struggle against the demons lent the concept of the Devil particularity, immediacy, and an intensely threatening nearness. The Evil One is present at each moment, ready and eager to attack us with every weapon from false intellectual sophistication through lewd thoughts and physical assaults to petty distractions. Behind these attacks lurks a cold, heavy, monstrous presence, clever yet idiotic, weighing the world down toward darkness.

7 *The Classical Christian View*

Saint Augustine of Hippo (354–430) synthesized and developed the diabology of the fathers. Augustine lived in Roman North Africa and wrote in Latin. The Latin West and Greek East had already begun to diverge during his lifetime, and Augustine's influence on the East does not compare with his immense impact on Western thought, both Catholic and Protestant. Augustinian, Western thought tends to "positive theology," using reason to construct a detailed, logically organized, and structured view of the world. Typically it begins by using philosophy— "natural theology"—to proceed as far as possible on the road to truth without recourse to revelation; then it introduces revelation (mainly the Bible) as the next step to truth; and finally it uses reason again to build upon revelation in "revealed theology."

The Syrian monk known as Dionysius the Areopagite, writing about 500, typified the tradition of "negative theology" more typical in the East. Negative theology affirms that the greatness of God is so far beyond the powers of human reason that rational systems have very limited value. Truth is pursued less through logic than through prayer and contemplation. Still, many of these contemplative, "mystical" elements exist in Western thought, and Eastern Orthodoxy is no stranger to positive theology. The two approaches are more complementary than competing. Taken together, Augustine's and Dionysius' views completed the basic structure of Christian diabology for more than a millennium.

Augustine and Dionysius based their formulation of Christian theology upon the tradition of New Testament, the fathers, and the creeds. This traditional theology begins with God, the eternal and timeless. God has no beginning and no end; he has no cause; he is Being itself. God is one and indivisible. But this eternal, timeless unity is not static; it is dynamic, seething with power. The dynamism is expressed in the three Persons of God, Father, Son, and Holy Spirit. These are not three gods or even three functions of one God, but three aspects of the one, unified God. The Son is the Father's Thought of Himself, the Word; the Holy Spirit is the Love that the Father and the Son have for each other.

The boiling dynamism of God pours itself out beyond itself into the cosmos. This is a pouring out of both the Word and the Spirit, of both reason and love. If the cosmos had been created only with love, it would be unformed; if only with reason, it would be a machine. But the cosmos is created with both reason and love and pulses with both.

The universe was not created out of any preexisting substance, for there was nothing other than God for it to be created from. God creates the cosmos because it is his nature to do so; he also creates it to increase the sum total of goodness in existence. In order to increase goodness, he creates beings with free will, for without free will there can be no moral choice of good. The creation of the cosmos was a creation of both space and time. What is in modern terms called the space/time continuum has a beginning and an end. There is no sense talking about space and time except within the continuum. God does not exist in space or time; space and time are properties of the cosmos that God creates. God was not "doing anything" "before" the cosmos existed, for there was no time "before" the cosmos. The cosmos exists eternally in the mind of God; in this sense it has no end. From the point of view of creatures dwelling within the cosmos, however, the world has both a beginning and an end.

The first beings that God created are the angels, enormously powerful and intelligent creatures, to whom God gave free will. Directly after their creation, the angels used their free will to make a moral choice. Most of them chose to love God; some, led by Satan, chose to put their own wills in place of God's. These sinful angels were cast out of heaven. God then created the material world, including human beings, to whom he also gave the gift of free will. Satan, envying the happiness of Adam and Eve, went and tempted them. The first parents were in no way compelled to sin by Satan; they exercised their free will in yielding to his temptation. Their sin alienated humanity from God and left us under the Devil's dominion.

From the moment of humanity's original sin until the Incarnation, Satan ruled the world. The Incarnation broke his power, restored human freedom, and opened the way to reconciliation with God. Christ and his community are now waging a difficult but ultimately victorious struggle against the power of the Devil, which will finally and permanently be broken at the second coming, when all things will be brought back to harmony with God. This was the outline of Christian theology that Augustine and Dionysius inherited; it left them with a number of unresolved problems, the most important of which was the problem of evil.

Augustine was deeply occupied with that problem from his youth; it was his sensitivity to it that prompted him to accept Manicheism for a while; and the question continued to absorb him after he became a settled Christian. Although he was always more concerned with the sinfulness of human nature and its redemption by Christ than with Satan, the Devil was an integral part of his theology.

Augustine began his dialogue *The Free Choice of the Will* with the question of evil. Evodius, his partner in the dialogue, inquires, "Tell me, please, whether God is not the cause of evil." The idea of evil in the cosmos was puzzling. Augustine regarded the cosmos as a book by a perfect poet who has shaped his plot from its beginning to its end and has perfectly chosen every word, syllable, and letter. The universe exists eternally in the mind of God; nothing that happens in the cosmos is unknown to its Creator. God as it were sang the universe into existence and sustains it in counterpoint through its coda. God's poem is harmonious, beautiful, full of joy, the expression of God's perfect love, and worthy of all our admiration, gratitude, and enjoyment. Then why and how did the perfect poet introduce, or at least permit, evil in this harmony?

Augustine's answers varied during the course of his life. After his early obsession with evil and his temporary Manicheism, he converted to Christianity and from then through middle age generally expressed a confident, optimistic view. God's narration moves in stately measures from the alpha to the omega, the beginning to the end. Time has intrinsic meaning. God could have redeemed humanity immediately after our fall; Christ could have returned the moment after his ascension. The fact that God allowed time to elapse between the fall of Adam and the first coming of Christ meant that he was using time for a purpose: to prepare humanity to the point that at least some would be able to recognize and accept their Savior. He has a similar purpose in allowing time to elapse between the first and the second coming of the Lord: to allow as many people as possible to accept Christ and be reconciled with God before the end comes.

In this optimistic view, pain and suffering are mercies sent by God to teach us the wisdom, humility, and kindness that we need to overcome our alienation and help God build a Christian community. Because pain is part of the learning process that prepares the way of God, God permits demons to afflict humans—even children—with temptation and suffering. In this stage, Augustine was offering two basic explanations of evil. First, free will is the most important reason for the creation of the cosmos, since it is the greatest good; but free will implies that some will choose evil; so evil is a necessary corollary of creation. Second, God uses both moral and natural evil to refine our souls by teaching us wisdom through experience. This "soul-building" theodicy, supposes that humanity makes a steady (though painfully difficult) progress toward the omega point, when all will be reconciled with God.

The fall of the city of Rome to the Visigoths in 410 shocked every civilized person in the empire, not least Augustine. In addition, he was increasingly appalled and depressed by the persistent heresies and schisms of the church. As he grew older, the ancient pessimism and fear of evil that had nagged him since adolescence reemerged and became dominant. Now he saw the cosmos as incurable. Humanity had been totally corrupted by original sin and thrust under the Devil's dominion. No intrinsically good community could be constructed in a world so riddled with evil. Suffering now appeared less an instruction than a punishment, a prelude to the pains of hell. The world was lost in darkness, and to refuse to face the vast dimensions of the shadow was an evasion. "This is the Christian view," he wrote toward the end of his life, "a view that can show a just God in so many pains and in such agonies of tiny babies." The stare Augustine leveled unflinchingly at pain and death became so dark and somber that Peter Brown, his biographer, speaks of "the fearsome intensity with which he had driven the problem of evil into the heart of Christianity."

This is radical, hideous evil. Where does it come from? How can it be reconciled with a good God? The dualist solution Augustine had once embraced as a Manichean had long ceased to interest him. A principle of evil, a being absolutely evil in itself, a lord of evil independent of God— such a thing could not exist, for it would constitute a limitation of God, God the eternal, omniscient, and omnipotent. No aspect of the cosmos, whether spirit or matter, no devil, no unformed primal matter, could resist, deflect, alter, or defer God's plan. The book is written, the poem complete. God has devised its ending as its beginning, in all eternity, and not a letter can be altered. Everything that God makes is good and according to his loving plan.

The horned helmet worn by warriors to obtain magical power made the warrior a symbol of ferocity that merged with the Devil. The Finglesham Buckle from Anglo-Saxon Kent, sixth century. Courtesy Institute of Archaeology, Oxford.

But if everything God makes is good, how can evil exist? Because it is not created at all; it does not truly exist; it is essentially privation, lack of being; it has no intrinsic reality. Nothing is by nature evil, and nothing is by nature evil: both meanings of the phrase apply. Evil is simply lack of good. Yes, but why is there this lack? Why did God make the cosmos with holes in it? Augustine distinguished at the outset between natural and moral evil. Although natural evils—tornadoes or cancer—are truly painful and terrifying, they are part of a divine plan whose outlines are hidden from our limited vision. Natural evils appear evil because we cannot fully understand the cosmos. If we could, we would see how these apparent gaps in being fit the divine plan. And, imperfectly though we see, we do have some hint of the reasons for suffering and pain: they exist to teach us wisdom, to warn us of the dangers of sin, or to ensure just punishment for sin. For sinners, adversity is a punishment; for the innocent, it is a divine gift of warning; what it is for babies or animals Augustine did not know, but God's providence turns the worst evils, even moral sin, to ultimate good.

Moral evil is far worse than natural evil, for it not only harms its victims but also eats away the soul of the sinner. What is the cause of moral evil? Augustine suggested that it is the result of free-will choice on the part of intelligent beings such as angels or humans. Unfortunately he went on to explore the question of what might cause such a choice of evil—unfortunately, because any answer to that question is inherently illogical, since nothing can cause a free-will choice.

Augustine's scheme has only an anomalous place for the Devil. If we are concerned with explaining the moral evil in the world, what we observe is human evil, and human evil can be accounted for by original sin. Since Adam and Eve were free to sin without the Devil's intervention, and since the Devil had no power to compel them to sin, the Devil's role is unnecessary to explain human sin. Further, if we try to attribute evil to the Devil, we are left with God's responsibility for creating a cosmos with the Devil in it. Positing the Devil's role in order to remove responsibility for evil from God fails. Augustine did not acknowledge these anomalies, because they were forced on him by Scripture and tradition. If revelation did not attest Satan's existence, Augustine's system would have had no need for him.

Augustine's most important contribution to diabology was his discussion of free will and predestination. The problem is this. We experience the sense that we are free to choose, and the Bible seems to imply that we are responsible for choosing. Yet both reason and revelation also indicate that God is the all-knowing and all-powerful sovereign of the cosmos. If God is omnipotent, how can angels and humans really be free to choose or be responsible for their choices? Augustine was the first to pose the question explicitly in all its complexity, though he never resolved it, and the debate continues today among philosophers, physicists, biologists, and psychologists, as well as theologians. Einstein observed, "What I am really interested in is whether God could have made this world in a different way; that is, whether the necessity of logical simplicity leaves any freedom at all."

Augustine always asserted the truth of both propositions: that humans and angels are free, but that God's power is unlimited by any principle, including our freedom. Sometimes it is difficult to see any *real* freedom in Augustine's use of the term. In his early life, when he was a Manichean, Augustine tended toward the determinism typical of Gnostic dualism. Then, after his conversion, he wrote *The Free Choice of the Will*, affirming against both Manicheans and pagans a real role for free will. Later, when he confronted the Pelagians, who exaggerated free will, he returned to a more deterministic stance. Toward the end of his life, Augustine affirmed predestination with such severity that his opponents accused him of reverting to pagan fatalism.

He affirmed predestination for three reasons. First, God's utter sovereignty implies an utterly determined cosmos. Second, although Augustine allowed (somewhat inconsistently) that the original choice of Adam and Eve was truly free, once humanity had chosen evil we were bound to sin and lacked true freedom. Third, since we are unfree, we have no way of choosing to change without the intervention of the Incarnation, from which grace flows to free us from sin; but since grace irresistibly binds us to Christ, we again have no true freedom of choice. Yet Augustine continued to insist that free will must somehow exist, even in the context of a totally determined universe, an incoherency that he could wriggle out of only by declaring it a mystery impenetrable to the human intellect. He thus spanned a whole spectrum of views on the subject, but his later, predestinarian ideas were more influential with later theologians, including Aquinas, Luther, and Calvin.

The most important logical options on freedom and determinism—then as now—are the following. (1) The cosmos is meaningless, random, moving in no planned or discernible direction. (2) The cosmos is determined by fixed natural laws arising from the structure of space/time. (3) The cosmos is determined by one or more unexplained, mysterious forces such as "fate" or Marxist "history." (4) The cosmos is predetermined and completely mapped by God. (5) Intelligent creatures have at least some limited power to shape their own lives. Options four and five were open to Augustine and the Christian tradition.

Within the framework of these two options a variety of positions is possible, depending on one's view of time. (1) All time and space exist eternally in an unchanging four-dimensional whole. Time appears to be moving; things appear to be changing. In a sense they do change, because we perceive them to, and our perceptions are themselves real. But to God, all time and space exist at once; past and future are equally real and present. In this Augustine's views are similar to those of modern relativity and quantum physics. In both views the space/time continuum exists as a whole; its coordinates can be mapped in four dimensions; past and future are merely our perceptual terms for something that is in a larger sense unchanging. (2) The future does not exist, but, as the philosopher Brian Hebblethwaite put it, "each state of the universe uniquely determines the next state, so that if one knew all the causes operating at any one time, one would know precisely what their outcome would be in the future." This view, which prevailed in the natural sciences until quite recently, is theologically only slightly removed from the first view, for with a "temporally structured deterministic universe," Hebblethwaite observed, God will know "precisely what will come to pass, since a deterministic universe is . . . present in its causes." Theologically this view is weaker than the first, because it seems to muddle space/time with eternity, as if God were imprisoned in space/time and could not see what we call the future. (3) God's omniscience is conditional. He may know all there is to know without knowing a future that does not yet exist. This position allows both for the freedom of intelligent beings and for true randomness in physical events. As Hebblethwaite puts it, God knows "every possibility and what to do in respect of each eventuality," but he leaves this "a genuinely open-structured world." Although this third position also somewhat muddles time and eternity, it provided Augustine and later theologians with the only way of reconciling predestination and free will.

Although Augustine tended to predestination, he sometimes felt his way toward a reconciliation that goes like this: Nothing could exist that could limit God's omnipotence—nothing, that is, except God himself. God chooses freely, in eternity, to suspend his omnipotence in certain areas of the continuum so as to allow for free will. He does this because his purpose in creating the cosmos is to increase the good, and it can increase only if some creatures freely choose it. God withholds or withdraws his omnipotence from free-will acts, so he does not cause them. When you are faced with a genuine moral choice, you have genuine free will to choose good or evil. Still, God knows in all eternity what your choice is and has eternally designed the cosmos to account for it. In contemporary terms, God "programs" the cosmos to include both free will and the adjustments to free-will choices. The scheme is workable if time and eternity are not confused. God does not rush around like a plumber frantically plugging leaks whenever they occur. God knows every leak in all eternity; in the very act of creation he adjusts the cosmos to take care of those leaks. He cannot prevent sin without abrogating free will, but he adjusts for sin so that every event fits his providential purpose. God's eternal knowledge of the free choices we make does not cause us to make those choices. God grants free will to intelligent creatures—humans and angels—and supports them in their search for the good by giving them a special energy called grace.

The original state of Satan and that of Adam were similar in that before sinning both were completely free. Both possessed basic character and will that were free and undistorted. But whereas Adam's original sin bent his will and that of his descendants until Christ freed us from our bondage, the original sin of Satan did worse, for it tied him to sin and ruin forever. Once having sinned, the Devil and his angels are bound forever to the shadows; no possibility exists that they will ever repent. Their punishment is harsher than that of humans because they were originally higher beings entrusted with greater responsibility. Their high intelligence and knowledge did not allow for the mitigating circumstances of weakness and ignorance that applied to the first humans.

Later Christian theologians and poets attempted to deepen this explanation, but none was wholly successful. The basic idea is that original sin, whether angelic or human, bends the will in such a way that it cannot be straightened without God's grace. But there is no compelling reason why God should extend that saving grace to humanity and withhold it forever from the fallen angels. Nonetheless, the Christian tradition, supported by the vast majority of theologians, is that the sin of the fallen angels is indelible.

Why did the angels fall? Augustine offered two explanations. The first is ontological. God alone is perfect and unchanging. The angels are not coeternal with God but creatures whom he made at the beginning of time, and all created beings are subject to change and corruption. The second is moral. The angels freely chose, without any cause of their choice, to prefer the limited good of their own will to the infinite good of

God's will. These explanations seemed sufficient to Augustine while in his moderate stage, but as he grew more predestinarian toward the end of his life, he pondered the possibility that God had created two different classes of angels. His dilemma was this: On the one hand, both sets of angels (that is, all the angels) must have been created absolutely equal, or else God would be responsible for their inequality and thus the ultimate cause of the sin of those who fell. But on the other hand, if there was no initial difference between them, no cause of their fall could be discerned, and the only explanation would be absolute freedom. In his predestinarian phase Augustine could not allow this, since it seemed to limit the absolute sovereignty of God.

He attempted to explain the matter as follows. The angels, being limited and fallible as well as free, are capable of sinning if left to their own devices. But God did not wish them to fall. He therefore decided to strengthen them, to confirm them in their goodness by a gratuitous act of grace. This confirmation brought the angels a deep understanding of God, the cosmos, and their own condition. Since they understood reality so completely, they became incapable of violating its principles, of sinning. These angels formed one group. Another group was also created good in nature and with freedom to choose, but from this group God withheld the grace that confirms in goodness, leaving them capable of sin. They freely chose to sin and thereby became demons. God did not cause this defect of will, but he permitted it. He could have confirmed all the angels in goodness, but he preferred to leave some to their own devices.

One problem with this scenario is that for God to decide to save some of the angels and not others is an inexplicable act of apparent injustice. Moreover, the analysis does not succeed in shifting the responsibility for evil away from God, as Augustine intended that it should. Even if God did not actually create two varieties of angels, the effect is the same if God chooses to discriminate between two groups so that by his choice two varieties came to exist.

The whole blundered argument might have been avoided had Augustine stuck to the simplest and most elegant explanation: some angels chose God and others chose sin, both with an absolutely free motion of the will that had no cause. The blunder arose from Augustine's lack of consistency on which of two fundamental positions on evil to take. Either one views God's omnipotence and sovereignty as absolute, or else one tries to put a distance between God and moral evil by positing real freedom on the part of intelligent creatures. Augustine tried to have it both ways. Still, there is a way to reconcile the sovereignty of God with free will. Augustine saw the way—God's omnipotent withdrawal of his own omnipotence from the sphere of creaturely freedom—but he abandoned it for a more predestinarian view that shifted responsibility for moral evil directly onto God, and then refused to make that responsibility explicit.

When the angel named Lucifer fell, Augustine's explanation continued, he became the Devil, and the other fallen angels became the demons. The good angels, remaining with God, retained their natural intelligence enhanced by illumination, but the evil angels, shadowed by sin, lost the light of intelligence along with the light of love. The rational powers they did retain were darkened by folly. The demons became stupid as well as evil—providentially for us, because God takes advantage of their stupidity to protect us from them. The higher an angel stood in the ranks of heaven, the farther it plunged into hell; thus Lucifer, prince of angels, sank to the lowest point of the universe. From this ruin he cannot rise. "No new Devil will ever arise from among the good angels," Augustine wrote. "This present Devil will never return to the fellowship of the good."

Whether or not the Devil's sin can be said to have a cause, it did have a specific character: pride. When Satan's will sinned, the first sin it seized was pride. His pride consisted of love of self above love of God: Satan wished not to owe anything to God, preferring to be the agent of his own glory. From pride sprang envy of God and, after humanity was created, of the happy relationship with God that humans enjoyed in Paradise. From pride and envy followed lying and all the other sins.

Before the original sin of humanity, the Devil had no power over us. But after we freely chose to alienate ourselves from God, God permitted the Devil to exercise certain rights over us. The Devil could not claim these rights on his own, for as the greatest of sinners he possessed no rights of any kind. But God in his justice gave the Devil power to tempt, test, and punish us. In strict justice, God could have left us in the Devil's power forever, for it was our own free choice to alienate ourselves from happiness. Not in justice obliged but in mercy sustained, God took on human nature in order to reconcile us with him. He did this out of love, not out of need. He had given us into the hands of Satan and could have taken us back by any means he chose. But he preferred justice to force; he preferred to pay the Devil his due; and so he delivered himself up to Satan, who hastily and greedily seized him.

But Jesus, being divine as well as sinless, was in no way the Devil's due. By seizing him, Satan transgressed justice, violated the contract he had with God, and so lost his claim on us. God eternally knows the whole story. Augustine produced an image as colorful as the bait and hook: Christ was the cheese in the mousetrap, placed there by God to induce the devil to make the grab and so lose the prize. It was not so much that God planned to trick Satan as that he knew that Satan would be so overwhelmed with hatred and envy at the thought of God's love for humanity that he would hurl himself upon Christ with needless fury. Satan's attack on Christ was an inevitable result of God's decision to take human nature upon himself.

Augustine mingled this expression of ransom theory with sacrifice theory. Christ's sacrifice was an act of infinite generosity having infinite potential effects. Yet those effects were immediately limited, because the act saved some humans and not others. Two cities exist on earth. One is the city of God, the community whose inhabitants long for God and goodness. The inhabitants of this city view the world as a temporary lodging on the road to their true native land. The other is the worldly city, whose inhabitants, ruled by greed, lust, and avarice, scuttle about after power, deluding themselves that such poor fare provides true nourishment. The worldly city is occupied by evil angels and evil humans; the heavenly city by good angels and good humans. The world and the society in which we live is a mixture. Some of us are citizens of heaven and some of hell, and it is difficult to discern saints from sinners, difficult even to be sure to which city we ourselves belong.

Though Christ died for all and wishes that everyone would inhabit the heavenly city, he compels no one to enter, and many people are so perverse that they choose not to live there, preferring the pleasures of the worldly city. Therefore, said Augustine, Christ's Passion does not realize its full potential: it does not deplete the earthly city and fill the heavenly one. God repeatedly offers humanity the chance; the majority have always refused citizenship in the heavenly city and remain unsaved.

Jesus, a man, died for his brother and sister humans, but he did not die for the fallen angels, who were set immovably in their sin. Though his death removed some of the consequences of the angels' fall, it did not remove their own alienation from God. Neither did it save humans who refuse to participate in Christ's saving sacrifice. Sinners, including infidels and heretics, are citizens of the worldly city, walking the downward way. They are cells of Satan's body. Over these Satan did not lose his rights; he holds them firmly, justly, and for as long as their sin shall last. Fallen angels and fallen humans may know that Christ is God, but if

An angel and a demon dispute over the soul of a dead man, which is being weighed in the balance. The angel cautions the demon not to cheat. Courtesy Museu d'Art de Catalunya, Barcelona.

they do, their knowledge engenders fear rather than love, and they derive no benefit from it. They know the cosmos only to hate it and its maker.

The power, intensity, and quantity of Augustine's work ensured that most of his ideas would be fixed in the diabology of the Western church. Yet the incoherence of some of his arguments illustrates the difficulty of trying to encapsulate truth in a purely rational approach. The mystical theology of the Syrian monk known as pseudo-Dionysius the Areopagite (to distinguish him from the person whose conversion is recorded in Acts 17:34) brought another dimension to diabology.

Dionysius, writing about 500, distinguished between positive and negative theology, emphasizing the negative way to God through contemplation and prayer over the positive way of reason. The negative way combines the idea of the individual's kinship and intense closeness with God with the idea that God is intellectually unknowable. We can know nothing about God through reason, for God is completely beyond anything that we might understand about him. "My ways are not your ways, and my thoughts are not your thoughts," says the Lord; "As far as the heavens are above the earth are my thoughts above your thoughts and my ways above your ways" (Isa. 55: 8–9). Our own reason is infinitely tiny and restricted by comparison to God. An ant has more understanding of Plato than the human mind can have of God. More important, God is in himself greater than reason itself and unlimited by any rational category. If we are to have a glimmering, we must understand God with an understanding that surpasses reason, an understanding given by God and drawing us by desire irresistibly toward that which is the source of all.

Dionysius did not reject reason altogether, for although the essence of God—God-in-himself—is forever hidden, God's "energies"—his manifestations or actions, or his extension in the cosmos—can be partially known. God can be seen in the things of this world, even though they refract or distort his image. Further, reason tells us that some statements are more untrue than others. The first step of negative theology is to negate qualities in God that differ most from his infinity. "Surely it is truer to affirm that God is life and goodness than that he is air or stone," said Dionysius, "and truer to deny that drunkenness or fury can be attributed to him than to deny that we may apply to him the categories of human thought." Thought can take you a little bit of the way. But the next step of negative theology is to understand that no quality whatever can be assigned to God, for qualities are inventions of the limited human mind. Even negative statements are illegitimate. For example, it cannot be said that God is great or God is small, nor can it be said that God is not great or small, for those statements impose limitations on God, limitations derived from our fallible reason. The essence of negative theology is that no categories whatever can comprehend God. Dionysius' theology is minimal, experiential, and limited to God's manifestations in the cosmos, not daring to speak of God-in-himself.

God-in-himself, God's essence, produces his actions or manifestations, which are the cosmos. Things are not external to God. God knows everything that exists, but not in the sense that things exist prior to or separate from his knowledge and then he knows them. Whatever exists has existence for the reason that God knows it. Whatever does not exist lacks existence for the very reason that he does not know it. Things truly exist because they exist in God, as part of his energy.

God produces the world from nothing in the sense that he does not produce it out of anything that preexists it. There is nothing but God; nothing other than God from which things can come; God produces the cosmos out of his own being. Later theologians, not grasping Dionysius' point, thought his views pantheistic, but they misunderstood both pantheism and ex nihilo theology. Pantheism is the doctrine that the cosmos is God and God is the cosmos; God and the cosmos are coextensive, identical. This was far from Dionysius' insight: he was not a pantheist but a panentheist. Panentheism is the view that the cosmos is God in the sense of being God's manifestation of himself, but that the cosmos is infinitely transcended by God-in-himself. The cosmos is in God as a sponge is in a vast sea. Ex nihilo theology was invented by the fathers to reject the idea that any prime matter or other principle or stuff existed independent of God; it was not invented to deny that God produced the cosmos out of his own stuff. Later theologians have often argued as if there was God, and there was also Nothing, and God made the cosmos from that Nothing. The image is of God sitting in the midst of a vast Nothing and then creating the world out of it. But this implies that God is subject to time and that Nothing is really a kind of something. In fact nothing is not anything. It is no thing at all. There is God; that is all that is; there is nothing at all outside God, not even Nothing. The cosmos is God's manifestation of himself.

God is what is. Everything that is comes from him, and everything yearns to return to him. "All things are moved by a longing for the Beautiful and the Good," said Dionysius. Things without will or intelligence seek him naturally through natural processes; beings with will and intelligence seek him through conscious desire. The whole cosmos longs to be united with God, and God longs to gather it to him. God's first creative act is an act of desire that spills the cosmos out; his last creative act is to draw back in desire what he has produced in desire. The universe originates in the infinite creative energy inherent in God's nature. He bursts with energy, radiating in abandon an unlimited bounty. With the same energy and desire he draws the cosmos back into himself. The cosmos exists in a state of creative tension between the energy that exhaled it and the energy that draws it back in. The purpose of the cosmos is the dynamic expression of God's energy.

The cosmos consists of a glittering hierarchy stretching from those entities that are closest to God to those farthest from him. The hierarchy is not static, but a dynamic, moving scale or ladder on which the intelligences may be drawn upward on their way to union with God. Dionysius' is the first detailed description of the celestial hierarchy, in which the angels are arranged into three levels of three ranks each. The highest triad—the Seraphim, Cherubim, and Thrones—receive direct illumination from the divine principle that illuminates the cosmos. The middle triad—the Dominations, Virtues, and Powers—receive the divine illumination from the first triad and in turn transmit it to the lowest triad—Principalities, Archangels, and Angels. Archangels and Angels then convey God's will to humanity. This hierarchical arrangement was widely adopted in both Eastern and Western churches.

The idea that the seraphim are at the pinnacle of the angelic hierarchy combined with the idea that the Devil had been the highest angel led many writers to assume that Lucifer had been a seraph. Dionysius could not himself adopt the view, since in his system the highest orders of angels had no contact with the earth; the great tempter had to be from one of the lower orders of angels, for it was these who communicated with humans. In fact, the Evil One played little role in this system. Dionysius constructed no evil hierarchy to mirror the heavenly one.

Then how, in a world made with divine desire, a world in which all things have their being in God, can evil exist? The answer, Dionysius thought, lay in understanding the nature of goodness. God is love, but he is the furthest thing from meek or mild. God is love, but his love is like the cold winter wind that bites and penetrates and shakes and terrifies. God is what he is; what is, is. It is no limitation on God that he is not as we would prefer him to be; it is our limitation that we wish God to conform to what we desire. God is love, but God is also the God of Abraham, Isaac, Jacob, and Moses, whose face one cannot look upon and live. God is both, and more. God's love and God's goodness are beyond all human conception of love and goodness.

Dionysius had to face a dilemma. His system is essentially monistic, for there is no room in it for anything but God. Now, a thoroughgoing monistic position must maintain that even evil is part of God. Consistency demanded that Dionysius argue that evil proceeds from God and, however transformed, is drawn back into him. But Dionysius could not face this; he had to find a way to preserve the goodness of God. He found his way out in the theory of privation. Evil is only a lack of good; it has no substantial being but only a shadow of being. In one of his great showers of words, Dionysius says that evil is "a lack, a deficiency, a weakness, a disproportion, an error, purposeless, unlovely, lifeless, unwise, unreasonable, imperfect, unreal, causeless, indeterminate, sterile, inert, powerless, disordered, incongruous, indefinite, dark, unsubstantial, and never in itself possessed of any existence whatever."

All things are God, but evil is not God, since evil is not anything, only lack of being, lack of Godness. That is the argument from privation. It is a noble intellectual effort and a courageous logical defense of the all-good, all-powerful God. Most of the fathers, including Augustine, had stood by that defense. But for Dionysius and his followers it was even more necessary. Since the universe is not only created by God but is itself God, the question was how evil can exist in God himself. What is, is God; the cosmos is God; but there is evil in the cosmos. How resolve this painful problem? By denying real existence to evil. It is an elegant, logically beautiful solution. But it does not work, it fails to account for the suffering of countless men, women, children, and animals; real pain is not mere privation. Moreover, even if evil is lack of good as cold is lack of heat, we must still ask whence that cold, whence that lack, whence that evil, in the body of God that is the cosmos.

Still, Dionysius' cosmos reminds us that the world cannot be seen as wholly evil, that goodness is more fundamental, more real, and more powerful. It also reminds us of the intensity of our longing for harmony, as if we were being drawn up toward a unity that somehow forever escapes our grasp. Dionysius' cosmos is a holy order, unchangeable, absolute. No disorderly thing can exist in it. Harmony is the concord of all creatures with this cosmos, whose unity is progressively realized as all creatures are drawn gradually to God.

Evil therefore is not inherent in the cosmos or in anything at all that exists. But "how is it that the demons, if they have been brought forth from the good, are not themselves good?" Dionysius asks. The Devil's nature is real and good, since it is created by God. But to the degree that the Devil turns his will away from the reality of God toward the unreality of his own selfish desires, he moves away from goodness, being, and reality toward privation of reality. Of all creatures, the Devil has moved farthest from God and closest to the void. Eastern orthodoxy followed Dionysius in explaining evil by this combination of privation and free will, as Western theology followed Augustine's similar explanation. Thus rational theology and mystical theology came up with similar answers that later theologians, such as Aquinas, tried to weave together in a coherent fabric.

The classical Christian tradition had now been established. The frame had been constructed and the canvas stretched. The succeeding centuries would paint in the details. And yet the metaphor is not quite correct, for the framework was subject to strain and stress; it needed repairs and eventually rebuilding. The classical structure lacked the consistency of a purely monist or a purely dualist view; its semidualist nature contained inconsistencies that constantly challenged Christian thinkers. Most Christians ignored or evaded these inconsistencies, consciously or unconsciously. The best and most thoughtful struggled with them, releasing enormous creative power in the process. For the inconsistency of the classical view is its ultimate strength. Simpler, more consistent systems fail to deal with the ambiguity of the real world as we experience it; they are brittler, more easily broken. The inconsistencies of the classical structure lent it flexibility, subtlety, give; they allowed for a continuous tugging and tension, an unceasing struggle to understand that makes the Christian effort to cope with evil creative, open-ended, and liberating.

Although this book is not concerned with the Muslim tradition, it should be remarked that the Muslim view of evil and the Devil offers similar creative tension. Although Islam is more monistic than Christianity, Muslim theologians also faced the problem of evil in a world created by an infinitely good and powerful God, and Islam adopted many of its approaches to the problem from the early Christian fathers. Muslim theologians evolved both rational and mystical approaches similar to those appearing in the Christian tradition. Muslim theodicy is richly textured and shares with Christianity and Judaism the same faithfulness to human experience and the same courage in confronting the challenge of evil.

8 *Lucifer Popular and Elite*

POPULAR religion—the religion of the uneducated—consisted of theological ideas that had percolated down (usually with distortions) from the elite, combined with legendary and folklore elements.

In the early Middle Ages, theology, learning, and education were dominated by monasteries. The monks, training the clergy in the monastic schools and teaching the laity through homilies, derived their diabology from the desert fathers' fierce and colorful emphasis on the ubiquity and tangibility of demons. Homilists dwelt on demons for the express purpose of frightening their congregations into avoiding sin. The monastic tendency to emphasize the Devil's power was balanced by the opposite tendency of folklore and legend to make Satan seem ridiculous and impotent. This was a natural psychological reaction against the terrors of the monastic view. The more threatening Satan's power, the more comedy was needed to tame him and relieve the threat. In the tension between these contradictory tendencies, popular opinion oscillated between perceiving Satan as a lord of dark and terrible power and perceiving him as a fool.

Popular and folklore beliefs were defined less sharply than those of theology; the folklore Devil shades into other negative power figures such as giants, dragons, ghosts, monsters, weranimals, and "the little people." Over generations folklore supplied the tradition with many trivial details: what clothes the Devil wears, how he dances, how cold and hairy he is, and how he may be tricked or evaded. Some of these details gained wide credence and established themselves in art and literature. Few, however, became important elements in the tradition, since none addressed the core question of the nature of evil. Serious treatment of evil percolated down from elite religion far more than it rose from the popular. Indeed, the popular trivialization of the Prince of Darkness blurred and undermined the human effort to understand and cope with the power of destruction.

Folklore often split the Devil into more than one personality. From the time of Jewish Apocalyptic literature, the Devil had many names, such as Satan, Sammael, Asmodeus, Satanael, Belial, and Beelzebub, and the Apocalyptic stories sometimes assigned these names to different characters. Medieval folklore and literature sometimes revived this dramatic device: for example, the character Lucifer may appear as prince of hell and Satan as his henchman. But such distinctions lacked consistency and coherence; ignored in most legend and literature, they were flatly rejected by theology. The deepest and clearest theological and psychological perception has always been that the Devil is a single personality directing the forces of evil.

In addition to the ancient names deriving from the Judeo-Christian-Gnostic traditions, the Evil One attracted a host of popular nicknames that increased through time in number and variety. He was Old Horny, Old Hairy, Black Bogey, Lusty Dick, Dickon, or Dickens, Gentleman Jack, the Good Fellow, Old Nick, and Old Scratch, with comparable names in other languages. Such names shade into those of minor demons, themselves identified with the sprites or "little people" of paganism—spirits such as trolls, goblins, leprechauns, and kobolds. Hundreds of such names exist, such as Terrytop, Charlot, Federwisch, Hinkebein, Heinekin, Rumpelstiltskin, Haussibut, Hämmerlein, Robin Hood, Robin Goodfellow, and Knecht Ruprecht. Giving the Evil One an absurd name was a popular antidote to the terror he struck.

Satan's appearance, according to the tradition of folklore, varied as widely as his name. He was frequently identified or associated with animals, partly because animals had been sacred to the pagan gods, whom the Christians identified with demons. The Devil could appear as almost any animal except the lamb, ass, or ox (because Christ is the "Lamb of God" and the ox and ass were by tradition at the manger.) Most frequently he appeared as a serpent, dragon, goat, or dog. He took on a variety of human forms as well: an old man or woman, an attractive youth or girl, a servant, pauper, fisherman, merchant, student, shoemaker, or peasant. He frequently made his appearance as a priest, monk, pilgrim, or other holy man. He could be a theologian, mathematician, physician, or grammarian, and he proved highly skilled in persuasion and debate. He could appear as an angel of light, as Saint Paul had

Hieronymus Bosch, *Christ Carrying the Cross*, detail. The faces of people mocking the suffering Christ are demonic. Oil on wood. Courtesy Museum voor Schone Kunsten, Ghent.

warned, and occasionally he even dared masquerade as Christ or the Blessed Mother of God. He might appear as a threatening giant, idol, or whirlwind. His proper form is invisible or amorphous, but he can shift his shape to suit his purpose.

Often the Devil appears monstrous and deformed, his outward shape betraying his inner defect. He is lame because of his fall from heaven; his knees are backward; he has an extra face on his belly, knees, or buttocks; he is blind; he has horns and a tail; he has no nostrils or only one; he has no eyebrows; his saucerlike eyes shoot fire; he has cloven hooves; he emits sulphurous stenches; he is covered with coarse, black hair; he has misshapen, batlike wings. In artistic representation he resembled the pagan god Pan, horned, hooved, covered with goat hair, and equipped with oversized nose and phallus.

The Devil is usually black, symbolizing the absence of light and goodness. His skin is black, or he is a black animal, or his clothing is black. Sometimes he is a black rider on a black horse. His next most common hue is red, the color of blood and fire; he dresses in red or has a red or flaming beard; redheaded men and women are more subject to his influence than others. Occasionally he is green, owing to his association with the powers of vegetation, of forest wilderness, and of the hunt. He carries a fiery sword or an iron bar, or he wears clanking chains. He sometimes gives money away, but it inevitably changes sooner or later into something gross. The same is true of his other gifts: a knight invited to a mysterious banquet found that the succulent dishes and fine wines placed before him turned suddenly into excrement.

The Devil comes from the north, domain of darkness and punishing cold. Curious connections exist between Satan and Santa Claus (Saint Nicholas). The Devil lives in the far north and drives reindeer; he wears a suit of red fur; he goes down chimneys in the guise of Black Jack or the Black Man covered in soot; as Black Peter he carries a large sack into which he pops sins or sinners (including naughty children); he carries a stick or cane to thrash the guilty (now he merely brings candy canes); he flies through the air with the help of strange animals; food and wine are left out for him as a bribe to secure his favors. The Devil's nickname (!) "Old Nick" derives directly from Saint Nicholas. Nicholas was often associated with fertility cults, hence with fruit, nuts, and fruitcake, his characteristic gifts. This odd connection indicates how freely associative folklore becomes and how tangential to the essential point. The permutations of the folklore Devil are almost limitless; for the most part they do little to penetrate the problem of evil.

Anything that had been consecrated to the pagan gods became sacred to Satan. Pagan temples were his dwelling places: Christians either pulled them down or sanctified them as churches. Trees, springs, mountains, stiles, caves, and ruins (especially megaliths), groves, streams, and woods were haunts of the Prince of Darkness. The Devil favors the hours of noon and midnight, but he also likes dusk; he flees at dawn when the cock crows. The air is so full of demons that a needle dropped from heaven to earth will necessarily strike one; they swarm in the air like flies. The Devil usually dwells in the underworld, often at the center of the earth; a minor tradition placed hell in Iceland, whose extreme cold, groaning glaciers, and active volcanoes suggested a place of torment.

Lucifer and his followers are active always and everywhere. They cause mental and physical illness; they steal children, shoot arrows at people, attack them with cudgels, or leap upon their backs. They enter the body through every orifice, especially the mouth during yawning and the nose during sneezing. They haunt graveyards, ruins, and houses. Ghosts appeared in medieval folklore as souls on leave from purgatory, but Christian theology more commonly assumed that they were actually demons taking on the shapes of the dead.

The Devil rides out at night as leader of a wild hunt. Surrounded by demonic, baying dogs, Satan and his followers ride ghostly horses through the forests, winding their hollow horns. Anyone unfortunate enough to hear the dreadful sound in the wilderness at night must fall on his face at once, for to see the wild hunt is to die. The hunt may also appear as a rout of wild women led by a demoness (an ancient fertility goddess), a motif that became one of the elements in witch lore. Like his manifestation the dragon, Satan guards underground treasures. He and his followers ride animals backward. Having taken the place of the Teutonic giants, who constructed huge monuments, the demons build gigantic artifices. Any huge, mysterious object of stone was supposed to have been thrown down, built, or dug out by the Evil One. There are Devil's ditches, dikes, bridges, gorges, and towers. Lucifer hurls down meteorites; he piles up sandbars in harbors so that ships will run aground. He constructs piers, houses, roads, even church towers. His favorite engineering feats are bridges. The following story is typical. Jack and the Devil build a bridge near Kentmouth. Whatever they build up by night falls down by day. Finally Satan completes the bridge with the understanding that he will obtain the soul of the first living creature to cross the bridge, but Jack tricks him by throwing a bone onto the roadway, so that the first creature to pass is a dog.

Theology insisted that the Devil could be defeated only by calling upon Christ, but folklore tamed the terror by allowing humans to dupe the Prince of Darkness with native wit and guile. The Devil built a house for a cobbler after the cobbler promised that he could have his soul as soon as a lighted candle guttered out, but the cobbler blew out the candle before it burned down. Lucifer could be defeated in wrestling matches, mowing or sowing contests, drinking bouts, gambling wagers, or debates. Sometimes Satan's humiliation was satisfyingly grotesque, as when he attempted to prevent Saint Theobald from attending a council by removing a wheel from his cart. The saint forced him to take the wheel's place and went contentedly on his way with Lucifer rolling on the road beneath him. Schoolboys, farmers, shoemakers, smiths, farmhands, servant girls, cobblers, and monks are common heroes of such tales; rarely is the victor a priest or a gentleman. The stories convey the idea that the poor and humble are wiser than the rich and proud. They bring down the arrogant—including Lucifer himself—with their practical wit and common sense. The point of contact between this popular religion and theology is that the Devil, however crafty, is at bottom a fool who understands nothing.

Folkstories were usually aimed at cutting the Evil One down to size, but some frightening tales reveal the other side of folk ambiguity: the real terror of the dark power. Jack of France encountered a monk who was standing by the road reciting the names of those who would die in the year to come; Jack heard his own name called; horrified, he peered under the monk's cowl—and saw the hideous, leering face of Satan. One must never call upon the Devil in anger, for he may surprise you by answering. A man irritated by his whining little daughter exclaimed that he wished the Devil would carry her off; he did. An innkeeper vowing "May the Devil take me if this be not true" soon wished that he had kept quiet.

The Devil is almost always male. He has a powerful grandmother, probably an avatar of an ancient fertility goddess; he also has a wife and seven daughters representing the seven cardinal sins. He is the father of Antichrist, whom he begets on a Babylonian whore; he also engenders other evil or numinous figures such as Merlin, Attila, Caliban, and giants. The Devil's impregnation of a mortal woman, particularly his fathering of Antichrist, is a parody of the divine Incarnation. Since the Devil as an angel has no sex and can take on whatever form he pleases, "she" could have borne a child to a man, but that would have missed the mockery of the Holy Spirit's appearance to the Blessed Mother. Most basic is the sexist assumption that any figure of such enormous power has to be male. Lucifer's mother, sometimes called Lilith, is proud of "her son, the Devil." In a parody of Mary and the angels, she and the demons join in singing praises around her son's throne. In hell as on earth, the role of the female is to follow and admire the male. Folklore reflected not only contemporary society but the millennia-old assumptions of male supremacy and domination.

The line between the Devil, the prince of evil, and his followers the minor demons, occasionally blurred even in theology, is more muddled in folklore. The most important of Satan's many accomplices is the Antichrist, who will come at the end of the world to lead the forces of evil in a last, desperate battle against the good. Heretics, Jews, and (in the later Middle Ages) witches are the most prominent of Satan's human helpers. Jews and heretics may at least be unaware that they are serving Satan, but witches enlist knowingly in his ranks, worshiping him and offering him sacrifices.

One may deliberately summon the Devil in a number of ways, but most effectively by an incantation to Satan to appear, analogous to a prayer to God. One might also bind the Devil to come through magic, for which there is no analogy with the divine. God can only be asked; the Devil can be either asked or compelled. Satan is most seriously summoned for the purpose of making a formal pact. The idea of pact goes back to a story about Saint Basil circulated in the fifth century and to an even more influential story about Theophilus of Cilicia dating from the sixth.

As Hincmar of Reims retold the Basil story in the ninth century, a man wishing to obtain the favors of a pretty girl goes to a magician for help and as payment agrees to renounce Christ in writing. The magician, gratified at pleasing his Dark Master by making a new recruit, drafts a letter to Satan and orders the lecher to go out at night and thrust the message up into the air. This he does, calling upon the powers of evil. Dark spirits descend upon him and guide him into the very presence of Lucifer. "Do you believe in me?" asks the Dark Lord upon his throne. "Yes, I do believe." "Do you renounce Christ?" "I do renounce him," the lecher replies in a blasphemous parody of baptism. Then Satan complains, "You Christians always come to me when you need help but then try to repent later, presuming upon the mercy of Christ. I want you to pledge allegiance in writing." The man agrees, and the Devil, satisfied with the bargain, causes the girl to fall in love with the lecher and ask her father for permission to marry him. Her father, who wishes her to become a nun, refuses. The girl struggles against the Devil's temptations but is finally unable to resist any longer. But just before she surrenders her virtue, the pact comes to light, and with the aid of Saint Basil the man repents and the girl is saved from a fate worse than death.

The other story, the legend of Theophilus, one of the most popular of all European tales, eventually fathered the legend of Faust. Theophilus, a clergyman in Asia Minor, was offered a bishopric at the death of the previous bishop. Theophilus declined, but later regretted it, for the new bishop deprived him of his offices and dignities. Enraged, Theophilus plotted to regain his influence and obtain revenge. He consulted a Jewish magician, who took him out at night to a secret place where they encountered the Devil surrounded by his worshipers bearing torches and candles. The Devil asked him what he wanted, and Theophilus agreed to become his servant in return for his lost perquisites. Taking an oath of allegiance to Lucifer, he renounced his fealty to God and promised to lead a life of lust, scorn, and pride. He signed a formal pact to this effect and handed it over to the Devil, giving him a kiss in sign of submission. The Devil gave him great wealth and power, but at last he arrived to claim payment. Terrified, Theophilus repented and called upon the Blessed Mother for help. Mary descended into hell, seized the contract from Satan, and returned it to Theophilus, who destroyed it.

The legend, containing infernal reflections of both Christian baptism and feudal homage, spread rapidly across Europe and firmly established the notion of pact. It is one of the few examples of a popular idea changing the course of elite theology. The fathers had argued that all evildoers had implicitly agreed to be servants of Satan, but the idea of an explicit pact with homage to the Devil was new. By the fifteenth century, pact was the central accusation against alleged witches, and by the seventeenth century, documents allegedly constituting such formal pacts were brought as evidence into courts of law.

Pact was one of the keystones in the demonization of minorities—the transformation in the Christian mind of heretics, Jews, and Muslims into conscious minions of the Prince of Darkness. Total misunderstanding of the religion of others led Christians to make the most improbable assumptions. The Jews, who did not believe in the Incarnation or the Eucharist, were believed to steal Eucharistic hosts, take them home, and stab them until they bled; the rigidly monotheistic Muslims were believed to worship idols. The German version of *The Song of Roland* is explicit: the Muslims are pagans who worship 700 idols, the chief of which are Apollo and Muhammad. Muhammad, a human prophet to the

Theophilus gives the Devil the written pact (left) and on the right places his hands between Satan's in the sign of feudal homage. Abbey church of Souillac, twelfth century. Courtesy Lefèvre-Pontalis/© Arch. Phot. Paris/ S.P.A.D.E.M.

Muslims, was in the Christian mind the chief god of the idolatrous Muslims, barely distinct from Satan himself. It followed that Christians had both the right and the duty to stamp out these monsters. The same was true of the Jews, for Jews not only desecrated the host but kidnaped and sacrificed Christian children. Their synagogues were temples to Satan; they practiced evil magic; the Antichrist would be a Jew of the tribe of Dan. The relative toleration of Jews that existed in the early Middle Ages was replaced from the eleventh century by a fierce anti-semitism expressing itself in massacres, murders, and mass expulsions.

A much more constructive role played by the Devil in popular religion was that of a vehicle for ironic criticism of Christian society itself. Letters from the Devil became a popular genre in the later Middle Ages. Their purpose was threefold: to satirize corrupt ecclesiastics, particularly at the papal court; to amuse; and finally to offer instruction in rhetoric. The form of the letter was often a legal grant or charter in which Lucifer bestowed rewards for services rendered. He thanked the clergy for their greed, drunkenness, and worldly ambition, all of which brought him many recruits in hell. The salutations of such letters parodied legal charters: "Satan, emperor of all the realms of hell, king of shadows, duke of the damned, to his most faithful servant John Dominici, archbishop of Ragusa and abettor of all our works, sends good health and eternal pride." "The Letter of Lucifer" composed in 1351 was widely copied and adapted. After the salutation to "all the members of our kingdom, the sons of pride, particularly the princes of the modern church," it goes on to say, "we are sending some of the eminent demons and nobles of hell to counsel and aid you; your cleverness knows very well how to acquiesce in their suggestions and add to their treacherous inventions." After a long satire on the state of the church, the letter concludes, "dated at the center of the earth in our shadowy kingdom, in the presence of hordes of demons specially summoned for this purpose in our treacherous consistory."

Christian liturgy was linked to popular religion because most people encountered Christianity in the rites of the church more than in theology. The Devil, however, played little part in the liturgy, with the one major exception of the rite of baptism. By the third century the Western church commonly administered baptism at Easter. A series of scrutinies—masses during which exorcisms were administered to catechumens seeking admission to the church—were conducted in the weeks before Easter. Exorcism became an invariable part of baptism. Before the candidate could be received into the Christian community and the Body of Christ, the dark lord had to be exorcized from his soul.

The term "exorcism" had its origins in Greek paganism and derives from the Greek *exorkizo*, "to secure by oath" or "to ask or pray deeply." In its root meaning it was a solemn, intense address to someone or something and was not necessarily connected with demons. Among the pagan Greeks and even the early Christians, exorcism could be addressed to good as well as to evil powers. The New Testament uses the word "exorcize" twice to characterize earnest entreaties to Jesus.

By the third century the meaning of exorcism had narrowed: it was an indirect prayer to Christ to expel harmful spirits from persons or objects. The water, incense, salt, and oil used at baptism needed exorcism: "I exorcize you, creature salt . . . that this creature salt may in the name of the Trinity become an effective sacrament to put the Enemy to flight." The Devil or demons could also be addressed directly, and the two modes combined, as in this exorcism of water: "I exorcize you, creature water; I exorcize you, all you hosts of the Devil." Unbaptized persons needed exorcizing because Satan held lordship over humanity from the time of Adam and Eve. Underlying exorcism is the assumption that even after the Incarnation Satan retains certain powers over the material world as well as over fallen humans.

In addition to exorcism, the baptismal scrutinies included other confrontations with the Evil One. The Devil was sternly admonished to acknowledge the justice of the sentence of doom passed on him, to do homage to the Trinity, and to depart from the catechumen. The usual formula was "Therefore, accursed Devil, depart," but some wordings, such as the following, from the Gallican liturgy, were masterpieces of anathema.

I accost you, damned and most impure spirit, cause of malice, essence of crimes, origin of sins, you who revel in deceit, sacrilege, adultery, and murder! I adjure you in Christ's name that, in whatsoever part of the body you are hiding you declare yourself, that you flee the body that you are occupying and from which we drive you with spiritual whips and invisible torments. I demand that you leave this body, which has been cleansed by the Lord. Let it be enough for you that in earlier ages you dominated almost the entire world through your action on the hearts of human beings. Now day by day your kingdom is being destroyed, your arms weakening. Your punishment has been prefigured as of old. For you were stricken down in the plagues of Egypt, drowned in Pharaoh, torn down with Jericho, laid low with the seven tribes of Canaan, subjugated with the gentiles by Samson, slain by David in Goliath, hanged by Mordecai in the person of Haman, cast down in Bel by Daniel and punished in the person of the dragon, beheaded in Holofernes by Judith, subjugated in sinners, burned in the viper, blinded in the seer, and discountenanced by Peter in Simon Magus. Through the power of all the saints you are tormented, crushed, and sent down to eternal flames and underworld shadows. . . . Depart, depart, wheresoever you lurk, and never more seek out bodies dedicated to God; let them be forbidden you for ever, in the name of the Father, the Son, and the Holy Spirit.

The scrutinies included the "exsufflation," in which the priest blew into the candidate's face to express contempt for the demons and drive them away. The priest also touched the catechumen's ears with spittle in imitation of Jesus' healing. He marked the sign of the cross on the candidate's brow to keep demons away. During the Easter vigil, the catechumen would face the west, the region of darkness and death, and make a formal threefold renunciation of Satan. Then he turned toward the east, the direction of light and resurrection, and formally transferred his allegiance to Christ. He was anointed with holy oil as a seal against further assaults by the Prince of Darkness. In the central act of baptism, the descent into water symbolized descent into the underworld of death, and emergence from the water symbolized rebirth and resurrection. Baptism, the culmination of the individual's freedom from Satan, had powers to cure illness of body and mind as well as corruption of soul.

Aside from his general power over humanity, the Devil or his demons could possess any particular individual. The victim of such a possession was called an energumen. His body was under the temporary control of a demon, who could be expelled by exorcism. Such possession was in no way voluntary; the victim had not used his free will to invite the Devil in, and so an energumen was in no way a sinner; he was totally different from one who called voluntarily upon demons with incantations. Once the demon was expelled, the energumen would return to his normal life, usually without memory of the period in which his body was out of his control.

The elite theology of the Devil in the early Middle Ages followed that of the fathers. The only thoroughly original theologian of the period was John Scottus Eriugena (c. 820–c. 877), whose greatest work, *The Division of Nature*, composed between 862 and 867, stood in the tradition of negative theology. God is absolutely incomprehensible both to us and to himself. To know something is to define it, but God cannot be defined. More than that: God is not anything at all. It is absurd to say that God is something, for that puts him in the same category as created things. Nothing can be affirmed about God, for whatever is affirmed about him

denies its contrary. If we say that God is great, tha\
small; if we say that he is light, that denies that he is d\
God is beyond all categories, transcends all categories, anc\
categories. Any affirmation about God can be no more than a

God is not any substance or being. It is even absurd to main\
God "exists," as if God occupied the space/time continuum wit\
things that "exist." A dog, a table, a star, or a woman may exist, but\
does not exist if by existence we mean something present to the senses. If
a shirt exists, then God does not. But if by existence we mean uncon-
tingent being—eternal being dependent on no other being—then God
exists and the shirt does not. Whatever "being" may be for God, it is
totally different from what "being" is for a shirt.

Eriugena, like Dionysius, was a panentheist. The cosmos is God, but
God also transcends the cosmos. All things are in God, and all things are
God, but God is also beyond all things. Each creature that exists exists
for the reason that God thinks it and acts in it; its existence lies in God. If
we could penetrate to the deepest level of any creature, we would find
that that deepest level is God: "We should not understand God and the
creature as two things removed from one another, but as one and the
same thing." God is above, and below, and inside, and outside, of all
things; he is the beginning, the middle, and the end. The cosmos is God
in that it exists within God, but God infinitely transcends the cosmos.

> Every creature lives in God,
> And God is himself created in every creature
> In a way that we cannot grasp.
> Unreachable, he offers himself to us,
> Unseeable, he shows himself,
> Unthinkable, he enters our minds,
> Hidden, he uncovers himself,
> Unknown, he makes himself known,
> The unutterable Name utters the Word in which each thing is.
> Infinite and finite, complex and simple,
> He is nature above nature, being above being.
> Maker of all, he is made in all,
> Unmoving, he enters the world,
> Timeless in time, unlimited in limited space,
> And he who is no thing becomes all things.

There was never a time when the cosmos was not. God creates space
and time when he creates the cosmos. It makes no sense to imagine God

waiting for a while with things in potential before he actualizes them. God is in eternity; what he does, he does eternally. The universe is therefore both created and eternal. It has a true beginning and a true end for creatures dwelling within it, but it is truly eternal in the Word of God. The Word—Christ—is the link between God and creation. In Christ the Word lie all the causes, essences, ideas, predestinations, and seeds of the entire cosmos. When does God make this act of creation? At the beginning of time, from our point of view; in all eternity, from God's. Out of what does he make it? Out of nothing, that is to say, out of himself, for there is nothing other than him.

The physical world is God, but in a less direct sense than the ideal world: it is cloudy, shadowed, and ignorant. This is the nature of evil: lack of knowledge, lack of being. Evil has real effects, but in the deepest sense of existence it does not exist. It is nothing. Whatever has real being has it because God knows it. God does not know evil, so evil has no real being. If God knew evil, then evil would come from God, and this was not an alternative for Eriugena. The evil in creatures springs from their desire to cling to what comes from ignorance rather than what comes from reality.

The temptation of Adam and Eve by Satan was a historical event occurring in time. For Eriugena, the Devil's presence was unnecessary. Humanity was free to choose ignorance over reality and would probably have done so even if untempted by the Devil. The sense of a brooding, powerful, omnipresent Devil that dominated so much of medieval thought is not present in Eriugena. At the end of the world, everything will return to God, and the illusions of evil, privation, and ignorance will disappear. Even the Devil will be purged of sin, and his true, created nature will be drawn back to God. He will not cease to be, but he will cease to be the Devil. The sting of evil is drawn, and the world is made whole.

Christian art was able to get inside Lucifer's character in a way that neither folklore nor theology was able to do. The more dramatic moments of Lucifer's story—his original rebellion, his expulsion from heaven, his temptation of Christ, Christ's descent into Hell, and the end of the world—lent themselves to artistic treatments that explored the psychology of the fallen angel. Ironically, such explorations led to a degree of empathy. The rich literature of Old English, which introduced Teutonic ideas into the Judeo-Christian story, presented the Germanic hero, struggling alone, often against overwhelming odds. Proud and unbeholden to anyone, the Teutonic hero did not quite fit the pattern of

Christ or a saint. The most apposite figure in Christian tradition was Lucifer, proudly standing alone in hopeless battle, unyielding to the end against an implacable foe. For the first time, Lucifer seemed worthy of a kind of grudging admiration. The Teutonic conception of lordship, in which a military leader is surrounded by retainers bound to him in mutual loyalty, honor, and commitment, was also adapted to diabology. Christ was the lawful lord of heaven, whose trust Lucifer (and Adam) violated. The Teutonic punishment for denial of one's lord was to cut the traitor off from the community to wander as a lordless outlaw without a protector. Christ thrust Lucifer lonely into a lordless world: Teutonic peoples could grasp both the rightness of his punishment and the pathos of his wretchedness. The Devil also provided an inverted illustration of the values of Germanic feudalism: the bonds of loyalty between lord and retainers are twisted and perverted in hell, where Satan rules his vassals.

The Old English poem *Genesis* (eleventh-century in its final form) presents a dramatically detailed account of the rebellion and fall of the angels that goes far beyond the biblical story. God created the angels before making the material universe and its inhabitants. He gave the angels free will, expecting them to be his loyal vassals. But one of the angels, full of pride and envy, boasted that he need not serve God. Admiring the brightness and beauty of his own countenance, he turned his thoughts from contemplation of God to contemplation of himself. A rebellious vassal, he imagined that he could renounce his rightful lord and set up a fief in heaven for himself. "I can become God just like him!" he boasted. In the northwest of heaven he established a rebel stronghold and built a throne for himself, summoning the other angels to rally round his banner. But God, whose rights as lord had been violated, hurled Lucifer and his followers down to the dark dales. The rebel angels fell for three days and nights into the pit, where they lost their angelic dignity and became wretched outlaws.

Satan, once the most beautiful of the angels, now found himself in hell's stinking shadows. Undaunted, the rebel hero raised a castle in the darkness. There, rising from his accursed throne, he delivered a defiant speech to his retainers, reporting that he had heard that the Lord was unjustly planning to give the empty seats the rebels had vacated in heaven to a race of contemptible villeins, mere humans made of base earth and soil. Already God had prepared Eden for the first of these miserable creatures. Oh, Satan exclaimed in anguish, if I could just free myself for one winter hour, what I could accomplish with this host of hell!

In his heart Satan knew that he had no hope of defeating God in open battle. He therefore suggested a new plan to his thanes. If we cannot attack directly, we can at least pervert these humans, turn them against their Lord, and bring them down here to hell to be our slaves. I shall rest more comfortably in my chains knowing that humans too have lost the kingdom of God. One of the demon thanes volunteered for the mission, donned his war helmet, and ventured upward to Eden, where grew two trees, one of life, the other of death. (Two trees unambiguously good and evil suited Teutonic sensibilities better than did the ambiguities of biblical flora.)

Taking a serpent's shape, the demon tempted Adam first. The Anglo-Saxon audience was much more comfortable with the idea of a great lord (good or evil) approaching the lord and master of humanity rather than his wife on important business. The demon told Adam that he bore the message that God in fact wished Adam to pick the fruit of the tree of death and eat it. Adam, astutely observing that this thane looked little like an angelic messenger, declined, and the demon turned his attentions to the weaker sex. Complaining to Eve that Adam had misunderstood him, he guilefully insisted, "I am not like the Devil." He cleverly appealed to Eve's love for Adam to persuade her that she would be helping her husband by eating the fruit. Eve ate, and immediately received what she took to be a beautiful vision of heaven. The messenger congratulated her on her changed appearance, and her delusion was now so deep that she imagined both him and herself to shine with angelic beauty. She then persuaded Adam to join her in eating the fruit, and the demon's hopes were fulfilled. Laughing and capering, he prepared to return to hell with the news of his success. Adam and Eve, human, fallible, inexperienced, had believed the lies, but now that the deed was done, they realized that they had betrayed their Lord. It is strange that God "would let so many people be tricked by lies masquerading as wisdom," the poet puzzled.

Another Old English poem, *Christ and Satan*, proceeds quickly through the story to the moment when the fallen angels find themselves established in hell. Here Satan's speech from the throne is pathetic as well as defiant. We have lost our glory, he tells his retainers, and exchanged it for the shadows of hell, bound in torment among fires that give no light. Once we sang amid the joys of heaven; now we pine in this poisonous place. The other cruel spirits blame their lord for leading them into the disastrous rebellion. You lied, they complain, in making us think that we could become our own lords and not serve the Savior. Well, here you are now, an outlaw bound fast in fire, and we your followers have to

Mouth of hell swallowing the damned, who are tormented by demons as Christ locks them in. Cotton MS Nero IV fol. 39. Courtesy of The British Library.

suffer with you. Throughout their wretched colloquy Satan and his thanes rage against the reality of the world as it is constructed; their rage is a perfect artistic expression of the demonic temperament and of Satan's predicament. The wretched spirits refuse to accept the world as God has created it, yet they can never change it. The Devil's refusal to accept reality produces the eternal misery in which he dwells: he constructs his own hell. Defeated yet proud, the hero faces his *wyrd*, his implacable fate.

Sparking fire and poison as he speaks in the dark cavern, Satan makes his report to his thanes, rehearsing his reasons for rebelling. I used to be a high angel in heaven, he mourns, but I plotted to overthrow the light of glory. Now God has thrust me down here; very well: he has merely confirmed me in my hatred. There is no place in this deep darkness for us to hide from God, for though we cannot see him any longer, he can see us. It would be better had I never known the brightness of heaven, which is now taken from me and given to Christ. God at least grants me the power to fly up from this prison and visit earth to tempt humans, but only those souls that he does not wish to keep for himself, for he has given all the authority of heaven and earth to his Son. Satan ends by uttering a dirge of sheer misery: "Alas for lordship's misery, alas the protection of God's power, alas the might of the Maker, alas earth, alas light of day, alas God's joy, alas angelic host, alas heaven! Alas that I am deprived of eternal joy!" The passage concludes with a description of Christ resplendent in the glory that Lucifer had craved for himself.

The second portion of *Christ and Satan* deals with the harrowing of hell, where the holy dead are waiting for Christ to come to free them. He breaks down the doors, and a great light pierces the darkness, accompanied by angel song as if at daybreak. The third portion treats Satan's temptation of Christ. The Devil hoists Jesus mockingly onto his shoulders in order to show him the whole world. I will grant you dominion over peoples and lands, he promises: receive from me cities, broad palaces, and even the kingdom of heaven. Satan's theology is faulty, for he has no right or power to offer Christ dominion in heaven; the biblical accounts had Satan offering Christ only the earth, over which God had given the Devil temporary power. Christ responds scornfully, setting Satan the task of returning to the darkness and measuring the length and breadth of hell with his own hands. Satan obeys sullenly and reports to his thanes that the grim gravehouse measures a hundred thousand miles—probably the largest number the poet could conceive.

Taken together, the three parts of *Christ and Satan* take Lucifer from his proud boasts in the first through his shocking defeat in the second to his utter humiliation in the third. It is a historical drama of Christ's progressive victory over the power of evil. Early medieval literature filled in the tradition with rich detail. Theologians could draw upon this richer, fuller tradition in their own speculations.

9 *Scholastics, Poets, and Dramatists*

BEGINNING in the eleventh century the rapid spread of literacy led to a wide shift in cultural attitudes, including the growth of individual self-consciousness and critical awareness. Intellectual life from 1050 to 1300 was dominated by scholasticism, a method characterized by a strict and formal application of reason to theology, philosophy, and law. In the twelfth century scholasticism developed its characteristic dialectical method: a question was posed, passages from Scripture and tradition were cited on both sides, and logic was summoned to resolve the question. In theology, scholasticism sharpened doctrines to a fine edge in order to establish well-defined boundaries between truth and error, orthodoxy and heresy. Though great scholastics such as Aquinas knew the limitations of reason, the thrust of scholasticism as a whole was toward building certain knowledge as an intellectual stronghold from which orthodoxy could be defended.

The analytical interpretation of Scripture and tradition using logic and Greek philosophy changed diabology by freeing theology from the dependence upon tradition that had characterized most of the early medieval period. At the same time, it raised new dangers. It constructed elaborate rational superstructures upon weak epistemological bases and eventually moved too far away from experience.

Wide shifts in attitudes toward the Devil sometimes moved in contradictory directions. Satan continued to become more and more colorful and immediate in art, literature, sermons, and popular consciousness. This change was part of a general tendency to solidify religious figures: both Christ and Mary became more present and immediate during this time, Mary becoming Satan's most vigorous opponent in popular legend.

On the whole, people seem to prefer to believe in a conscious source of evil rather than in blind fate or chance. Yet the Devil's function in theology declined. Humanism, the scholastic attack on Cathar dualism, the satisfaction theory of Saint Anselm (1033–1109), and the revival of Aristotelian ethics all lessened Lucifer's role in theology to the extent that he sometimes degenerated into a caricature of rhetoric or propaganda, as when papalists referred to the antipope Clement III as a "messenger of Satan and lackey of Antichrist," or as when trivial debates were set: "Are we to hate the Devil as much as we love Christ?"

Anselm did much to reduce the Devil's role in theology. In his book *The Fall of the Devil*, he concentrated on the fall of Lucifer rather than on that of Adam because Adam's fall can be indirectly and partially explained by the temptation offered by the serpent, but no preexistent evil existed to tempt Lucifer. Thus the analysis of his fall is essentially a discussion of the origin and nature of evil.

Anselm believed that God is responsible for natural evil, for he created a cosmos with ontological deficiencies: blind cows and crippled babies exist. Even if such privation is somehow necessary for the ultimate good of the cosmos, God still has responsibility for it. When a baby lacks limbs or a woman with cancer lacks health, these privations cause real suffering. Moral evil, which also causes real suffering, can be assigned either to free-will choice or to a cause. But if moral evil is assigned a cause, then it is merely another variety of ontological evil, and God is again directly responsible for it. The actions of the Devil's will are part of the cosmos that God constructs and causes knowing in all eternity its every detail, its every event. We may say that he wills only the good and merely permits evil, but this permission itself seems to imply that God created the conditions that caused Lucifer's fall.

Thus Anselm investigated God's responsibility for evil by analyzing the fall of Lucifer. If the Devil invented evil, God permitted him to do so. But how could Lucifer will the wrong thing? Since God gave him his will, it could not itself be evil. Anselm's analysis proceeded on the lines of the medieval theory of justice. When Lucifer's will turned from what it should desire to what it should not, it unbalanced the harmony of the cosmos, introducing injustice, and it is in this injustice that evil consists. God has his plan for the cosmos. Humans and angels must act in accordance with this plan. When laws and actions accord with the divine harmony, justice prevails; when they do not, injustice prevails. By introducing the dissonance of his selfishness into the cosmos, Lucifer twisted the original harmony into a state of injustice. How to assess the relative responsibility of Satan and of God? Anselm faced the question more resolutely than anyone else before Luther.

In explaining the Devil's fall, Anselm cut through the old knot that had stuck at the center of the question since the time of Augustine. The conditions that surround an evil action are in no way its cause. No preconditions caused Lucifer's fall, none at all. Why did Lucifer sin? For the reason that he willed to. If any condition causing a free-will choice existed, the choice would not be entirely free. Free will is not a mere appearance; it is not compelled; it is not caused; it is really, truly, and absolutely free. The answer is psychologically satisfying, for we do experience having freedom of choice, and we also experience the sense of sometimes making evil choices. It became the classic free-will defense freeing God from the onus of causing moral evil.

In retrospect, Anselm's answer seems like the invention of the wheel, but earlier theologians missed the solution on account of the heavy weight of Augustine's predestinarian ideas. Anselm argued that the terms "predestination" and "foreknowledge" were misnomers, for God is not situated in time looking ahead. Rather, all moments are an eternal now for God: he sees the whole cosmos from alpha to omega. God is omniscient, knowing every detail of his cosmos, and he is omnipotent, responsible for every detail. God's own freedom is complete. His responsibility for most things is direct: the orbits of the planets, the flight of birds, even ontological evils such as cancer. For free-will choices he is only indirectly responsible. Since God constructs the cosmos not as a mechanical toy but as a forum for morally responsible creatures, he wills that certain creatures—humans and angels, for example—have true freedom to choose either good or evil. God destines the entire cosmos to be what it is. But he wills some things for themselves; other things, such as moral evil, he wills only indirectly in the sense that he creates a cosmos in which they inhere. "Although God destines these things caused by free-will action, he does not cause them by compelling the will or restraining it, but by leaving it to its own power. . . . Some things are predestined to occur through free choice."

This answer, which anticipated Luther's doctrine of the two wills of God, achieves a resolution of the ancient contradiction between predestination and free will and removes God's responsibility for sin. It does nothing, however, to relieve God of responsibility for ontological evil: indeed, it makes him directly responsible for cancer and blindness. Further, it does not explain why, if moral evil must exist, it must cause the amount and degree of suffering that it does.

Having introduced injustice into the world, Satan tempted Adam and Eve in order to spread injustice. Because Adam and Eve are fully responsible for their own choice, original sin could have occurred without any intervention by Satan. Anselm, respecting tradition, never thought of removing Satan from the scene, but elsewhere he was able to describe original sin and its effects without any reference to the Devil. God creates human nature to conform to justice and to be in harmony with the cosmos and with him. In effect a kind of contract existed, where God promised us happiness if we acted in accordance with justice. But we broke the contract by original sin, failing to render God his just due. Though we have no power to harm God in himself, we do have the power to harm him by alienating ourselves from the just order that God wills for us.

Though God allows Lucifer certain powers over humanity because of our sin, the Devil has no rights over us at all. Whatever we owe as a result of our sin we owe to God and not to the Devil. Rejecting ransom theory, Anselm formulated an original variant of sacrifice theory known as satisfaction theory. In this theory Lucifer plays a little role. Because we violated our contract unjustly, God in justice is under no obligation to save us. But his mercy and love make it fitting and proper for him to do so. God therefore chooses to save us. But he cannot restore alienated humanity by force or by fiat without violating justice himself. We humans had unbalanced the scales of justice; we now had to restore the balance by offering compensation. But we have nothing to offer God, because everything that we have is his own gift to us. Humanity thus owes God a great debt that it has no means to pay; God has the means to pay but owes no debt. It follows that the only being who can make the appropriate sacrifice is one who is both God and man. As a man representing the whole human race, Christ owes the debt; being God, he can pay it. Christ's sacrifice satisfies the demands of justice.

Legalistic though it was, satisfaction theory presented a coherent theory of redemption. Gradually it came to replace ransom theory completely among theologians (although not in literature or legend). As ransom theory faded, so the role of the Devil in theology diminished.

Scholastic arguments clarified other problems of diabology. When did Lucifer fall? Scripture and tradition agreed that he was corrupt "from the beginning," but Peter Lombard (1100–1160) and others observed that if he had really been evil from the moment of his creation, God would have created him evil, which is absurd. On the other hand, Lucifer could not long have delayed making his choice, for angelic intelligences grasp the

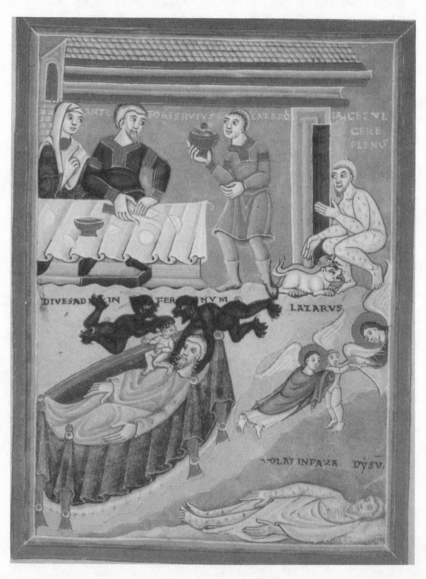

The parable of Lazarus and the rich man. Lazarus is saved while the soul of the rich man is taken from his coffin by two coal-black demons. Manuscript illumination from the Pericope Book of Henry II, Germany, eleventh century. Courtesy Dr. Ludwig Reichert Verlag, publisher of the 1981 facsimile edition.

nature of the cosmos intuitively and immediately; they do not learn over time by sensory observation and reason, so no new information can enter their minds to change them. Therefore a delay, albeit a very small one, must have intervened between Lucifer's creation and his fall.

The scholastics established why the Devil cannot be saved. First, unlike Adam and Eve, he cannot plead the extenuation of having been tempted by someone else. Second, since his natural intellect was so much greater than that of humans, his fault was proportionately greater. Third, since angels cannot learn anything new, they cannot change their minds or repent. Fourth, after their fall, their angelic qualities are diminished. They retain their intellects in only an impaired, diminished form, and though they do not lose their free will, they lose the power actually to choose between good and evil. Fifth, Lucifer and his angels derive no benefit from the sacrifice of Christ, for they are not humans. It would require one of his own species to redeem Lucifer, but this is impossible, for each angel constitutes its own species. Sixth, since the Devil fell untempted, he would have to return to grace unaided, which is impossible.

The revival of dualism by the Cathar heretics had an important impact on diabology. The Cathars, whose deep roots were in Gnosticism, entered the West in the 1140s and spread from northern Italy into southern France, Aragon, the Rhineland, and the Low Countries. Cathar dualism, the most dangerous heretical challenge to the medieval church, was finally exterminated only by crusade and inquisition. Essentially the Cathar view of the Devil was intended to save the goodness of God by limiting God's power and to account for and respond to the conflict between good and evil that we observe in ourselves and in others. Catharism was a poignant yearning to transcend this hopelessly ruined world in a beautiful and perfect world beyond.

The dualist doctrines of the Cathars varied from group to group; the largest general difference was between the absolute dualists, who held that the Devil was a principle completely independent of God, and the mitigated dualists, who believed that he was a creature who had usurped God's powers. The absolute dualists argued that there must be two independent principles, since we observe both good and evil in the world. If only one principle exists, it must be either good or evil, since one principle cannot embrace opposites. If the one principle is evil, where does good come from? If it is good, where does evil come from? It is impossible that a God who is all-good and all-powerful should construct a cosmos such that he regrets what occurs in it. This approach was so abstract that many Cathars adopted more moderate and more concrete views. One such view was that Lucifer was a son of God, a brother of Christ; another was that Lucifer was the son of the abstract evil principle. Neither of these views truly exonerated God from responsibility. Only the absolute view seemed to offer a consistent answer.

Whatever the Devil's origin, the Cathars agreed that he is the prince of this material world, its maker and its ruler. All agreed that the true God created only spirit. The absolutists said that the Devil created the material world at the same time as God created the spiritual world or earlier; the mitigated dualists said that God created the spiritual cosmos first and then the Devil imitated it crudely by making formless matter and molding it into creatures; he could give these unfortunate things no life, so he went to heaven to seduce the angels so that he might stuff them into inanimate matter and procure a captive population for himself on earth.

The God of the Old Testament is not the true, good God, for he is changeable, cruel, and, above all, the creator of this evil material world. The personage who fits the qualities of the Old Testament God is not God at all, but Satan. Christ's saving mission was to come in the appearance of a body to warn us that in order to return to God we must free our spirits from the gross flesh in which the false God, Satan, has imprisoned them.

The Catholic response to dualism was summed up in the influential Fourth Lateran Council of 1215, which treated the Cathar threat so seriously that it addressed it in its very first canon. The assembled bishops declared that the true, good God created all things from nothing. The Devil and the other demons were created good in nature but made themselves evil by their own free will. At the resurrection at the end of the world all persons will receive their just deserts, evil humans and angels suffering perpetual torment with the Devil, while the good enjoy eternity with Christ. The council and the scholastics argued against the dualists that evil is nonbeing and that two opposed beings are logically impossible: (1) Since evil has no essence it cannot be the source of anything. (2) Evil may diminish good but cannot consume it, for otherwise nothing real would be left, nothing in which evil could reside, and it would eliminate itself. (3) Since evil has no being, it cannot cause anything except "accidentally" in that it resides in a good that causes something. (4) A principle of incoherence and disorder cannot exist, since these are mere negations of coherence and order. (5) If two eternal principles were absolutely balanced, the cosmos would be in stasis between them, but if they were *not* absolutely balanced, one would eternally exclude the other. (6) An absolutely evil being cannot exist, because absolute evil is absolute nothing; further such a being would be self-contradictory, since it would hate and cancel out its own essence; if it loved and cherished anything in itself, then it would not be entirely evil.

The Catholic and Cathar arguments sailed past each other, never in contact except to fire salvos. The Cathars insisted upon the ultimate reality of evil; the Catholics denied it on the ground that evil was mere privation. The Catholics insisted that nothing could limit the sovereignty of God; the Cathars believed that God was limited by something external to him: matter and evil. Yet, oddly, these views converged at a deeper level. Both sides were affirming, each in its own way, the utterly alien, non-Godness of evil. For the Cathars, it is non-God because it is a different god. For the Catholics, it is non-God because it lacks God's being. The two sides were too hostile ever to find any mutual ground, and as Catholic doctrine and organization grew more rigid, it tended more and more to associate heretics with Satan. Having been demonized, heretics were subject to legal prosecution and societally sanctioned persecution.

In the mid-thirteenth century, when these turmoils were in temporary abeyance, the most influential of the scholastics appeared, Thomas Aquinas (1225–1274). Thomas distinguished among four kinds of evil. Of these he dismissed absolute evil as an abstraction having no referent in reality, since absolute evil is absolutely nothing. He also objected to calling "metaphysical" evil an evil at all, because the inferiority of creation to God is a logical necessity. This left him with natural evil and moral evil. In natural evil Thomas distinguished between privation and negation. Some lacks in creatures are not properly privation and therefore not natural evils. That a pig lacks wings or a stone lacks gills is not *privation*, but *negation*, and in no sense evil. Real privation, natural evil, occurs only when a creature is deprived of something properly belonging to it: "Evil is a given subject's failure to reach its full actuality." Each creature is drawn to realize itself fully in God/being/goodness, and evil is the measure of the extent to which this realization is obstructed. A deaf woman is not a fully realized woman, so the woman's deafness is a natural evil.

Now, how to reconcile the existence of natural evil with that of a good God? Why are there women lacking hearing, men lacking sight, children lacking limbs? At the beginning of his *Summa theologiae* Thomas admitted that the existence of evil is the best argument against the existence of God. After undertaking to refute atheism with his famous five proofs of God's existence, he turned to face the problem of evil squarely.

God is responsible for the entire cosmos. No other principle can exist, no independent cause of evil, no *summum malum*. Total evil is total privation and nonbeing. God makes all things good. Anything that exists, including Satan, is good because God created it. Evil could not exist without good, for evil does not exist in itself and so must be a defect in an inherently good being. To what extent is God responsible for the privations of natural evil and moral evil?

Every evil has a cause. Using Aristotelian terms, Thomas argues that evil lacks a formal or final cause, since it is nothing in itself, but it does have a material cause—the good in which it resides—and an efficient cause—the agent that brings out the defect. Natural evil always has a natural cause. Any defect in nature is caused by some preceding defect. It might be thought that God is the original cause of such defects, if only because he must have introduced the first one. But defects are only accidental byproducts of a good. Bacteria cause suffering in other creatures only "by accident": they are good in themselves. A boulder, good in itself, causes pain "by accident" when it rolls down onto a passerby. God never wills the defect, but only the good in which the defect resides. Thus God can be said to be the cause of natural evil only "by accident." He creates the man and he creates the bacteria; both are good; the bacteria deprive the man of health only "by accident."

Having no defect himself, God cannot be the cause of any. He wills no evil. It is true that he also does not eradicate evils; he permits them to occur for a greater good; his providence extracts good from every evil. Sometimes this is obvious, as when pain causes us to withdraw our hand from the hot stove. Often it is not at all clear, as when a child is run over. But the perishability and corruptibility of creatures are necessary in a cosmos diverse enough to express and reflect its divine creator fully. A cosmos in which nothing was perishable would be static and monolithic. Defect and evil are contingent upon and subordinate to the greater good. The spider could not live without eating the fly; the weasel would perish unless it devoured the mouse. "Tell that to the mouse" is not an adequate retort, because the theory takes the mouse's suffering fully into account. It is logically impossible to build a cosmos bursting with life and vigor without corruptibility and perishability and the suffering they entail.

Thomas's God, then, does not will natural evil but accepts it as the necessary price for the existence of the cosmos. Is that existence worth so much suffering, or is so much suffering compatible with the existence of a good God? Thomas assumed so, but the argument that evils are only "apparent" since they are part of a great order whose perfect goodness is hidden from us has never been satisfying. Still, even if the existence of God were denied, the problem would remain; the argument against the existence of God on the ground that evil exists strikes not only at God but at any idea of any rational, orderly, or purposive cosmos. The argument from evil, if it is valid, destroys the notion of all order and all cosmic principles, not just the one we call God. By destroying order and principle it renders all value judgments completely subjective. In the eighteenth century the Marquis de Sade would see this very clearly. But then a curious thing happens: the original argument is destroyed by a paradox. If no order or purpose exist, then all human values and aspirations are absurd, and consequently good and evil are only subjective constructs. But since evil then cannot exist objectively, it cannot be adduced against the existence of God. Still, anyone maintaining the existence of God must cope honestly with natural evil.

Moral evil raised other problems. On the one hand Thomas wanted to assert that everything in an ordered cosmos has a cause, but on the other he wanted to affirm free will, both to provide a reason for the creation of the cosmos and to restrict God's responsibility for sin. Thomas used privation to restrict God's responsibility for natural evil, and he used free will to restrict God's responsibility for moral evil. In his solution, God is not responsible for moral evil, because moral evil is the free and direct choice of the agent. God's predestination and providence govern the entire cosmos, but his providential plan embraces free will and its consequences.

Like Eriugena, Anselm, and other leading scholastics, Aquinas was thus able to address the problem of evil without assigning the Devil a necessary role. Still, he assumed the existence of the Devil as a given of revelation, and he helped refine some points of diabology. At the beginning of the cosmos, God offered Lucifer a gift of supernatural grace that would have conferred beatitude upon him had he accepted it. Satan understood that this was the highest good, better than any natural happiness, but he chose to set that consideration aside. Satan's sin has both content and quality. The content is his choice to reject beatitude in order to seek what he believed to be his natural happiness. With his angelic intelligence and knowledge, he could not have believed that he could actually equal God, but he wanted to be *like* God in the sense of being free to command his own happiness by his own resources and thus to owe no debt of gratitude to the Lord. Satan's sin occurred soon after the moment of creation, at the point when he realized that he was not God, that he was dependent upon God, and that he had the choice of accepting this state of dependence or not.

The Devil's action upon us is only external. He can persuade and tempt us, but he can never infringe upon our freedom by causing us to sin. Since he can tempt, he is an indirect cause of sin, but the sinner himself or herself is always the direct cause.

If the Devil is not necessary to explain either sin or temptation, what is his function? Thomas's answer is that he is the head, chief, prince, ruler and lord of all evil creatures, incorporating them into one entity with him. As the faithful are members of Christ's mystical body, so sinners are members of Satan's mystical body, united with him in alienation.

The scholastics thus refined certain points of diabology but found in their tightly logical systems little need for the figure of the Prince of Darkness. Theologically, Satan was in decline. In European culture as a whole, however—in legend and literature—the figure of Satan grew in strength. In the effort to create artistic unity, to make the story of salvation more dramatic and the development of the plot more compelling, writers of literature constructed an elaborate scenario more gripping than that of the theologians.

One of the most powerful representations of Satan occurred in visions of the other world, a literary genre that went back to the third century and in the eleventh produced *The Vision of Tundale*. This minor masterpiece, which influenced subsequent artistic and literary representations of the Evil One, including Dante's, describes the torments of the damned in the fiery pit. It presents two striking pictures of demons and one of Lucifer himself. Tundale saw "a beast of unbelievable size and inexpressible horror. This beast exceeded the size of any mountain he had ever seen. His eyes were shining like burning coals, his mouth yawned wide, and an unquenchable flame streamed from his face." He saw another demon having two feet and two wings, with a long neck, iron beak, and iron talons. The beast sat atop a pool of ice, devouring as many souls as he could seize in his talons. These souls, as soon as they were digested in his belly, were excreted onto the ice, where they were revived to face new torments. And at last Tundale saw Satan himself:

the prince of darkness, the enemy of the human race, who was bigger even than any of the beasts he had seen in hell before. . . . For this beast was black as a crow, having the shape of a human body from head to toe except that it had a tail and many hands. Indeed, the horrible monster had thousands of hands, each one

Satan, king of hell, tortures the damned while bound to a fiery grill as in the *Vision of Tundale*. Illumination from the *Très riches heures du Duc de Berry*, Burgundy, fifteenth century. Courtesy Musée de Condé, Chantilly, and Photographie Giraudon.

of which was a hundred cubits long and ten cubits thick. Each hand had twenty fingers, which were each a hundred palms long and ten palms wide, with fingernails longer than knights' lances, and toenails much the same. The beast also had a long, thick beak, and a long, sharp tail fitted with spikes to hurt the damned souls. This horrible being lay prone on an iron grate over burning coals fanned by a great throng of demons. . . . This enemy of the human race was bound in all his members and joints with iron and bronze chains burning and thick. . . . Whenever he breathed, he blew out and scattered the souls of the damned throughout all the regions of hell. . . . And when he breathed back in, he sucked all the souls back and, when they had fallen into the sulphurous smoke of his maw, he chewed them up. . . . This beast is called Lucifer and is the first creature that God made.

The most important development of the Devil in literature appeared in the work of Dante (1265–1321), the greatest medieval poet and lay theologian. His *Divine Comedy*, written in the last fifteen years of his life, is a complex mystical poem in which the Devil, though seldom "on stage," is a powerful force operating throughout both hell and earth. Dante did not mean to write a scientific treatise on the physical universe. Rather, he wished to portray the cosmos according to its moral design. For Dante and his contemporaries, the deepest meaning of the cosmos was ethical, not physical, although as a careful artist he wished this ethical world to be analogous to the physical universe as it was understood in his time. In the *Comedy*, the physical universe is a metaphor for the ethical cosmos rather than the other way round.

Like Ptolemy's, Dante's universe was arranged in a series of concentric spheres, the earth being the sphere at the center. Above and around the earth was the sphere of the moon and then in order those of Mercury, Venus, the sun, Mars, Jupiter, Saturn, the fixed stars, and the *primum mobile*, the sphere that moves the whole universe. Beyond and above these was heaven, the abode of God, the angels, and the blessed souls. In the center of the earth was hell, and at the very center of hell, imprisoned in darkness and ice, was Satan.

Dante worked out a mystical vision not unlike that of Dionysius. Every being in the cosmos moves either toward God or toward the Devil. God is ultimately far up and out; the Devil is ultimately far down and in. When we are filled with our true human nature, which is made in the image of God and buoyed by the action of the Holy Spirit within us, we rise naturally up toward God, we spread out, widen our vision, open ourselves to light, truth, and love, with wide vistas in fresh air, clean, beautiful, and true. The mystic rose at the threshold of heaven opens out for us. But when we are diverted by illusion and weighed down by sin and stupidity, we sink downward and inward, away from God, ever more narrowly confined, our eyes gummed shut and our vision turned in upon ourselves, drawn down, heavy, closed off from reality, bound by ourselves to ourselves, shut in and shut off, shrouded in darkness and sightlessness, angry, hating, and isolated. Each circle of hell as we descend is narrower and darker. There is nothing in that direction, literally nothing: silence, lack, privation, emptiness. God is expansion, being, light; Satan, drawn in upon himself, is nothingness, hatred, darkness, and despair. His isolation stands in utter contrast to the community of love in which God joins our minds with the first star.

On one level this system places the Devil rather than God at the center of the universe. On a deeper level, however, Dante meant God to be placed at the real, moral center of the cosmos, though he could not represent this in spatial terms. Indeed, he took pains to insist that the moral center cannot be located in space or time. It is not in space and has no pole; heaven has no other "where" than in the mind of God; it is the point at which all times are present, the point at which every "where" and every "when" converge. Like Nicholas of Cusa in the fifteenth century, and like twentieth-century physicists, Dante could say that the universe has its center everywhere and its circumference nowhere. Dante represented his cosmos according to the only scheme available to him, the Ptolemaic and patristic model that placed the earth at the center, but he knew that the real center is the life and light of God, which is everywhere. The pathos and horror of Dante's Satan is that he is forever blind to that light, isolated from God's love.

Dante addressed the problem of Satan's geographical location at the center of the universe by referring to Aristotelian physics, in which everything in the universe seeks its natural place (see Figure 2). From the sphere of the moon upward, natural movement is curvilinear, orbital; below the moon, and on and inside the earth, movement is rectilinear. Fire moves naturally upward, water naturally downward. When this view of physics is translated into ethical terms, love is seen as rising naturally upward, sin as sinking naturally downward. The love that rules the cosmos raises it with its light. The center of the cosmos is the point toward which all heavy, sinful things sink. It is the point farthest away from God, the logical place for the Devil to dwell.

As the result of their prideful sin, Satan and his angels were exiled from their native land above; they rained down from heaven, a despised crew driven down from bliss. One tenth of the angels fell in ruin, a

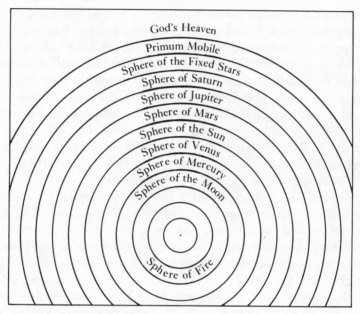

Figure 2. The heavenly spheres (adapted from William Anderson, *Dante the Maker,* 1980)

number that God makes up by the creation of humanity and the salvation of the saints. Satan had been the highest of the angels, a mighty six-winged seraph. But he fell like lightning from heaven, plunging through the spheres and hurtling toward earth. When he struck the earth, the impact opened a huge crevasse into which he hurtled all the way to the center of the globe. Satan was so ponderous with sin that he sank into creation like a plumb into pudding. A cave or "tomb" was hollowed out by his fall, a tomb that became hell. The earth from this giant excavation was thrust out onto the surface, where it formed the mountain of purgatory.

Satan is at the dead center of the universe, his head sticking up toward Jerusalem and the north, his buttocks frozen in the ice, his huge, hairy legs rearing up toward purgatory and the south. Vergil, Dante's guide, is obliged to turn himself laboriously with Dante on his back while clinging to Satan's furry hide, in order for them to direct their course toward the clear stars above.

The Devil's cold and heavy power is a dreadful thing in the cosmos, but when we see Satan himself at the center of hell he appears more pathetic than terrifying. Dante specifically intended Satan to be empty and contemptible, a futile contrast to God's energy. The absence of dramatic action here expresses Satan's essential lack of being. He is frozen at the dead point of the turning world, where all the heaviest sins have sunk and converged. At that point there can be no more motion; the heaviest weights crush together in an eternally immobile mass, where Satan is compressed by all the weight of the cosmos. If all things are drawn to God, what is left to be drawn to Satan? Nothing: only the nothingness and meaningless of sin. As we close in upon ourselves when we turn away from God toward unreality, so the center of hell is a dark mass turned infinitely in upon itself, cut off completely and forever from reality. Satan, the symbol of this nothingness, can have no real character except negation, and his futile immobility is precisely what Dante wished to portray. The icy lake that holds him immobile is frozen too hard to crack, a sign of death and an antinomy of the life-giving waters of baptism. Satan's immobility is the opposite of the freedom of the angels, his frozen hatred the opposite of God's love, which quickens creation. His forced motionlessness contrasts with God's voluntary serenity, which, without itself moving, moves the world.

Satan's nothingness permeates everywhere, a cold counterpart to the warm presence of the Dove. Empty and idiotic, it emanates out from the dead center, seeping through all the cracks of hell onto the sinful earth, leaching warmth and light away. Satan's force acts like gravity, weighting men and women down toward hell. This weighting is the exact opposite of the force exerted by God, who draws things toward him to the extent that they are light, spirit, and good.

The lowest pit of hell is designed for traitors, and there Satan, the betrayer of God the Father and the apotheosis of all treason, dwells. With his three hideous mouths he chews on Brutus and Cassius, who betrayed their ruler, and upon Judas, who betrayed Christ. Below each of his three grotesque faces Satan has a pair of huge wings, six in all to show that he had once been a seraph. These are not the feathery wings of angels, burning with living gold, but leathery batwings, which beat the frozen air vainly, unable to take off, stirring up winds that freeze the streams of hell and seep up through the earth to stir mortal minds to sin. This frozen wind is the opposite of the fire of love that breathes from the Holy Spirit.

The Devil is a towering mass of moribund matter. Theology held that angels remained angels after their fall. But Dante presented Satan as a gross incarnation mocking the true Incarnation of Christ and as the absolute opposite of spirit. Dante interpreted the Christian Platonist tradition that pure matter is furthest from God and closest to nonbeing to make his Satan, with his shaggy, bestial body, almost pure matter.

The impotent ugliness of this hulking, pathetic creature stands in complete contrast to the beauty of God. The eternal mastication of the three traitors is futile as well as hideous. As he chews on his human prey, he weeps tears of frustrated rage, and the tears mingle with the traitors' blood and drool down his chin. The bloody weeping of the hideous giant serves not to save; it only repels—and parodies the blood, water, and tears shed by the heavenly Lord upon his cross.

The Devil was a major character in other literary works of the later Middle Ages, as well, and in the theater. The mystery and miracle plays were written mostly by clerics for the purpose of edifying (or terrifying) as well as entertaining a large, uneducated audience for whom the Devil had acquired a stark immediacy in this time of plague, famine, and wars. These playwrights' efforts to achieve dramatic unity produced the first coherent chronological accounts of the Devil's activities from his creation to his final ruin. The rest of this chapter follows this chronology and illustrates it with quotations from a number of plays.

The history of the world begins at the instant when space and time are created. Immediately after, according to medieval drama, God made nine orders of angels and created Lucifer the highest angel of the highest order, second in glory only to God himself. "I make you closest to me of all the powers, master and mirror of my might; I create you beautiful in bliss and name you Lucifer, the bearer of light." When God appoints Lucifer the "governor" of the whole host of heaven, the bright angel's head is turned. We see God's throne center stage, with the angels grouped around it singing their songs of praise. When God rises and proceeds to exit, Lucifer contemplates the vacant throne and muses upon his own glory:

> Aha, that I am wondrous bright . . .
> All in this throne if that I were,
> then I should be as wise as he.

Lucifer scorns the angels' dutiful praises of God and bids them look at him instead and "see the beauty I bear. Shall you sing your song to God or to me? For I am the worthiest that ever may be."

The good angels recoil in horror: "We will not connive at your pride." Lucifer is undeterred:

> A worthier lord forsooth am I
> and ever worthier than he.
> In evidence that I am worthier
> I will go sit in God's throne.

Lucifer's accomplice, the angel Lightborne, encourages him with gross flattery: "The brightness of your body clear is brighter than God a thousandfold." The good angels make a last effort: Stop, they cry, or "Alas, that beauty you will spill." Contemptuous of their caution, Lucifer takes the throne, savoring the fullness of his pride: "All the world's joy is marked in me, for the beams of my brightness are burning so bright. In glorious glee my glittering gleams: I shall be like him who is highest on high." These anthropomorphic angels quarreling around God's throne contrast with the theological idea of a single moment of cold choice made at the beginning of time by a great cosmic power. Lucifer's grab for power was too colorful, too familiar to human nature, for the dramatists to resist.

Lucifer, shining splendid in the chair of God, invites the angels to worship him: "All angels, turn to me, I advise, and to your sovereign bend your knee." The good angels refuse, but the weaker fall at his feet, and Satan, Beelzebub, Astaroth, and the others welcome him as their leader. Literature sometimes diverged from theology in applying the different names of the Evil One to separate characters, blurring the essential distinction between the Devil and his subordinate demons. Such separation enabled the writers to express dramatic tensions within the Devil through dialogues. When Lucifer and Satan were distinguished from each other, Lucifer usually held pride of place, for that was the name the Devil had borne before his fall.

Lucifer now utters his proudest blasphemy: "If God should return, I will not leave, but sit right here before his face." That seals his doom. When God does appear, he is furious:

> Lucifer, who set you here while I was gone?
> How have I offended you?
> I made you my friend; you became my foe;
> why did you thus offend me?

"Lucifer, for your great pride I condemn you to fall from heaven to hell, and with you all who take your part; never more will they dwell in bliss with me." Lucifer's abrupt and undignified expulsion from heaven accentuates the transformation from beautiful angel to ugly fiend: "Now will I make my way to be thrust into endless torment. For fear of fire I crack a fart."

God proceeds to fashion the material world while the fallen angels in hell, shocked by their sudden ruin, lament their fate. They are horrified to discover that they have turned into "black fiends," and one of them cries out:

> Alas, alas, and woe! ·
> Lucifer, why did you fall so?
> We who were angels so fair
> and sat so high above the air,
> now we've become as black as any coal,
> ugly and tattered as a fool.

Lucifer himself bemoans his fate in a dirge that is a pathetic inversion of the angelic litany in Daniel 3.52–92:

I complain to you, wind and air, I complain to you, rain, dew, and mist, I complain to you, heat, cold, and snow, I complain to you, flowers and green meadows. . . . I complain to you, sweet song of birds, I complain to you, hills and deep valleys, I complain to you, rocks and stones, I complain to the whole world that God has created. I beg them to pray for me to the Almighty.

The Devil's view is that God has unjustly hurled him from heaven and humiliated him by creating humanity to take his place in the heavenly ranks. God has, moreover, intensified the insult by creating humanity in his own image and taking on human rather than angelic form. Satan complains: "Since we were fair and bright, I thought that he would take our shape; but I was disappointed; he plans to take human form instead, and that makes me envious." Why should a crude creature made of clay enjoy such bliss?

As the fallen angels discuss their predicament in an infernal council or parliament, their thoughts turn to revenge. They decide to attempt to destroy the new creation with its precious jewels Adam and Eve. Satan says that he will

> show mankind great envy.
> As soon as ever God creates him,
> I shall send one of my order
> to destroy him,
> to make mankind do wrong.

The parliament chooses one of its number—in most versions Satan—to go up to Eden. He plans his strategy: "I shall take a virgin's face and the body and feet of a serpent."

> I will go in a worm's likeness.
> A kind of adder is in this place,
> which has wings like a bird's,
> feet like an adder, a maiden's face;
> her appearance shall I take.

The Devil tempts Adam unsuccessfully before trying Eve. He first offers Adam knowledge. He approaches his intended victim with an offhand question, "How are you doing, Adam?" Adam replies that he is getting along very well. Ah, the tempter replies, but you could be doing even better, and I can tell you how. Adam admits that he does not know why God has forbidden the fruit, and the Devil explains that it yields knowledge of all things. If you eat it, you will become God's equal, he lies. He then shifts to tempting Adam with power, telling him that if he eats the fruit he will no longer need a lord. The medieval Adam readily recognizes the folly of losing a lord's protection. Realizing the identity of the tempter, he accuses him of the worst of feudal crimes, disloyalty and treason. "Get out of here," Adam shouts, "you are Satan!"

The Devil then turns his attention to Eve. Eve also recognizes him but naively fails to grasp that he is evil. He offers her a bouquet of temptations: he wants to help her and her husband; God has selfishly denied them the fruit because if they eat it they will become his equals; Adam is too insensitive to understand what is good for them both; he is not good enough for his beautiful, delicate wife; he is stupid and needs her help; since she is more capable than her husband she must become his equal; she can satisfy her curiosity by consuming the fruit; she will become queen of the world if only she will taste it; when all is said and done it has a marvelous taste. God "cleverly keeps you from eating the fruit because he wants no one else to enjoy the great powers that it bestows." Like Adam, Eve remarks that they seem to be happy as they are, but Satan brushes this aside:

> To greater state you may be brought.
> Yes, gods shall you be!
> of good and ill to have knowledge,
> and so to be as wise as he.

Satan invites Eve to precisely the same sin of pride that had brought him down himself. "If you will bite into this apple, you will be just like God" and wear the crown of heaven as the Creator's equal.

In shameless flattery Satan admires Eve's face, her figure, her eyes, her hair; he behaves like a courtly lover insinuating himself between husband and wife. With Eve still undecided, the Devil departs, only to return in the shape of a serpent. She goes to the serpent, listens to it silently, and then abruptly bites into the fruit. After eating, Eve experiences a vision that the audience is intended to recognize as a delusion sent by the Devil, and then she returns to Adam, repeating Satan's arguments: "Bite on boldly, for it is true: we shall be gods and know everything." Adam quickly yields.

God returns, reproaching Adam and Eve and cursing Satan roundly: "You wicked worm full of pride!" The Devil tries to explain himself to God:

> For I am full of great envy,
> of wrath and wicked hate
> that man should live above the sky
> where once I used to dwell.

God sends him packing back to hell, but Satan is pleased to have accomplished his mission: "I have played my part well and can go home, for no devil will ever do such a good day's work as I have done." When he returns to hell to make his report to Lucifer, his reward is according to the inverted values of hell: only further punishment. "Praise me, Lucifer," Satan exclaims, "for I have just caused the worst disaster that ever may be." Splendid, Lucifer replies, we'll make you a crown. "What shall we make it of, roses?" asks Ashtaroth. "Why no," Lucifer replies, "of thick irons burning like lightning."

How did the terrifying prince of this world, the mighty enemy of God, become a figure for parody, satire, and even broad humor? A tendency toward the comic Devil began in the theater as early as the twelfth century under the influence of folklore and the folk performances of mimes, jugglers, and maskers. The function of the funny demon was to produce comic relief, both to entertain the audience and to relax and prepare them for the next tragic action. Medieval demon plays had several levels of comedy. The lowest was slapstick, in which the demons ran about the stage leaping, farting, shouting oaths and insults, making obscene gestures, and executing pratfalls. The second level was a broad satire reserved for the higher demons. Lucifer blesses his demons by placing his hand on their groins while insulting them in parody of priestly benediction. Hell is the place where all values are inverted: every praise is a curse, every song a cacaphony. The third level was satire of demonic human behavior. Sebastian Brandt's *Ship of Fools* (1484) portrayed a ship captained by a fool with fools as passengers, representing the follies and vices of humanity, the vices being identified with demons. The fourth level was elevated irony. The Devil is truly powerful and terrifying, but God brings his grandiose plans to nothing. When Satan is portrayed as God's great adversary, his ruin provokes a kind of mystical hilarity, a sense of release and joy. We know that his doom is sure, that his twisting of justice will at last pass away into the night without a trace. The cosmic joke is always on the Devil, and he refuses to have it any other way.

The dramatic history of the Devil continued with the story of the Old Testament, in which God and Satan are pitted against each other in a number of incidents. The Devil claims that because of original sin his power over the human race is absolute and eternal, but dramatic tension builds continually during the Old Testament scenes, because the audience knows that Lucifer is mistaken and that the Savior will soon come to free all God's children from their grasp.

The Annunciation by the angel to Mary is the first hint the demons have that the Savior may be about to appear, and when they hear the news they call another dark council to argue over its meaning. The Devil's parliament is a perfect occasion for a comedy of inversion. "God curse you," Lucifer screams at Satan, and Ashtaroth shouts, "Get the devil out of here!" Lucifer bewails the inversion's effects: "My nobility and beauty have become deformity, my song a lament, my laughter desolation, my light a shadow, my glory sorrowful rage, my joy incurable mourning." Satan insults Lucifer, observing that whenever he tries to sing or laugh he howls like a famished wolf. Lucifer orders his lieutenants to entertain him with song, and Ashtaroth, Satan, Beelzebub, and Berich make up a little ditty about death and damnation. Their singing is so hideous that even the Dark Lord cannot bear it: "Hey, you clowns," he calls out, "you're killing me with that noise. By the devil stop it! You're all off key."

Finally the demons get down to the business of discussing the Annunciation, and Lucifer asks if they think that anyone would be able to wrest the imprisoned souls from their grasp. Ashtaroth and Berich assure him that this could never be, while the audience smiles grimly, knowing that the harrowing of hell is in store. Berich insists that the lost souls will never escape, but Satan is not so sure, for he remembers the Old Testament prophecies about the Messiah, and Lucifer muses that Mary's pregnancy may have some bearing on the question. The council sends Satan up to tempt the Virgin, but after failing a hundred thousand times he reports back to Lucifer that she is incorruptible. And, he cautions, "it just gets worse." This virgin has had a fine baby son who will cause us even more trouble, for rumor has it that he is the Messiah himself come to redeem humanity. Lucifer orders Satan punished for bringing such bad news, and Satan pleads for mercy. Thinking fast, he proposes to save the situation and his own hide by going back up to tempt King Herod to massacre the children, and Lucifer's mood changes immediately. "What an outstanding idea!" he cries. Later the Evil One encourages the younger Herod to execute John the Baptist and tempts Mary Magdalene to a life of prostitution.

The demons are still unsure whether Jesus is a magician, a prophet, the Messiah, or God himself. "What the devil kind of man is this Jesus?" Berich exclaims. "This is giving me a stomachache," Satan moans. "I am very worried about this Christ. I would really like to know who his father is. If he is God's child and born of a virgin, then we have been badly outmaneuvered, and our success will be short." The demonic parliament discusses the Incarnation with hopeless stupidity: the prophets foretold that Christ was coming, but not to worry, because Mary's son is named Jesus, not Christ.

Belial and Beelzebub beg their prince to go and tempt Christ in order to find out who he really is. Satan tempts the second Adam in much the same way that he tempted the first, but with the opposite outcome. Christ refuses to allow him to learn the truth. If the Devil were to persuade Jesus to hurl himself from the pinnacle of the temple, either Jesus would die, showing that he was not God, or he would be held up by the angels, proving that he was. By refusing to respond, Jesus both shows his contempt for the Devil and keeps him in suspense. Satan skulks home to hell:

> What he is I cannot see;
> whether he be God or man
> I can tell in no degree;
> In sorrow I let a fart.

The harrowing of hell. Christ lances the bestial Satan while drawing the just out of the mouth of hell. From the Miniatures of the Life of Christ, France, c. 1200. Courtesy The Pierpont Morgan Library, New York.

When he returns, Lucifer rages at him: "Go away, Satan! May God curse you! May the Devil carry you off!" Astaroth still blusters that Jesus is nothing but a false prophet, but Lucifer's fear, which originated at the time of the Annunciation, is slowly growing. The monstrous stupidity of the demons as they try to provoke, and then to stop, the crucifixion illustrates their failure to understand that whatever they do, God's will and providence cannot be thwarted.

When Jesus begins his ministry, the demons cannot keep track of him; he seems to be everywhere at once. Lucifer asks, "Satan, tell me where Jesus is now." Satan replies, "The devil *I* know: he's getting worse every day with his teaching and preaching." The raising of Lazarus and his liberation from hell serve to warn the demons that Christ's power may be unstoppable, for if he can save one soul from hell he can save all. Yet the Devil's empire on earth has lasted so long that he cannot really believe that its ruin is now at hand.

Increasingly desperate and still unsure as to the nature of their adversary, the demons plan to kill him. They send Lucifer's daughter Despair up to Judas to persuade him to betray his master and then prompt his suicide. Meanwhile Christ is being led before the Sanhedrin and Pilate for judgment, an event that delights Satan. He rushes down to hell to tell Lucifer the good news. But Lucifer has been struck by second thoughts: if Jesus really is divine, then their plan to kill him will only bring down worse ruin on their heads. "False Satan," he bellows ungratefully, "you've wrecked everything." Lucifer sends Satan back up to earth in a desperate attempt to stop the crucifixion; Satan appears to Pilate's wife in a dream and tells her that a calamity awaits her husband if he condemns this innocent man. Pilate's wife warns Pilate, but he responds that he cannot falter in Caesar's service.

The demons do not appear at the crucifixion, because the playwrights considered the comic side of their character too pronounced to introduce into such a solemn moment. But they are right there after Christ's death, carrying off the soul of the unrepentant thief. Satan attempts to seize the soul of Jesus as well, but the archangel Gabriel repels him with a flaming sword. This is a turning point. Up till now, the Devil has been on the offensive; from now on he is in ignominious retreat.

Driven back to the hold of hell, the demons deploy their defenses. Yet they are still boasting stupidly. Satan exclaims, "If Jesus comes down here and dares say one single word, I'll singe his hair off." He still refuses to grasp who Jesus is: "I knew his father by sight; he earned his living as a craftsman; so what makes this Jesus so high and mighty? He's nothing but a man really, so go on, you demons, get that boaster and bind him in hell. We hanged him on the cross, and we'll take care of him now. Go get him and knock that dastard down." But into the depths of hell's darkness a great light shines, and the unaccustomed sound of souls rejoicing penetrates the dark council. "What is that noise?" Lucifer demands, and Berich replies, "It is the human race; their salvation is at hand." Lucifer groans: "I knew it; I always knew that man would come and steal our inheritance."

The decisive moment in the history of salvation is now at hand. The soul of Jesus comes to the gates of hell and utters the great words from Psalm 24:7–10: OPEN UP YOUR GATES! At long last the demons know the truth for sure. "Alas, oh no," groans Belial, "we must bow to your orders; we know now that you are God." The Devil tries to stave off ruin by arguing with Jesus. Wait! he cries. Look here, I was promised that I could keep the damned souls! All right, Jesus replies, go ahead and keep Cain, Judas, and all sinners and unbelievers. Yes, Satan pursues, but if you get to steal my other souls, then I get to continue to wander the world and corrupt your servants. Christ's majesty refuses this bargain: No, fiend, you shall not, for I will bind you fast in hell. Michael puts Satan in chains, and the Lord leads the happy souls in triumph out of the pit.

The crisis is now passed. At the time of Jesus' resurrection, the demons are still scurrying foolishly around trying to regain control of events, but the Devil's doom is sure. The final act in salvation history is the last judgment. Just before the second coming of Christ, Satan mounts one last doomed assault on the kingdom of God. The demons hold a final council and decide that their only hope is for the Devil to beget a child, the Antichrist. When they hear that the Antichrist is born, the dark parliament rejoices. The Devil visits his young son on earth and offers him the kingdoms of this world, a temptation to which the false messiah, unlike the true one, eagerly assents. Antichrist roams the world, working spurious miracles, deluding the people, persecuting the saints, encouraging unjust rulers, and preparing for the final battle.

The battle is swift and decisive. Antichrist calls out in vain:

> Help, Satan and Lucifer,
> Beelzebub, proud knight!
> I am suffering terrible pain . . .
> I fear for my body and soul,
> And now all is going to the Devil.

When he dies, two demons carry him down to the underworld. "With Lucifer his lord long shall he lie; in a seat of sorrow shall he sit." The reaction of the demons to Antichrist's descent is ironically mixed. They rejoice to see their comrade; they are pleased to see him damned, for he adds to their soul hoard; yet they know that his ruin brings theirs ever nearer.

It is now doomsday, and still the demons are confused. They are happy because hell will now be eternally filled with all the damned souls. Rushing here and there with books listing sinners and bags full of documentation, they welcome the arrival of each prisoner. It is an exciting time, an inverted Christmas feast. Yet it is now that Satan is bound finally and forever. God announces it: "Lucifer, you have never been willing to take responsibility for your sins. Instead you have daily persisted in your malevolence. . . . Therefore I curse you." The demons are horrified. Lost is their kingdom, lost their power to obstruct the kingdom of God. The cosmos is restored to harmony; death, sorrow, and sin are no more. The last action on the stage of the world is abrupt and final: Christ shuts the door of hell, locks it, and takes away the key.

10 *Nominalists, Mystics, and Witches*

THE fourteenth, fifteenth, and sixteenth centuries—traditionally called the late Middle Ages and Reformation—are best taken as a single period, some of whose characteristics in literature, popular legend, homiletics, and the witch craze encouraged belief in Satan, while others, such as nominalism, weakened its influence. Nominalism, the dominant intellectual trend, was based on the rejection of the Platonic, idealist belief—known as *realism*—that abstract ideas have an intrinsic *reality* over and above the reality of individuals. William of Ockham (c. 1285–1347), the Oxford Franciscan and nominalist leader, held that realism was not only false but also a source of unnecessary complications. Ockham's "Razor"—the principle that the simplest explanation that accords with the evidence is usually the best—slashed away at the abstract "realities" that earlier philosophers had invented. We know that Socrates and Plato are both human, Ockham observed, by direct experience and intuition. We do not need to refer to an abstract quality "humanity" to know this. People could tell a man from a finback whale before Plato invented realism. We have no evidence that "humanity" exists, only individual humans; no evidence that "finback whaleness" exists, only individual finback whales. Knowledge of abstract qualities is therefore a creation of human beings rather than a reflection of the external world itself.

When applied to God himself, nominalism had several effects. First, it meant that whatever we say about God is a human proposition that cannot be assumed to describe the true nature of God. All human categories, including "being," "power," and "knowledge" are *equivocal*, that is, they mean something quite different applied to God from what they mean applied to a human, a horse, or a star. We can know God by experience and intuition, but as soon as we try to construct a rational theology to get at the nature of God we are obliged to use equivocal terms and thus get no closer to God rationally than human rational conceptions of him.

For Ockham, universal ideas are human constructions. There are no ideas in the mind of God, no prototypes that the Deity had to choose among for use as patterns. God's freedom is absolute, unbounded by any necessity, including logic. Every event in the cosmos is immediately contingent upon God. The nominalists distinguished between God's "absolute power" to do whatever he wishes and his "ordained power"— the way he has in fact set the cosmos up. God could have made the physical and moral laws of the cosmos quite different; he has the absolute power to do things he has never done and will never do: it is in God's absolute power to make hydrogen and oxygen combine into fruitcake. It is not, however, in his ordained power to do so. His absolute power is unlimited, but his ordained power is what God actually chooses for the cosmos. It is limited and fixed, not because of any limitation inherent in God, but because God eternally and freely chooses it to be so. Evil is evil because God declares it to be evil, not because God recognizes an intrinsic quality of evil that existed before he declared it so.

Nominalism led to two quite different positions on free will and determinism. The absolute freedom and inscrutability of God led some nominalists to emphasize determinism. God may save or damn according to whatever principle he chooses or according to no principle at all. The predestinarian view made God responsible for evil, for he could have given the Devil the grace to confirm him in goodness and chose not to do so. The majority of nominalists, however, emphasized God's faithfulness to the "ordained power," the order that he in fact creates, an order in which he includes free will. Ockham himself strongly believed in free will, though emphasizing that it in no way limited the absolutely unrestrained power of God. Evil is evil because God ordains it so; God could have made lying good and friendship evil. But if God thus creates the alternatives of good and evil, he must be at least the partial cause of evil. Still, Ockham reminds us, what we humans call "evil" is not necessarily "evil" to God; we must not imagine that any such category that we invent corresponds to ultimate reality.

Nicholas of Cusa (1401–1464) came closer to imputing evil to God. Nicholas's central assumptions were nominalist, and he also drew upon the mystical tradition stemming from Dionysius. Humans cannot know anything in itself. Absolute truth, whatever that may be, is forever beyond our grasp. Of God we know only that he is *maximum*, totally exceeding every object of experience and therefore incomprehensible in himself, although we can know a little about the cosmos, which is a manifestation of God. "All affirmations that are made about God by theology are anthropomorphic." We cannot even say that God is maximum *being*, for he transcends our conception of being. Since God has no proportional relationship with anything finite, whatever we say about him is merely equivocal, and the only way we can grasp anything about God is to understand that we must deny any disjunctive proposition about him—any proposition that denies its opposite. We cannot say that God is the beginning if by that we exclude the end, or that he is great, if by that we exclude the small.

Since God is absolutely without restriction, there is no quality that his nature excludes. All opposites are united in God. God exists and does not exist; he is being and not being; he is greatest and smallest; he is transcendent and immanent; he is beginning and end; he creates the cosmos from nothing, yet it extends from himself; he is unity and diversity; he is simple yet embraces all distinctions. God is a "coincidence of opposites," a union of contraries, beyond the grasp of human reason, and Nicholas affirmed that it is the only thing we are entitled to say about God. We can never define God, for God is his own definition and it is by him that all things are defined. We are completely ignorant of God. "Yet in a way that we cannot comprehend, absolute truth enlightens the darkness of our ignorance." For although God cannot be known intellectually, he can be experienced, directly intuited, and by the simple as well as the learned. Since God gives us minds, we must use them to try to understand him, but love brings us infinitely closer to God than the most subtle reasoning.

This is close to an absolutely monistic view, allowing no limitations on God, permitting nothing outside the totality that is God. But what then of evil? Nicholas was on the verge of taking the final step and perceiving good and evil as another coincidence of opposites inherent in God. He might have done so while making clear that "good" and "evil" are merely human categories. To say that God includes both *what we call good* and *what we call evil* would allow for God's being wholly good with a goodness differing from and transcending our own. Our hatred of evil and our courageous will to overcome evil would also be part of the coincidence of opposites in God, part of his "ordained power." This theory would have been consistent with the Hebrew and Christian tradition that always perceived the Devil as the creature and servant of God as well as God's enemy. But Nicholas looked at this logical consequence of his theory, flinched, and retreated into the old view of evil as privation.   .

The revival of Christian mysticism in the fourteenth, fifteenth, and sixteenth centuries drew strength from the rise of nominalism. Nominalism and mysticism shared the assumption that God could be reached through experience, intuition, and love rather than through reason. The mystical intuition is that everything lives, moves, and has its being in God. One who understands, Ray C. Petry observed, "has *only* God and thinks only God, and everything is nothing but God to him. He discloses God in every act and in every place. The whole business of his person adds up to God."

The mystics' intuition that the cosmos is an aspect of God himself, produced by God in love and drawn back lovingly to God, raises the question of evil more poignantly than any other Christian tradition. If everything is God, and the cosmos is overflowing with divine love, there seems to be no room at all for evil and the Devil. The mystics were tempted to explain evil in terms of privation. For Meister Eckhart (c. 1260–1327), only God is absolute being; creatures have being only insofar as they exist in God; otherwise they are a "pure nothing." If evil does not have its being in God, it can be regarded as pure nothingness. Elsewhere, however, Eckhart faces the problem more squarely. We cannot assume that the goodness of God is the same as our goodness, for we have no right to impose human conceptions upon God. One who calls God good is as wrong as one who calls God evil. The existence of what we call evil "is required by the perfection of the universe, and evil exists in what is good and is ordered to the good of the universe."

The fourteenth-century contemplative Julian of Norwich also saw that God's goodness transcends our ability to understand good and evil: "For a man regards some deeds as well done and some as evil, and our Lord does not regard them so, for everything which exists in nature is of God's creation, so that everything which is done has the property of being of God's doing. Our God does everything that is good, and tolerates what is evil. I do not say that evil is honorable, but I say that our Lord God's toleration [of evil] is honorable." Ultimately God includes what we call evil in himself, but God himself suffers the same evil that he asks us to suffer. The Incarnation and passion of Jesus Christ are signs of God's willingness to share with us in the terrible effects of evil. Our limited minds cannot grasp the sense of it, but God makes all things right: "See, I am God. See, I am in all things. See, I do all things. See, I never remove my hands from my works, nor ever shall without end. See,

I guide all things to the end that I ordain them for, before time began, with the same power and wisdom and love in which I made them; how should anything be amiss?"

The mystics' fundamental vision was unitive: all things, including all sinful creatures, are united with God. The Devil can have no ultimate significance in the cosmos. Ultimately the Devil is nothing, emptiness. Emptiness has three meanings for the mystics. One meaning is positive: the emptying of all attachments from the soul so that the soul can encounter God. The second is ontological: the nonbeing of that which is not God. The third is moral: the nonbeing and meaninglessness of whatever is directed away from God. For the mystics, the Devil is a moral vacuum pulling us away from reality. The contemplatives' desire to avoid definitions and their hesitation to press for rational explanations deterred them from dwelling on the Devil intellectually. Yet in practice they felt his presence more often and more immediately than most.

The contemplatives believed that the Devil bent his evil attention on them more than upon others because the soul's union with God is what the Devil hates most intensely. The Devil was the source of all that obstructed contemplation. The Devil suggests that we have no time for prayer and contemplation, that they are illusions, that they lead nowhere, that they are a waste of time, that we are not worthy of them, that it is better to do good works, that we look foolish to others when we pray. Or, even worse, he makes us proud of our spiritual achievements, making us feel superior and giving us false sensations of warmth or lightness or visual or auditory hallucinations. The more we overcome spiritual obstacles, the more severely he exerts himself to block us from the unitive path. His attacks on the contemplatives ranged from spiritual temptation to physical assault: Julian of Norwich gives a detailed picture of the fiend who tried to choke her to death. The spiritual temptations were worse. As Julian observed, "everything opposed to love and peace is from the Fiend."

The contemplatives urged those feeling demonic temptations not to try to resist directly but rather to turn their thoughts away and pray for God's grace, for the Devil has no real power against us. As one put it, "For a man to let the Devil get the better of him is just like a well armed soldier letting an insect sting him to death." Protected by God's grace, we fend off the Devil with faith and joy. Walter Hilton (d. 1396) said, "It gives us the hilarity and joy of one who sees evil overthrown to see the Devil, the chief of all evil, shown as a clumsy scoundrel bound by the power of Jesus, whom he cannot injure." And Julian saw "our Lord scorn his malice and despise him as nothing, and the Lord wants us to do so. Because of this sight I laughed greatly. I see sport, that the Devil is overcome, and I see scorn, that God scorns him, and he will be scorned, and I see seriousness, that he is overcome by the blessed Passion and death of our Lord Jesus Christ." The ultimate answer to evil is not to cudgel the brain but to live a life of love and laughter.

Direct experience of the Devil could also take quite a different form. Although nominalism and mysticism tended to downplay the Devil's power, another, much more popular phenomenon of the fourteenth, fifteenth, and sixteenth centuries raised his powers to unprecedented heights. This was witchcraft. "Witchcraft" has three quite different meanings. It sometimes means simple sorcery, the charms or spells used in many societies worldwide to accomplish such practical ends as healing a child, assuring the fertility of crops, or warding off an enemy. Recently it has referred to modern neopaganism, a late-twentieth-century religion limited to small groups mainly in the Anglo-Saxon countries. The third meaning is the only important one for the history of the Devil: the allegedly Satanic witchcraft of the period of about 1400–1700. Whether the accused witches ever believed or practiced the Satanism attributed to them or whether it was projected upon them by their enemies, the conviction that Satanic witchcraft was real pervaded Western society for three centuries.

By the fifteenth century a stereotype of diabolical witchcraft had emerged: on a Thursday or Saturday night, some men, but more women, creep silently from their beds in order to avoid disturbing their spouses. The witches who are near enough to the meeting place make their way on foot, but those who live at a distance rub their bodies with an ointment that enables them to fly off in the shape of animals, or else astride broomsticks or fences. Ten or twenty witches attend the meeting, later called the "sabbat." The ceremony begins with any new witches swearing to keep the group's secrets and promising to kill a child and bring its body to the next meeting. The neophytes renounce the Christian faith and insult a crucifix or Eucharistic host. They proceed to worship the Devil or his representative by kissing his genitals or backside. After the initiation, the witches bring children to be sacrificed to the Devil, and the babies' fat is used to confect the ointment used for flying or for poison. The witches partake of the child's body and blood in a blasphemous parody of the Eucharist. After supper, the lights are extinguished, and the witches fall to an indiscriminate sexual orgy, sometimes having intercourse with the Devil himself.

Witches bestow the "obscene kiss" on the Devil while their fellows ride through the air on the way to a "sabbat" or "synagogue." Illumination from a fifteenth-century French manuscript. Courtesy Bibliothèque Nationale, Paris.

How did such fantastic ideas gain credence? The phenomenon of diabolical witchcraft developed over the centuries from many sources. In the earlier Middle Ages, numerous incantations and spells were used to affect sexual desire, exact revenge, or obtain riches, but they were not assumed to involve demons; rather, they were supposed to manipulate hidden natural forces. But later, under the influence of Aristotelian scholasticism, it was believed that natural magic did not exist and that magic could be effective only through the aid of Lucifer and his minions. A woman named Bardonneche, wife of Lorent Moti of Chaumont, called up a demon named Guilleme to help her blunt her husband's sexual appetite; the Devil appeared to her as a pale young man in a long tunic, and on another occasion as a rooster. One Marguerite summoned a demon named Griffart, who helped her revenge herself on her enemies; he took the shape of a black rooster or a ruddy man in a black hood and red tunic. A Michel Ruffier summoned "Lucifel" who, in the form of a huge black man, helped him get rich.

The second ingredient of witchcraft consisted of elements derived from paganism and folklore, for example the bloodsucking female demons who have the double function of seducing sleeping men and killing infants. The third element was medieval heresy. Heretics, persons persistently denying accepted Christian doctrine, were deemed to be in Satan's service and subject to accusations of orgy, infanticide, and other obscene outrages against God and the church. From the 1140s, Cathar dualism, with its insistence upon the enormous powers of Satan, increased the widespread terror of his ubiquitous presence.

Scholastic theology was the fourth element. Witchcraft was less a popular movement than an imposition of ideas by the intellectual elite upon the uneducated. All who oppose Christ's saving mission on earth, whether pagans, sinners, Jews, heretics, or sorcerers, are limbs of Satan. Christians are by duty obliged to reform them if possible and eliminate them if necessary. Lucifer's powers to protect his followers were so mighty that fire and sword were often deemed necessary to overcome them. The central stone in the scholastic edifice of witch beliefs was the idea of pact, which went back as far as the story of Theophilus. In that case the pact was a simple contract between two consenting parties assumed to be almost equal, and it was explicit: Theophilus signed a written contract with Satan. Now, in the scholastic theory of pact, these two elements changed. It was now assumed that the person making the pact did so as a groveling slave, renouncing Christ, offering the Devil homage on bended knee, and even submitting to sexual intercourse with him. The scholastics argued that where pact was not made explicitly, it was implicit, for heretics and other evildoers had put themselves under Lucifer's command whether or not they had made a conscious and deliberate submission to him.

The fifth element, almost as important as theology itself, was judicial oppression, by both secular and ecclesiastical courts, particularly the inquisition. Witchcraft implied pact, and pact implied the most serious of all heresies: the belief that Satan is worthy of worship. The definition of witchcraft as heresy brought it under the jurisdiction of the inquisition. Although the inquisition was never an organized bureaucracy directed from Rome or anywhere else, inquisitors in various regions kept one another informed. Eventually a body of assumptions about witches was collected in inquisitors' manuals in the form of lists of leading questions to be put to the accused. Under threat of torture, many readily confessed to these stock accusations; then, each confession was used as further evidence for the validity of the assumptions. Thus a body of judicial precedent—based largely on illusion—was formed.

· The trial of an old man named Pierre Vallin in southern France in 1438 illustrates the process. Seized by the inquisition for witchcraft, he was repeatedly tortured, then removed from the place of torture and interrogated, and then given the choice of confessing or being returned for more torture. Under such pressure, Vallin confessed that he had been the Devil's servant for sixty-three years, during which time he had denied God, desecrated the cross, and sacrificed his own baby daughter. He went regularly to the witches' sabbat, where he copulated with Beelzebub and devoured the flesh of children. The inquisition condemned him for heresy, idolatry, apostasy, and the invocation of demons. He was then tortured for another week until he named a number of accomplices. Neither Vallin's fate nor that of the alleged accomplices he was forced to name is known, but typically their property would have been confiscated before they were burned at the stake.

Belief in diabolical witchcraft had its roots in the Middle Ages, but it became a true craze in the sixteenth and seventeenth centuries. Writers, judges, and theologians of those centuries assumed that witches existed all over Europe, in every neighborhood, all linked in one great conspiracy under Satan's rule. Though such a conspiracy never existed, papal pronouncements, Catholic councils, Protestant synods, secular courts, inquisitorial tribunals, and leading scholars all repeatedly proclaimed its reality. The craze began with the publication in 1486 of the *Hammer of Witches* (*Malleus maleficarum*), a book by two inquisitors that was quickly printed in so many editions that it outsold every book except the Bible. For the most part, witchcraft was an invention of the elite, gradually spreading down through pulpit and classroom to the people, who greedily accepted it as an explanation for their own personal troubles. Terror of a diabolical plot by witches against Christian society now spread through every level of that society. Aggravated by the religious and political tensions of the Reformation, witchcraft was both cause and result of the revival of the Devil, whose strength had been flagging but who now returned to his kingdom in full pomp and regalia. Terror of witchcraft provoked both judicial prosecution and popular persecution, and the victims numbered in the hundreds of thousands.

The witch craze was one of the most important episodes in the history of the Devil, reviving belief in his immediate and terrible powers to an extent unsurpassed since the time of the desert fathers. It also revealed the most terrible danger of belief in the Devil: the willingness to assume that those whom one distrusts or fears are servants of Satan and fitting targets of destructive hatred. Though the projection of absolute evil upon one's enemies is not the exclusive property of those who believe in the Devil—atheist commissars practice it with as much zeal as inquisitors—belief in Satan did lend itself handily to the particularly grotesque form of demonization that was witchcraft.

11 *The Devil and the Reformers*

T̶HE complex set of events called the Reformation can be divided into three: the Reformation of learned, relatively conservative Protestant leaders such as Martin Luther and John Calvin; the radical Reformation, including the Anabaptists; and the Catholic Reformation culminating in the Council of Trent. None of these however, resulted in ideas that diverged sharply from traditional diabology. The great change came not with the Reformation, but with the Enlightenment of the eighteenth century. Both Catholic and Protestant belief remained continuous with the Aristotelian, scholastic, Augustinian mode of thought that had characterized the later Middle Ages.

Underneath this conservative theology, nonetheless, social changes were slowly preparing a radical shift of attention from demonic to secular human evil. The growth of the towns encouraged the growth of literacy far beyond the priesthood, so that the urban middle classes became able to read and interpret the Bible on their own. At the same time, increasing numbers of literate people focused their attention on secular concerns such as making money, building businesses, and raising families. The rising nation-state advanced the needs of secular power against the claims of church and religion.

The Devil was not ready to retire in the face of the new concern with the things of this world, and he reached the height of his power just at the time when the intellectual structure supporting him began to crumble. Both the witch craze and Luther's Reformation encouraged his potency. Protestant emphasis upon the Bible as the sole source of authority meant renewed confidence in New Testament teaching on Satan. Moreover, because of the Protestants' fear of witchcraft and despite their enthusiasm for pruning out traditions they considered unrooted in Scripture, they accepted virtually all of medieval diabology. Further, they removed structures such as exorcism and private confession that helped individuals to feel that Satan was under control. Both Protestants and Catholics also enlisted the Devil in the propaganda war: for Protestant pastors, the pope was the Antichrist; in Catholic exorcisms the demons were reported to praise Protestant doctrines as they fled screaming from the bodies of their victims. The religious wars between Catholics and Protestants, and among varieties of Protestants, promoted the sense that the Devil was active everywhere.

Another reason for the growth of Satan's power was the turning inward of the Christian conscience, not only in Protestantism but in the new introspective character of Catholicism typified by Ignatius Loyola (1491–1556). In earlier ages, the Devil had been confronted by God, Christ, and the whole Christian community. If attacked by Satan, you could at least have felt part of a great host that closed protective ranks around you in the mists. But now you had the responsibility for fending him off as an individual, alone. No shining saints or angels armed with the sword of glory protected you now; you were left in your closet, solitary with your Bible, fearfully pondering your sins, exposed to evil's winter winds. No wonder that the literary heroes of the age were Faust alone at the midnight crossroads with Mephistopheles, and Macbeth alone on the blasted heath with the three witches. Isolation provokes terror, and terror lends itself to an exaggerated view of the Devil's powers.

The same century that saw such a vast increase in Satan's powers ironically also witnessed the beginnings of overt skepticism. The depths of terror brought on by introspective individualism provoked intense psychological reaction against belief in the powers of evil. In 1563 Johann Wier expressed his skepticism of witchcraft and diabology in his book *On Magic*, and Michel de Montaigne (1533–1592) argued that the evidence for witchcraft was surely too shaky to justify putting people to death. Intellectual skepticism was abetted by the stout incredulity of practical, uneducated laymen such as Brian Walker of Durham, who announced, "I do not believe there is either God or Devil, neither will I believe in anything but what I see." The response of believers to such skepticism was the retort: No Devil, no Redeemer. If the Devil, the second-best-known figure in Christianity, could be excised from the Christian tradition, then eventually even Christ might vanish. If Christ did not come to save us from the power of the Devil, perhaps he did not come to save us at

Goya, *Conjuro*, 1794/1795. Goya, himself a skeptic, painted grotesque scenes of witchcraft for satirical purposes. Here the stereotyped witches are accompanied by familiar spirits, stick pins in images, and carry a basket of murdered babies for use in their cannibalistic orgy. Oil on cloth. Courtesy Museo Lázaro Galdiano, Madrid.

all. A religious world view in which God and the Devil fitted coherently was gradually being replaced by a secular one in which they did not. The result was that the existence of God would eventually be questioned like that of the Devil; the process only took a bit longer with God.

Martin Luther (1483–1546) devoted more theological and personal concern to the Devil than anyone else since the desert fathers. For Luther any valid view must rest upon the Bible read in the light of faith. Next to the Bible his chief source was Augustine, though he contrasted his "true" Augustine to the Augustinian scholastics, who, he believed, had overextended the range of reason. Reason must be used only in its proper sphere, which is an aid to understanding the truth that we have already learned from the Bible.

From Augustine and the nominalists Luther learned to insist upon the absolute omnipotence of God and its corollary, predestination. Luther embraced absolute predestination, maintaining that anything else would be an illogical, blasphemous limitation on God's sovereign will. "Therefore," he said, "we must go to extremes, deny free will altogether, and ascribe everything to God." A human being has no power at all to achieve his own salvation; he is always either in God's power or in Satan's. God chooses those whom he saves and allows the others to follow the Devil. Christ did not die for all, but only for those he has specially chosen. In boldly grasping the nettle of predestination, Luther was aware of its pricks: if the cosmos is so closely determined, why do we need the sacraments, sermons, the Bible, or the Incarnation itself? Why does God not simply set things up the way he wants without further ado? Although unable to resolve these difficulties, Luther remained unflinching in allowing no limitation whatever on the power of God.

God has two kinds of omnipotence. As the originator of the cosmos, he is absolutely free to make the world exactly as he pleases. This, Luther said, is his "natural omnipotence." Everything in the cosmos *is* because he wills it to be; if he did not choose it, it would not exist. God also has "theological" omnipotence: he is not only the remote cause of everything that is, but also its immediate cause. He keeps every mote in the universe in his immediate gaze, directing heaven, hell, all creatures, the entire cosmos—and the Devil.

In such a world God is both remotely and immediately responsible for evil. Luther distinguished between two aspects of God, contrasting the just, stern, and apparently cruel face with the kind, merciful, loving one which we know through the Incarnation of Christ. Because there is evil in the world, it must be the will of God. Yet God also wills the good against the evil. Thus God wills good; God wills evil; God does not will evil: all the above are true. To our limited minds, some things appear good and others evil, but ultimately all apparent evils are good since all that God does is good.

From the mystics Luther drew the notion of God as a coincidence of opposites. God is wrath, and God is love. God is repudiation, and God is grace. God is law, and God is mercy. God wills wickedness and hates the wicked. Unaided reason cannot penetrate this mystery; without grace we see God as incompetent, terrifying, or cruel. Because our notions of good and evil are different from and infinitely inferior to God's, we cannot always grasp the good in his purposes. We perceive God as having a double will, willing both good and evil, but this apparently double will is actually one united will that we cannot understand. This hard doctrine, Luther saw, was a corollary of the absolute omnipotence of God.

The stern, wrathful face of God can appear to be the Devil's mask. But the Devil's will is only *apparently* the same as God's will; while the Devil and God may will the same thing, their purpose is never the same. The Devil is God's tool, like a pruning hook or a hoe that God uses to cultivate his garden. The hoe takes its own pleasure in destroying the weeds for its own purpose, but it can never move out of God's hands, or weed where he does not wish, or thwart his purpose of building a beautiful garden. The Devil, against his will, always does God's work. All evils come from both the Devil and God, but the Devil wills the evil in them and God wills the good that comes out of them. "God incites the Devil to evil, but he does not do evil himself." The knowledge that God works through the Devil may tempt us to hopelessness and horror; unaided by grace, we would doubt God's own goodness. But the Incarnation of Christ reveals the mercy and love of God. Through Christ's love we can understand that despite the apparent harshness of the world God's loving presence and purpose are never absent.

If all is from God, then evil and the Devil are from God. But Luther's unflinching monism does not lead to acquiescence in evil. Though the Devil does evil under God's command, God also hates the evil and wishes us to fight against it. God struggles mightily against Satan, with every moment of moral choice the battleground. In a cosmos ruled by absolute omnipotence, Luther argued, the individual has no freedom. He or she is subject to the will either of God or of Satan. The soul is like a horse: when God rides, it goes where God chooses, and when the Devil rides, it goes where the Devil chooses. The two riders dispute the mount between themselves, but the horse obeys whoever is in the saddle.

Luther felt this struggle intensely within his own soul. His diabology was based on personal experience as well as on Scripture and tradition. As Heiko Oberman put it, Luther's "whole life was a war against Satan." Like the desert fathers and the medieval contemplatives, Luther felt that the Devil attacks more intensely as one advances in faith. Satan attempted to deter him from God's work through temptations, distractions, and even physical manifestations. He rattled around behind Luther's stove; at the Warburg castle he pelted nuts at the roof and rolled casks down the stairwell; he grunted audibly like a pig; he disputed with Luther like a scholastic; he sometimes lodged in Luther's bowels. Satan kept so close that he "slept with Luther more than Luther's wife Katie did."

Yet Satan's power over us is shattered by the Incarnation of Jesus Christ. Christ has struck Satan blow after telling blow in his miracles, in his preaching, and in his Passion. The Devil plotted the Passion in unthinking rage against Christ, and God used it to overthrow him, the proof being the resurrection. The world, the flesh, and the Devil still tempt us, but one little word—the name of the Savior—can crush them.

The Devil still has power in the world, however, because so many choose to follow him. Some make a deliberate pact with him: Luther was no skeptic about witchcraft and once himself saved a student at Wittenberg who had made a formal renunciation of Christ. All sinners serve in the Devil's army, including pagans, heretics, Catholics, Turks, and radical Protestants. The pope is the Antichrist himself. Luther's view that the whole world was in tension between God and the Devil did not permit him to see ecclesiastical disputes as matters of honest disagreement or even politics: they were always aspects of the great cosmic war.

The Devil's power remains "as big as the world, as wide as the world, and he extends from heaven down into hell," yet "the evil spirit has not a hairbreadth more power over us than God's goodness permits." Against the Devil, Christ puts a great arsenal at the disposal of Christians, including baptism, the Bible, preaching, the sacraments, and song. Luther's best known contribution to popular diabology is his famous hymn "A Mighty Fortress Is Our God," which some modern versions strip of its main point, Christ's defeat of Satan. The original is:

> A mighty fortress is our God,
> A good weapon and defense;
> He helps us in every need
> That we encounter.
> The old, evil Enemy

Is determined to get us;
He makes his vicious plans
With great might and cruel cunning;
Nothing on earth is like him. . . .
But if the whole earth were full of demons
Eager to swallow us,
We would not fear,
For we should still be saved.
The Prince of this world,
However fierce he claims to be,
Can do us no harm;
His power is under judgment;
One little word can fell him.

Our every defense against Satan rests upon the power of Jesus Christ. Drawing upon that power, the Protestant Reformation itself is a mighty fortress. Luther also used more direct means of defense, such as cheerfulness, laughter, boisterous, bawdiness, scorn, insults, and obscenity. Everything active, assertive, earthy, and good humored fends off the depression on which the Prince of Darkness thrives. One of Luther's best defenses was to go to bed with Katie.

Luther's followers spread his views, discussing his ideas in sermons, popular books, and catechisms. The catechisms, some written to aid the clergy in instructing the laity, others directly for the laity, give us a glimpse of what the faithful were expected to believe. The place of the Devil in these documents is secure and seldom silent. His existence, his influence, and his threat to Christians were never discounted. In one catechism Satan appears 67 times, Jesus only 63. In Luther's Greater Catechism of 1529, the reformer discusses Satan in relation to the Lord's Prayer, the Creed, baptism, and the Eucharist. Still, attention to the Devil was never recommended; the Christian best protected himself by turning his gaze away from the shadow and toward the light of the Lord.

John Calvin (1509–1564), the second great Protestant reformer, offered a precise, rational statement of his views in *The Institutes of the Christian Religion*. Calvin enthusiastically subscribed to the principles of faith alone and Scripture alone. Because human nature had been completely deformed by original sin, natural reason was unable to obtain any truth without the illumination of faith. True knowledge comes from the Bible, which the Holy Spirit interprets for those whom faith has saved. Calvin shared Luther's view of God's total omnipotence. No fate, fortune, chance, or freedom limits this complete sovereignty. Why God ordains evil is a mystery that we are not permitted to unravel. Yet, Calvin insisted, God has only one united will; although he seems to our limited intelligence to do both good and evil, he always works for the ultimate good. God not only permits evil, he actively wills it, as when he turned Pharaoh over to the Evil One to be confirmed in his obstinacy. In every evil human act, three forces are working together: the human will to sin, the Devil's will to evil, and God's will to the ultimate good. In every evil person, Satan and the Lord are both at work for their own purpose.

The Devil's role in such a theology was similar to that in Luther's. Calvin firmly rejected the skeptical view that angels and demons are only human ideas. Still, he did not pay nearly as much attention to the Evil One as his German colleague did. Recognizing that the Bible offers few particulars on the Devil, Calvin insisted that a detailed diabology was inappropriate. Since he experienced the Devil's assaults less personally than Luther, Calvin assigned him a narrower place in the world. Satan is completely under God's command and cannot do any evil that God does not expressly assign him. "To carry out his judgements through Satan as the minister of his wrath, God destines men's purposes as he pleases, arouses their wills, and strengthens their endeavors."

Historians now understand the Protestant Reformation and the Catholic Reformation as two parts of a general movement of reform. Still, deep differences pitted the two reformations against each other, the result being that many ideas on both sides were formulated and hardened in opposition to the other. The systematic theology of the Catholic Reformation tended to revert to medieval realism, reviving and elevating the teachings of Thomas Aquinas almost to the realm of dogmatic truth. This new Thomism offered little new theology, merely refining details of the scholastic system in the conviction that reason, based on revelation and aided by God's grace, could construct an objectively true view of the cosmos.

The Catholic Council of Trent (1545–1563) set a tacit seal upon the Thomist view of the Devil. Modern Catholic theologians, respectful of councils yet leary of diabology, have tended to evade the issue of conciliar authority on this point. On the one hand, only two ecumenical councils—IV Lateran and Trent—made explicit statements about the Evil One. On the other hand, virtually all Christian theologians, popes, and councils from the beginning of the church into the present century have assumed his existence. Trent made no statement explicitly affirming Satan's existence for the simple reason that no one was challenging it.

Three of its decrees define aspects of the Devil's activities, affirming that his power over humanity results from original sin, and blaming him for the existence of old and new heresies.

The Devil was accorded his traditional powers by Reformation contemplatives and mystics, notably the Carmelites Teresa of Avila and John of the Cross, and the founder of the Jesuit order, Ignatius Loyola. Loyola, who proposed systematic rules for spiritual training, insisted that no one at any time is free from the temptations incessantly offered by the Evil One, who seeks to convince us that worldly pleasures and sensual delights will make us happy. Often we are deluded into yielding, but the results are always the same: anxiety, sadness, and desolation. Satan sometimes seems to console us, but whatever good he feigns is only for his own evil designs, never for our welfare. Ignatius refined the psychological insights of the desert fathers on the discernment of spirits. If we are pointed toward God, the action of a good spirit in our hearts will promote peace, joy, hope, faith, charity, and elevation of mind, whereas the action of an evil spirit will bring upset, depression, concern with worldly things, and aridity of soul. However, if we are steeped in habitual sin and pointed away from God, the action of a good spirit calling us to repentance will seem harsh, and the action of an evil spirit, lulling us into contentment with our evil life, will seem pleasant and easy. To discern good from evil, therefore, we need to understand our own basic orientation as well as the effects of the spirits themselves. Because all the Devil's powers and wiles yield when confronted with the superior strength of Christ, the way to defeat the Devil is through steadfast faith.

Teresa of Avila (1515–1582) distinguished sharply between the essence of mysticism, which is loving contemplation of God infused by God's own love and grace, and the tangential phenomena that may accompany the contemplative life, such as visions, audible sensations, rapture, levitation, and stigmata. The Evil One can easily manipulate such phenomena to his own ends: Satan may create illusions of such things in order to corrupt the gullible; even when they come from God, the Devil may twist them by making us proud of them or by causing us to care for them more than for the real experience of God that they accompany. The purpose of the contemplative life is not to obtain spiritual favors but to give oneself completely to God.

Although Teresa warned against taking the Devil too seriously and advised despising his powers, both she and John of the Cross (1542–

1591) perceived him as incessantly active against all Christians, especially the contemplatives, whom he seeks at all costs to bar from their
goal of union with God. Though always powerless against the defense
that Christ raises up in a faithful soul, at the least sign of weakness the
Evil One rushes in with suggestions that seem reasonable at the moment
but eventually produce confusion, upset, and disgust. The temptations
are ingeniously diverse: he encourages self-righteousness and false humility and discourages us from prayer; he causes us to feel exaggerated
guilt and to labor under the impossible burden of trying to earn grace. He
makes us ill-tempered toward others and inspires doubt and fear that the
understanding we gain through contemplation is illusion.

Satan can also make direct and visible assaults. He repeatedly visited
Teresa, usually invisibly as a manifestation of the living lie, deceit, and
hypocrisy, but sometimes he appeared visibly: he perched in repulsive
shape on her left hand; his body exuded a flame that cast no shadow; with
a hideously gaping mouth he warned her that though she had escaped so
far, he would have her yet. When she made the sign of the cross, he
disappeared, only to reappear again shortly. She finally banished him by
sprinkling holy water on him. The Devil frequently beat her, shaking
her body with invisible blows. In visions she saw battles between angels
and demons and the torments of hell. Satan also beat John of the Cross,
sometimes hurling the saint out of his bed onto the cold stone floor.

These accounts by Teresa and John, like those of Luther, indicate the
powerful hold that traditional diabology had upon sixteenth-century
thought. They also pose a problem for modern historians, for they
cannot be dismissed as legends; they are autobiographical accounts,
direct testimony by those who had the experiences themselves. What
could these experiences have been? Modern viewpoints such as depth
psychology permit new angles, but any interpretation that dismisses the
mystics' own perceptions of the phenomena would be guilty of un-
sophisticated reductionism.

Under the influence of Luther and the witch craze, and because of the
harsh religious tensions of the era, sixteenth-century literature tended to
take the Devil as a more powerful threat than did that of the later Middle
Ages. A favorite genre of the period was the epic poem or play portraying
the fall of the angels and the glorious victory of Christ or his representative the archangel Michael over the evil angels at the beginning of the
world. In magnificent battle scenes, Christ and Michael are epic heroes
locked in deadly combat with Satan. This war in heaven, for which there

is no clear biblical warrant, had seldom appeared in medieval drama and was specifically rejected by Luther and Calvin. Yet its inherent dramatic tension and its suitability to Greco-Roman martial imagery made it irresistible to poets and playwrights seeking to adapt the conventions of the classical epic to Christian myth.

The voices of satire and skepticism were faint in the early part of the sixteenth century, the great exception being François Rabelais (1494?–1553). Rabelais mocks the order of society through his giant protagonists Pantagruel, Gargantua, and Panurge, directing almost slapstick mockery against the Establishment—bishops, lawyers, scholars, monks, and friars. The names and characters of the protagonists are derived from those of demons, but their rebellion against the established order is good-humored and crude. The first major work to present demonic figures who are sympathetic in their rebellion, *Gargantua and Pantagruel* prefigured the dissociation of the Devil from genuine evil.

Pantagruel and his father Gargantua are giants, which links them in folklore to the demonic; their exploits, such as killing cattle and devouring pilgrims, connect them with traditional demonology. The Devil occasionally appears in his own form, but always in a satirical, comical light: Lucifer has intestinal problems because of his bad diet. Formerly he dined on students, but nowadays they read the Bible too much and he can't get them down; instead he consumes an unsavory fare of lawyers, gossips, usurers, false monks, apothecaries, forgers, and drunken servant girls.

The most demonic character is Panurge, whose name, "doer of all things," suggests the multifaceted personality of the Devil. Like the traditional Satan, and like the Devils of Goethe, Dostoevsky, and Mann later, Panurge shifts his appearance, costume, voice, and manner to fit the situation. He has been a student at Toledo, widely known as a center of magical lore, and there he has worked with "the rector of the faculty of diabology." Panurge is a prototype of the "slick" Mephistopheles of the later Faust literature, tall, handsome, elegant, and of noble lineage, though traces of his demonic origins appear in his pallor, his blemishes, and his great age of over three hundred years.

The story of Faust was a great watershed in the literature of the Devil. After Christ, Mary, and Satan, Faust became the single most popular character in ths history of Christian culture. Plays, paintings, poems, novels, operas, cantatas, and films have for centuries featured Faust and his diabolical companion Mephistopheles. The Faust legend is loosely based on the actual life of a student of philosophy and theology who later turned to magic and then degenerated to casting horoscopes and predicting the future for money.

The first book devoted entirely to Faust was a mixture of legend and fantasy written by an anonymous German Protestant in 1587. The Faustus of this book attempts to obtain knowledge by his own efforts rather than to receive it by grace. This individualistic rebellion ties him to the original pride of Adam and Eve—and of Satan. Faustus thus became the prototype of the Romantic and modern revolt against authority. In order to master magical lore, he determines to call up the Devil. Going to a crossroads at night, he inscribes magical circles and figures on the ground and invokes a spirit. The spirit appears, shifting through various forms: a dragon, a fiery globe, a burning man, and finally a friar, the last identifying him with monkery and popery, Satan's chief tools on earth. The spirit explains to Faustus that he is an officer of hell and under the command of the great prince Lucifer, whose express permission he needs before he can agree to help the scholar. The spirit's name, Mephistopheles, a purely modern invention of uncertain origins, first appears in this book.

Mephistopheles goes to Lucifer and obtains permission to serve Faustus if the scholar will promise to give himself body and soul to the prince of hell. Faustus makes a written pact in blood, denies Christ, and promises to be an enemy of the Christian people. Though this pact was modeled on that of the medieval Theophilus, its more immediate precedent was the pact attributed to contemporary witches. In 1587, during the height of the witch craze, the story of pact made it plain to the audience that the magician Faust was involved in diabolical witchcraft. The pact grants Faust twenty-four years of power in return for the surrender of his soul to Satan when the time is up.

At first contented with these arrangements, Faustus eagerly quizzes Mephisto about the nature of hell, so the demon takes him on a tour. Terrified by what he sees in the pit, Faustus wants to repent, but Mephistopheles convinces him that it is too late to change his mind. This is a lie, for God always accepts a repentant sinner—but Faustus adds to pride the final and unforgivable sin of despair. He can escape only by throwing himself upon the mercy of God, and when it comes to the crunch he prefers eternal torment and separation from God to humble submission.

Faustus' original desire for knowledge and power is slowly transmuted into adolescent fantasies of lust and domination. He journeys to Rome to feast at the pope's palace, jampacked (in this Protestant tale) with whores and drunkards, and shows his contempt for the pontiff by whistling in his face. Then he journeys to Constantinople, where, pretending to be the prophet Muhammad, he obtains access to the sultan's harem. He wanders over Europe selling horoscopes to emperors, bishops, and professors. His exploits are Rabelaisian: he devours a bale of hay; he summons up Helen of Troy and satisfies his lust with her, but she turns out to be a demonic succubus.

When his twenty-four years are about to expire, Faustus summons his colleagues and students and recounts the whole story, warning them against sin, temptation, evil companions, and the wiles of the Devil. He seems momentarily to hope that this act of piety may save his soul, but, realizing that the hope is vain, he yields finally and completely to despair. At midnight the students feel a great wind shaking the house; they hear a hissing noise and then Faustus screaming for help. Next morning they find the strangely mutilated body thrown upon the dungheap, his head twisted from front to back.

The story of Faustus has distinctly modern characteristics that distinguish it from the medieval Theophilus legend. First, the story is anthropocentric. The medieval stories pit the Devil against Christ, the Virgin, or another saint; with Faust, the tension is between Devil and man. Faustus creates his own predicament and must get himself out of it if he can. Second, anthropocentrism is closely tied to individualism. The Protestant emphasis upon the lonely struggle of the isolated individual against spiritual powers meant that Faust had no recourse to a community or to the communion of saints. He does not even think of confession or the Eucharist, and the Lutheran author was certainly having no Virgin Mary coming to save him. Third, the story is pessimistic. The medieval sinner repented and was saved; here, the individual hardens his heart against salvation. Fourth, the story expresses the modern conflict about knowledge between Protestantism and modern secularism. Faustus desires knowledge for the power it gives, a modern secular attitude contrasting with the Protestant view that the soul unaided by grace cannot obtain any true knowledge and that the search for knowledge for personal advantage is both an illusion and a sin. Fifth, Mephistopheles signals the beginning of a change in the Devil's character; he shows a hint of sympathy with his victim and a trace of regret for his own rebellion. These signs of introspection, internalization, and humanization in Satan's character became an important theme of post–Faustian literature.

The first great literary expression of the Faust legend was Christopher

Marlowe's *Doctor Faustus* (1588/1589). Marlowe's plot follows the Faust-book closely. Faustus' first sin is pride: in the beginning he imagines that he can manipulate Mephistopheles to fulfill his own immoderate ambitions:

> By him, I'le be great Emperour of the world,
> And make a bridge, through the moving Aire
> To passe the Ocean: with a band of men
> I'le joyne the Hills that bind the *Affrick* shore,
> And make that Country continent to Spaine,
> And both contributary to my Crowne.

Soon Mephisto, using flattery, false promises, and threats, gains the upper hand. Faust begins to grasp the enormity of the situation on his tour of hell and yields to despair. He refuses to believe that Christ can save him because he knows that repentance entails renouncing the power he has gained and is enjoying. "I do repent; and yet I do despair." In the end, the Devil drags him off shrieking, his limbs are torn asunder, and his body is mutilated.

Mephistopheles is partly the traditional Christian Devil, " a spiritual lunatic," as Dorothy Sayers put it, "but like many lunatics, he is extremely plausible and cunning." Marlowe adds psychological depth to the character: Mephisto is not entirely evil; moody and introspective, he regrets his loss of felicity:

> Hell hath no limits, nor is circumscrib'd
> In one selfe place: but where we are is hell.
> And where hell is there we must ever be.
> And to be short, when all the world dissolves,
> And every creature shall be purifi'd,
> All places shall be hell that are not heaven.

Where God is, is reality. All else, Mephisto knows, is illusion, nothingness, and that nothingness surrounds him always. "Why this is hell nor am I out of it."

For Marlowe the individual Christian is responsible for his own fate. The Devil does not even need to tempt Faustus, for the magician, awash in pride and desire, takes the initiative himself. Mephisto is merely a tool that Faustus uses to advance his own sin, and he grants Mephisto domination of his soul freely. This is not a medieval struggle between Christ and Satan, but a modern man's deliberate ruin of his own life.

This sixteenth-century engraving shows a pre-Goethean conception of Dr. Faustus.

At the end of the sixteenth century, just as the Devil's powers were reaching their zenith, the spirit of skepticism and irony revived. The comic Devil reappeared, and the focus on real evil shifted from Satan to the human personality, a process encouraged by the increasingly worldly nature of urban society.

In the work of William Shakespeare (1564–1616), the Evil One never appears in his own form, though spirits often make a direct appearance. The burden of evil and terror in Shakespeare lies far less in demonic spirits than in demonic humans, humans having an appetite for evil for its own sake: Aaron in *Titus Andronicus*, Richard III, Iago in *Othello*, Macbeth and Lady Macbeth, Goneril, Edmund, and Regan in *King Lear*. Aaron is the most crassly demonic. The "chief architect and plotter of these woes," he is "the incarnate Devil," and his own words betray a malice transcending human motivation:

> O, how this villainy
> Doth fat me with the very thought of it!
> Let fools do good, and fair men call for grace,
> Aaron will have his soul black like his face.

He murders with a cruel joke on his lips, and he boasts of his crimes: "Hell, let my deeds be witness to my worth." He refuses to repent:

> I am no baby, I, that with base prayers
> I should repent the evils I have done.
> Ten thousand worse than ever yet I did
> Would I perform if I might have my will.
> If one good deed in all my life I did,
> I do repent it from my very soul.

These are not the words of a Faustus, but of the Devil himself, bearing the marks of the same boasting hardness that Milton would place in Satan's mouth in hell. The only human motivation of Aaron's behavior is his bitterness about his color, but this resentment, like Lucifer's own resentment of being created dependent upon God, is vain, irrational hatred of the world as it is. Aaron freely chooses evil for the sake of evil.

In his late tragedies—*Hamlet, Othello, Lear,* and *Macbeth*—Shakespeare showed an increasing concern with radical evil and the demonic. Hamlet is no demon, yet once he opens himself to revenge, the Devil gradually shapes him to his purpose. Hamlet plots murder; he sends the lovely Ophelia away to madness and suicide; he dispatches the kindly if bungling Polonius with a quick swordthrust and a cruel jest; he plots the ruin and humiliation of his own mother. He rejects the opportunity of executing Claudius while the king is at prayer repenting his sins, lest death in a moment of grace should spare him damnation.

The key is the alleged ghost of Hamlet's father, whose brooding presence darkens the play from the outset, for the ghost is a manifestation of the Devil. Shakespeare intended the ghost's character to remain ambiguous to the audience as well as to the characters. From the moment when the ghost is first seen, the characters do not know what to make of him. Is he a ghost, or is he a demon? Shakespeare intended the ambiguity to remain. Shakespeare's audience would have reacted with the assumption that the ghost was likely a demon, and the characters share this view. Horatio challenges the ghost:

> What art thou that usurpst this time of night,
> Together with that fair and warlike form
> In which the majesty of Denmark
> Did sometimes march? By heaven, I charge thee, speak!

Horatio reports it to Hamlet as "a figure like your father," and before he encounters it himself, Hamlet is unsure and suspicious:

> If it assume my noble father's person,
> I'll speak to it though hell itself should gape.

When he sees it, he is bold to address it, but his mind remains unsettled:

> Be thou a spirit of health or a goblin damn'd,
> Bring with thee airs from heaven or blasts from hell,
> Be thy interests wicked or charitable,
> Thou comest in such questionable shape
> That I will speak to thee.

Immediately Hamlet makes his decision, a fatal one: "I'll call thee Hamlet, king, father, royal Dane." Horatio is terrified and warns the prince: what if it take you to the summit of the battlements and there "assume some other horrible form" that will drive you mad? But Hamlet has already made his act of faith in the thing, a tragically mistaken discernment that will lead him to ruin. He continues to harbor doubts:

> The spirit I have seen
> May be a devil, and the devil hath power
> T'assume a pleasing shape, yea, or perhaps
> Out of my weakness and my melancholy,
> As he is very potent with such spirits,
> Abuses me to damn me.

When he later discovers that his uncle really is his father's murderer, he sees that the ghost has spoken true, but he fails to recall that the Devil knows how to speak the truth in order to achieve the destruction of souls.

That the ghost is no herald from Purgatory but the Devil himself is apparent in his envy, jealousy, and arrogance, and in the coarse and bitter description he offers Hamlet of the crimes of Claudius and Gertrude. Speaking no word of love to Hamlet, he advises his son only to press for revenge. To underline the hints, Shakespeare has the ghost speak to Hamlet and Horatio from beneath the stage, signifying the underworld. The ghost's hollow voice from below bids Horatio swear secrecy and Hamlet revenge. No saved soul would demand such oaths, or indeed any oaths at all. The ghost keeps shifting his position under the stage (the Devil is the most notorious of shifters).

Shakespeare gives plenty of hints that the ghost is the Devil but never explicitly says so because he wants us to share the doubt and so understand the difficulty of discernment. The dramatic function of the ghost's ambivalence is clear. He must be ambivalent enough to fool the audience because he must be ambivalent enough to fool Hamlet. If the audience could without doubt identify the ghost as Satan, they would find Hamlet's own failure in discernment unconvincing and unsympathetic. The Devil must be convincing enough as a ghost to deceive Hamlet and make the point that he may deceive any human being, including the audience—and the critics. Discernment is the key. Discernment is centered on the knowledge that a good tree bears good fruit and an evil tree evil fruit. If the fruit is evil, the tree cannot be good. Hamlet should have been able to tell that a spirit who speaks grossly and demands revenge is not from God but from the Devil. The course of action that the specter urges leads to death, destruction, and the ruin of innocent lives. Yet Hamlet concludes with damnable error that "it is an honest ghost."

Shakespeare's villains allow transcendent evil to work in and through them, and sometimes to overwhelm them, but they are seldom demons themselves. The arena in which good struggled against evil was now less frequently the halls of heaven or the pit of hell than it was the human heart. Belief in the Devil remained strong in Shakespeare's day, but the world view that in Luther's time had supported such belief had already been shaken. Over subsequent centuries it would gradually subside. Yet its single most magnificent moment was yet to come.

High on a Throne
of Royal State

T HE most magnificent portrait of the traditional Devil ever composed,
Milton's *Paradise Lost*, was written in the mid-seventeenth century, when
Satan was already passing out of fashion. People had become weary of
being terrified of the immediate threatening presence of hostile spirits—
and of the prosecutions for witchcraft, which in some areas touched
almost every member of the community, including the governing elites.
When the elite found themselves in jeopardy, they responded more
readily to the growing urge for relief. Once the field was thus prepared
for change, theoretical arguments against belief in witchcraft and the
omnipresence of Satan began to flourish. Protestants belatedly realized
that there was little scriptural basis for belief in diabolical witchcraft.
Reginald Scot's *Discoverie of Witchcraft* (1584) argued vehemently against
the excesses of demonology and witchcraft theory. Scot was no scientific
materialist; he believed in Satan's existence; but he argued that neither
Scripture nor tradition warranted the belief that we are under constant
attack by evil spirits.

Such moderate skepticism was temporarily overwhelmed in the early
part of the century by impassioned defenses of witch beliefs by King
James VI of Scotland in 1597 and by Matthew Hopkins in 1647. Toward
the end of the century, learned and reasonable defenses of witch beliefs
continued to appear, including Joseph Glanvill's *Sadducismus triumpha-
tus*," "Skepticism Defeated" (1681). Glanvill, an open-minded seeker
who believed in the compatibility of science and religion, questioned
every kind of dogmatism, including the religious and the materialist
varieties. He refused to dismiss belief in the Devil and pleaded for
objective investigation of reports of demonic activity. Eventually, how-

ever, the more thorough variety of skepticism prevailed. The final blows to the intellectual defense of witchcraft were dealt by Francis Hutchinson's *Historical Essay Concerning Witchcraft* in 1718, by which time its author was preaching to an audience already largely converted. Increasing religious skepticism was augmented by philosophical, rationalist skepticism, which held that the existence of incorporeal spirits cannot be demonstrated. Cannot be, that is, in a world view using the rationalists' assumptions; the new skeptics were not skeptical enough to see that their own views were also precarious.

The tension between skepticism and credulity in the seventeenth century produced a new phenomenon, the black mass, a strange combination of disbelief in Christianity and belief in the Christian Devil. The atmosphere for the black mass had long been building because of belief in witchcraft and demonic possession, where the force of the demonic was connected with human sexual aberrations. Satan's sexuality had usually been a repressed undercurrent in diabology. A few commentators and dramatists had viewed Satan's seduction of Eve in sexual terms, even portraying the serpent twined lasciviously around her body, and it was believed that demons in the appearance of physical bodies could seduce sleeping men and women. But it was only during the witch craze that the sexual aspects of the Devil—the orgies and sexual submission to Satan—became both lurid and prominent. In all periods sexual repressions have doubtless engendered fantasies, but it is unclear why the Devil became especially sexualized in the sixteenth and seventeenth centuries. Part of the explanation may lie in the shift of attention (as in Shakespeare) from the demonic as an external force to the demonic within human nature.

Some seventeenth-century accounts of possession remained traditional, especially where the possession affected a single individual rather than a group. The Devil first attacked Catherine de Saint-Augustin (1632–1668), a nun of Quebec, when she was five, and for the rest of her life he assaulted her with despair, lust, gluttony, and other temptations. The assaults increased in severity as she grew older, and from the age of thirty-two she was possessed by a horde of demons who inflicted agonies upon her body and soul, leaving her in peace at last only shortly before her early death.

Possession was at its most grotesque when Satan's powers were combined with human sexuality in an atmosphere of collective frenzy and hallucination often exploited for political purposes. At the Ursuline convent of Loudun the frenzy centered on a priest named Urbain Grandier, a sexual libertine whose arrogance had earned him many enemies, some of whom concocted a plot to ruin him by accusing him of debauching the nuns. The nuns were worked into frenzies by the suggestions and accusations made during the inquiry, until some of them came really to believe that they had been sexually molested by demons. They began to exhibit the coarsest gestures and language. Even after Grandier had been convicted and burned in 1634, and in spite of all efforts to exorcise them, the nuns continued to behave as possessed until public attention finally waned.

At the convent of Saint Louis de Louviers, Sister Madeleine Bavent, who had been seduced by her confessor before entering the convent, was the focus of the group possession. Several elements distinguish such phenomena from witchcraft: first, the focus was more exclusively on sex; second, the obscene rites were presided over by a priest. Orgies, desecration of the Eucharist, and even the occasional attendance of clergy at the sabbat were all part of witch beliefs, but at the sabbats the clergy did not participate but were only part of the congregation. That the orgiastic and anticlerical elements now became central illustrates the rebellious anticlericalism of seventeenth-century psychology. Nothing could be more blasphemous in Catholic Europe than the sexual misuse of the Eucharist, the Body of Christ, by an ordained priest.

Such fantasies plumbed the lowest depths in the black masses of the 1670s. A brisk trade in fortunetelling, aphrodisiacs, and poisons was uncovered by the Paris police in 1678. As the scope of the crimes among reputable families and the nobility was revealed, a special court was established to deal with them. The investigations brought to light magic and black masses as well as drugs and poisons. The affair got out of hand as people began to see how they might use lurid accusations against their enemies for their own political and economic advantage. In 1680 a number of priests were indicted for saying mass on the bodies of naked women at the center of a ring of black candles, of leading the congregation in sexual intercourse, of ritual copulation on the altar, of sacrificing animals, of murdering children and using their blood in the preparation of aphrodisiacs, of desecrating the Eucharist, of using the chalice to mix children's blood with sexual fluids, of invoking the Devil, and of making written pact with him. These black masses were supposedly offered at the request of courtiers and other influential people in order to procure political or sexual favors. One of Louis XIV's mistresses was accused of seeking by magic to make the queen barren and to fix the king's attentions on herself. As in the witch craze, once delusion began to touch people of such power and rank it was doomed. The king terminated the proceedings of 1682, issuing an edict eliminating prosecution for witchcraft. The black mass, a product of the cynical, skeptical, yet credulous seventeenth century, was not revived until the late nineteenth century.

In contrast to the cynical black mass, serious and moral plays and poems dealing with the war in heaven, the fall of the angels, and the temptation of Adam and Eve continued to be popular all over Europe both before and after John Milton's *Paradise Lost*, but it was Milton who knit the traditional stories into a fabric so coherent and compelling that it became the standard account for all succeeding generations. Milton was born in 1608. Brought up a staunch Protestant, he eventually formulated a somewhat idiosyncratic theology of his own, which he expressed in his treatise *Christian Doctrine* (1655–1660) and his poems *Paradise Lost* (1667) and *Paradise Regained* (1674).

These two epic poems cover almost the entire span of Christian salvation history; their express purpose was to "justify the ways of God to men." God created the world good; moral goodness is impossible without free will; humans and angels are free to choose evil; some do so; God's providence, turning everything to good, makes our fall the occasion for teaching us wisdom through trials and suffering; God ultimately redeems us through the Incarnation and Passion of Jesus. Milton intended God and man—not Satan—to be the dramatic center of the poem.

Still, Satan seems to be the protagonist, the character that most moves the plot along. Milton also deliberately made Satan appear magnificent at the beginning so that his audience might feel all the glamour of evil. Only if readers are attracted by Satan can they recognize their own tendencies to evil and grasp the ignominy and pathos of Satan's eventual ruin. Milton also seems to have inadvertently made the characters of God and Christ less interesting and dramatic than that of the Evil One. But he had absolutely no intention of portraying Satan in a positive light.

Milton followed the traditional chronology of salvation history. "In the beginning is God," and in the moment after the initial act of creation and before making the material universe, God creates the angels through the power of his Son, the Word. Then, summoning all the hosts of heaven before his throne, he calls the angels to witness the exaltation of his Son. One of the greatest of these angels was Lucifer. Milton is deliberately unclear as to Lucifer's rank in heaven: he calls him an archangel yet sets him in command of seraphim and cherubim. Milton judged that the only point he needed to make was that Satan had such high dignity in heaven that after his fall he naturally became king of hell.

The poet took pains to describe his godlike, princely nature and his terrifying stature:

> On th'other side Satan alarm'd
> Collecting all his might dilated stood,
> Like Teneriff or Atlas unremov'd:
> His stature reached the Sky, and on his Crest
> Sat horror Plum'd.
>
> [He] extended long and large
> Lay floating many a rood, in bulk as huge
> As whom the Fables name of monstrous size.

This great power is moved to envy and anger at the elevation of the Son above himself:

> Fraught
> With envy against the Son of God, that day
> Honour'd by his great Father, and proclaim'd
> Messiah King anointed, could not bear
> Through pride that sight.
> [Therefore] he resolv'd
> With all his Legions to dislodge, and leave
> Unworship't, unobey'd the Throne supreme.

Satan's rebellion occurs before the creation of the material universe, including humanity.

On one level the Almighty is the cause of Satan's ruin, for God chooses to create the cosmos such as it is; the angel Abdiel tells Satan: "I see thy fall Determin'd." On a second level, however, God does not directly will things to be as they are, for he has given his creatures true freedom. The freedom he wills, but he does not rule what choice they make. What God says of humanity's original sin also applies to Satan:

> Whose fault?
> Whose but his own? ingrate, he had of mee
> All he could have; I made him just and right,
> Sufficient to have stood, though free to fall.

If Satan fell freely, there is no cause of his fall, for there can be no cause of a truly free-will act.

But though his fall had no cause, it had motives. In the course of the poem, Satan's motives deteriorate from pride to envy to revenge. His "obdurate pride" appears from the beginning:

> He trusted to have equall'd the most High,
> If he oppos'd; and with ambitious aim
> Against the Throne and Monarchy of God
> Rais'd impious War in Heav'n.

To pride, Satan added envy of the Son of God, which overwhelmed him at the dramatic moment of Christ's elevation by the Father. Satan felt a sense of "injur'd merit" at the Son's power, which seemed to him a novel point of law introduced by an arbitrary, tyrannical God. To Milton and his audience Satan had no claim to any merit, injured or otherwise, since whatever good one has comes from God's gift. At God's request that the angels glorify the Son, Satan scornfully addresses them: "Will ye submit your necks, and choose to bend/The supple knee?" Once having made his choice, Satan adds revenge to envy, and when humanity is created, he adds hatred of our happiness in Eden and hatred that God should create us in his own image.

Satan's choice to rebel was the first of all sins: at the moment of decision, his daughter, Sin, sprang from his forehead. Satan's first act as sinner is to persuade some of his fellow angels to rebel. Withdrawing his followers from the hosts surrounding God's throne, he set up his own seat in the north of heaven. With eloquent, twisted reasoning he argues that the angels need not obey God, for because they cannot remember the act of creation, God's claim to have made them may be a lie. They may not be created at all, but rather "self-begot, self-rais'd," unbeholden to Father or to Son:

> Our puissance is our own, our own right hand
> Shall teach us highest deeds, by proof to try
> Who is our equal.

The immediate effect of the rebellion is war in heaven, which Milton portrays in the epic language of the *Iliad* or the *Aeneid*. Satan's war against God is an insane action that can have only one conclusion, and the audience knows that. To make a war against an omnipotent divinity credible, Milton was obliged to give the rebellious angels a high degree of valor and courage. He did this so enthusiastically as to introduce a whole new scenario to the myth. Traditionally, the war was over in one mighty battle, but Milton protracted the conflict and made the first stage a stalemate between Satan's armies and those of Michael, so that God is obliged on the third day to send his own Son to cast the rebels down. Where Michael has been hard pressed, the Son triumphs easily, putting forth "not half his strength."

> Instead of annihilating the vanquished, God checks
> His Thunder in mid Volley, for he meant
> Not to destroy, but root them out of Heav'n.

God actually leaves them with the power to do more damage, which perplexes Satan, who would have shown them no mercy as victor himself:

> Let him surer bar
> His Iron Gates, if he intends our stay
> In that dark durance.

But God wishes to teach the Devil that his every effort to do evil is inevitably turned to good:

> And high permission of all-ruling Heaven
> Left him at large to his own dark designs,
> That with reiterated crimes he might
> Heap on himself damnation, while he sought
> Evil to others, and enrag'd might see
> How all his malice serv'd but to bring forth
> Infinite goodness, grace, and mercy shown
> On man by him seduc't, but on himself
> Treble confusion, wrath, and vengeance pour'd.

Whatever Satan does redounds upon his own head, and he can never be saved. Humanity was seduced by another being, but Satan has no excuse.

Satan is the author of evil as God is the author of the universe. As a result of Satan's sin, wretchedness enters the world.

> How hast thou disturb'd
> Heav'n's blessed peace, and into Nature brought
> Misery, uncreated till the crime
> Of thy Rebellion? how hast thou instill'd
> Thy malice into thousands?

Having fallen from grace by their own choice, Satan and his evil angels fall from heaven by God's:

> Him th'Almighty Power
> Hurl'd headlong flaming from th'Ethereal Sky
> With hideous ruin and combustion down
> To bottomless perdition, there to dwell
> In Adamantine Chains and penal fire.

With him fell the angels who had taken his side:

> Lucifer from Heav'n
> (So call him, brighter once amidst the Host
> Of Angels, than that Star the Stars among)
> Fell with his flaming Legions through the Deep
> Into his place.

They fell "thick as autumnal leaves . . . Cherub and Seraph rolling in the flood." Nine days they fell down through the air, down through chaos, and nine days lay prostrate on the fiery lake.

> Nine days they fell; confounded Chaos roar'd,
> And felt tenfold confusion in thir fall
> Through his wild Anarchy, so huge a rout
> Incomber'd him with ruin: Hell at last
> Yawning receiv'd them whole, and on them clos'd,
> Hell thir fit habitation fraught with fire
> Unquenchable, the house of woe and pain.

But where is hell? Milton seems to follow Dante and tradition in locating it at the center of the earth:

> Here thir Prison ordained
> In utter darkness, and thir portion set
> As far remov'd from God and light of Heav'n
> As from the Centre thrice to th'utmost Pole.

The problem is that in Milton's chronology the earth has yet to be created, so hell can scarcely be at its center! There appears to be another problem as well. Later in the action Milton describes Satan's voyage from hell across chaos toward heaven, from which the universe hangs pendant on a golden chain. If the universe hangs from heaven, and both are separated by chaos from hell, where can hell be? The answer is that although Milton describes hell with physical imagery of the interior of the planet, his hell is not really in the earth. Where is it then? It is nowhere: that is the beauty of Milton's conception. The place where Satan seeks to raise a new empire is nowhere at all, a perfect metaphor for the absolute nonbeing of evil. Hell is less a place where the fallen angels dwell than a state of soul that stays with them wherever they go: "Which way I fly is Hell; myself am Hell." It is a state "where all life dies, death lives." Hell, being nowhere, is the fit abode for those who choose nothingness over reality.

Now that the angels have fallen, God proceeds to his second creation, the material universe. He summons a new world into being to make up for Satan's depredations in heaven:

> But lest his heart exalt him in the harm
> Already done, to have dispeopled Heav'n,
> My damage fondly deem'd, I can repair
> That detriment, if such it be to lose
> Self-lost, and in a moment will create
> Another World, out of one man a Race
> Of men innumerable, there to dwell.

The human race will make up for the fallen angels; it is the crowning glory of the cosmos; but that glory Satan will soon seek to soil.

But first we see Satan, cast down into the fiery lake, surveying his dark dungeon. He spies his lieutenant Beelzebub and then the whole shadowed host. Their natures, created by God, remain angelic, but their wills have become evil, and their outward appearance gradually changes to match the distortion of their wills. The continuing deterioration of Satan's character is matched by the increasing grotesqueness of his appearance. His warping continues for ever and ever:

> And in the lowest deep a lower deep
> Still threat'ning to devour me opens wide,
> To which the Hell I suffer seems a Heav'n. . . .
> While they adore me on the Throne of Hell,
> With Diadem and Sceptre high advanc'd
> The lower still I fall.

Though at first "his form had yet not lost/All her original brightness, nor appear'd/Less than Arch Angel ruin'd," it already bore the terrible marks

Satan is chained for nine days in hell's burning pool. Gustave Doré, engraving, 1882, for *Paradise Lost*.

of decline. Upon seeing his comrade Beelzebub for the first time in hell, Satan gapes, "O how fall'n! how chang'd," sensing that the mark of ruin is already upon himself, and later an angelic messenger will confirm his fears:

> Think not, revolted Spirit, thy shape the same,
> Or undiminsh't brightness, to be known
> As when thou stood'st in Heav'n upright and pure;
> That Glory then, when thou no more wast good,
> Departed from thee, and thou resembl'st now
> Thy sin and place of doom obscure and foul.

In order to deceive angels and humans, Satan takes on a number of animal forms, including vulture and serpent, and then whines that he is being degraded by doing so:

> O foul descent! that I who erst contended
> With Gods to sit the highest, am now constrain'd
> Into a Beast, and mixt with bestial slime.

In the course of the poem Satan is gradually reduced from bright angel to a peeping, prying thing that ends as a writhing snake.

Rising from the fiery lake into which he has been pitched in his expulsion from heaven, Satan muses to Beelzebub about their present predicament and future prospects. Condemning God as a cruel tyrant, he calls for protracted warfare against the Deity. Beelzebub joins his master in the delusion that God can be resisted, pretending that they had nearly succeeded in toppling the heavenly despot. But in Beelzebub's thought runs an undercurrent of worry: he fears that God must really be almighty since nothing less than omnipotence could have overcome their angelic might. All the demons participating in the infernal discussions have glimpses into reality that Satan lacks, but Satan's greater blindness, which proceeds from his greater evil, causes him to ignore these insights and pursue his insane plan. His response to Beelzebub's caution exposes a completely corrupted will choosing evil for the sake of evil:

> To do aught good never will be our task,
> But ever to do ill our sole delight,
> As being contrary to his high will
> Whom we resist. If then his Providence

> Out of our evil seek to bring forth good,
> Our labor must be to pervert that end,
> And out of good still to find means of evil.

This is a blunt plan for a counter-providence: whatever is good we will attempt to twist to evil; we hate good for the pure and simple reason that it is good. Satan embraces his own evil:

> Farewell happy Fields
> Where Joy for ever dwells: Hail horrors, hail
> Infernal world, and thou profoundest Hell
> Receive thy new Possessor; One who brings
> A mind not to be chang'd by Place or Time.
> The mind is its own place, and in itself
> Can make a Heav'n of Hell, a Hell of Heav'n. . . .
> Better to reign in Hell, than serve in Heav'n.

I affirm, he says, that my sole purpose is to embrace nothingness and to obliterate whatever is good. Again, this is vain boasting, for his anti-providential schemes are nonsense: in reality divine providence will turn every evil into good. Belial and the other demons rush about with their plans to build an empire with Pandemonium as its capital, but the idea of making this stinking, filthy place, which is literally nowhere, into a comfortable kingdom is absurd.

Satan nurses his own private scheme: if God is planning a new world and a new race, this presents me with an opportunity to strike a blow against the divine oppressor by fraud and by guile. Satan calls a council and feigns allowing the demons freedom of debate, all the while planning to have Beelzebub impose the master plan at the end. Satan opens the parliament:

> High on a Throne of Royal State, which far
> Outshone the wealth of Ormus and of Ind,
> Or where the gorgeous East with richest hand
> Show'rs on her Kings Barbaric Pearl and Gold,
> Satan exalted sat.

The throne from which Satan apes the royal state of God in heaven is, like the rest of hell, a lunatic phantasm. His opening address to his followers is equally mad, for he suggests that they can defeat the Almighty and end up with greater glory than before their fall.

Each demon makes his speech on the basis of his own ruling vice, which each disguises as a virtue. The savage Moloch rises to counsel war at all costs; even if it cannot be won, he argues, it is better than crouching here in chains. The smooth-tongued Belial speaks next, using all the arts of rhetoric and charismatic charm to oppose Moloch and advance his own lazy, sensuous scheme. Let us settle down in hell, he counsels, wait till God's anger cools, and perhaps we will eventually feel comfortable here. Mammon's advice resembles Belial's, though based more on avarice than on sensuality: Let us build a city and an empire here in the underworld, he suggests, mining the rich earth to construct palaces and so profit from our fall.

The assembled demons are inclining to the side of Belial and Mammon, but now Beelzebub rises to promote Satan's plan as if it were his own. Courtly, grave, recognized as Satan's prime minister, he commands immediate respect. Calmly and politely he exposes the illusions of the previous speakers. We can never be happy in hell, he argues, because God is in reality absolute master here as he is of the whole cosmos. The conclusions that an unclouded mind would draw from that premise are obvious, but the demons no longer have clear intellects. And so Beelzebub, stirring them up to hatred and contempt of humanity, advances a plan even more insane than the others. If we cannot confront God directly, he says, we can get at him by corrupting these little pets of his. The demons enthusiastically embrace this scheme to:

> Confound the race
> Of mankind in one root, and Earth with Hell
> To mingle and involve, done all to spite
> The great Creator.

But the plan is vain from the outset:

> But thir spite still serves
> His glory to augment.

Now the demons must decide which will do the dirty work in Eden. Satan volunteers, vaunting his courage and his initiative to his followers—whereas his real motive is to escape, if only for a while, the punishment of hell. Sallying forth, Satan reaches the gate of hell and there encounters his daughter Sin, on whom he has incestuously begotten "the execrable shape" of his son Death, who in turn has raped his mother and produced a brood of monstrous offspring. The Devil, Sin, and Death parody the Holy Trinity; Sin addresses Satan in terms appropriate only to God:

> Thou art my Father, thou my Author, thou
> My being gav'st me; whom should I obey
> But thee, whom follow? thou wilt bring me soon
> To that new world of light and bliss.

The dark irony is that this new world that the perverted trio will soon make their home is the earth.

The Devil proceeds, issuing from the gate of hell into chaos, a nonplace separating the nonplace of hell from the reality that is heaven and the universe depending from it. Leaving chaos, he journeys toward the universe while God watches his course across the void and already plans his response: the Son's willing sacrifice of himself for a humanity that Father and Son know will fall and will need redemption. Satan finally reaches the outermost sphere of the cosmos and, perching there, peers down, scanning the vulnerable universe like a vulture looking for prey. Descending to the sphere of the sun, he disguises himself as a cherub; thence he comes to earth, alighting upon a mountain near the Garden of Eden, the same mountain (Milton feigns) as that on which Satan would tempt Christ.

Sitting on the mountain, Satan soliloquizes in terms that we might take as honest soul-searching if we did not know that here was a being wholly committed to evil. The soliloquy is another of Satan's impostures; and yet not entirely so. His intellect, though coarsened and weakened, still retains a tiny remnant of its angelic powers, and here he seems to glance sideways at reality before rejecting it yet again. Looking at the sun, Satan hates it for reminding him of what true light really is. He recognizes that the choice of darkness was his own and that he is the author of his own misery. The thought of repentance enters his mind only to be rejected immediately. He knows which way his will is bent.

> For never can true reconcilement grow
> Where wounds of deadly hate have pierc'd so deep:
> Which would but lead me to a worse relapse,
> And heavier fall: so should I purchase dear
> Short intermission bought with double smart.
> This knows my punisher; therefore as far

> From granting hee, as I from begging peace:
> All hope excluded thus.

The angel Uriel, who observes this soliloquy from afar, notices the contortions of Satan's face and realizes that here is no innocent cherub but a threat to the innocuous inhabitants of earth.

Satan continues on to Paradise, upon whose beauties he spies in the shape of a cormorant from a tree; with envious hatred he watches Adam and his wife embracing in innocent union. Meanwhile Gabriel sets an angelic watch over Eden to protect them, and two of their guardian angels, Ithuriel and Zephon, come across Satan squatting like a toad and whispering fantasies of corruption into Eve's sleeping ear. Ithuriel touches him lightly with his spear, and at the touch Lucifer leaps up in his own shape, but so changed from his original glory that they do not recognize him. When they do, Zephon rebukes him and tells him of his true appearance. Satan is taken aback:

> Abasht the Devil stood,
> And felt how awful goodness is, and saw
> Virtue in the shape how lovely, saw, and pin'd
> His loss.

Still, his regret is not so much for the harm he is doing as for the loss of his own beauty and prestige. The two angels bring Satan before Gabriel, and the great archangels—one fallen, one elect—begin a dialogue. Satan disdains Gabriel's loyalty and boasts of his own courage and faithfulness to his comrades. Gabriel's reply is crushingly direct:

> O sacred name of faithfulness profan'd!
> Faithful to whom? to thy rebellious crew?
> Army of Fiends, fit body to fit head. . . .
> And thou, sly hypocrite, who now wouldst seem
> Patron of liberty, who more than thou
> Once fawn'd, and cring'd, and servilely ador'd
> Heav'n's awful Monarch? wherefore but in hope
> To dispossess him, and thyself to reign?

As Satan sits whispering to Eve in the shape of a toad, she in her dream sees him in the form of a beautiful angel suggesting the joys that will be hers once she eats the forbidden fruit. Her husband warns her that the dream may proceed from an evil spirit, but the dream has had its effect on the first woman, grooming her for the final temptation. To accomplish this, Satan roams the earth in search of a perfect disguise and settles upon the serpent, voluntarily shifting his shape into a form into which he later would be forced. Finding the serpent, as yet an innocent beast, asleep, Satan creeps into his mouth and possesses him. Unaware of the horror awaiting them, yet warned of possible danger, Adam suggests to Eve that they stay together, but she determines to walk in the garden alone, a situation that Satan is quick to exploit. On beholding her again, the Evil One hesitates just for a moment; a remnant of his original intellect opens his eyes to the beauty and harmony of the universe and of this its fairest inhabitant:

> Her graceful Innocence, her every Air
> Of gesture or least action overaw'd
> His Malice, and with rapine sweet bereav'd
> His fierceness of the fierce intent it brought;
> That space the Evil One abstracted stood
> From his own evil, and for the time remain'd
> Stupidly good, of enmity disarm'd,
> Of guile, of hate, of envy, of revenge.

Then his twisted will draws him back away from reality:

> But the hot Hell that always in him burns,
> Though in mid Heav'n, soon ended his delight. . . .
> Fierce hate he recollects, and all his thoughts
> Of mischief, gratulating, thus excites.

He explains to Eve how he, a poor serpent, had obtained wisdom merely by eating the fruit of the wonderful tree. Eve objects that God has forbidden the fruit, but Satan expostulates against a tyrant who would block her from growth and fulfillment. The tree, he insinuates, will give her and her husband immortality, a happier life, and higher knowledge. It will make them like gods, and the Lord's only motive in prohibiting it must be his desire to hold them under his control. Eve yields, her senses urging her to taste the fruit, her intellect bent by Satan's false reasoning.

With Eve's fall, the moment of high drama is over, for Adam will soon follow his wife into ruin. When he learns what she has done he is horrified:

> O fairest of Creation, last and best
> Of all God's Works, Creature in whom excell'd

> Whatever can to sight or thought be form'd,
> Holy, divine, good, amiable, or sweet!
> How art thou lost, how on a sudden lost,
> Defac't, deflow'r'd, and now to Death devote?

But he is bone of Eve's bone and flesh of her flesh, and his immediate and resolute choice is to remain by her. Whatever his motives, Adam knowingly chooses to violate God's will, and the consequences are inescapable. The two first humans are driven out of Paradise to live a life of suffering and alienation, while the serpent is cursed. Satan understands that the curse means his eventual ruin when Christ, the second Adam and son of the second Eve, will come to crush him beneath his foot. But meanwhile he shortsightedly rejoices, and his offspring Sin and Death now build their highway from hell to earth, which they subject to Satan's rule until the moment of redemption.

Satan triumphantly returns to the underworld to boast to his followers. Shining in what shreds of starlike glory yet remain to him, he mounts his glittering throne, and the fallen angels prostrate themselves in wonder and praise. I have defeated God and opened the earth to Sin and Death, he vaunts; arise and take possession of this your domain. But all of a sudden his boasts are reduced to reality, for the angels ranked round the vast throneroom take on shapes more becoming to their true nature. Satan hears, not the shouts of praise that he expects, but the authentic voice of his attendant throng:

> So having said, a while he stood, expecting
> Thir universal shout and high applause
> To fill his ear, when contrary he hears
> On all sides, from innumerable tongues
> A dismal universal hiss, the sound
> Of public scorn; he wonder'd, but not long
> Had leisure, wond'ring at himself now more;
> His Visage drawn he felt to sharp and spare,
> His Arms clung to his Ribs, his Legs entwining
> Each other, till supplanted down he fell
> A monstrous Serpent on his Belly prone,
> Reluctant, but in vain, a greater power
> Now rul'd him, punisht in the shape he sinn'd,
> According to his doom; he would have spoke,
> But hiss for hiss return'd with forked tongue
> To forked tongue, for all were now transform'd

Satan planning to possess a serpent to tempt Adam and Eve. Engraving, 1882, by Gustave Doré for *Paradise Lost*.

> Alike to Serpents all as accessories
> To his bold Riot: dreadful was the din
> Of hissing through the Hall, thick swarming now
> With complicated monsters, head and tail.

Satan, who had taken the serpent's form to seduce humankind, is doomed forever to crawl upon his belly before the dreadful majesty of God.

In *Paradise Regained*, Milton described the healing of the alienation between God and humanity by the resistance of the second Adam, Christ, to a new temptation. Satan, who has lost all his majesty in his degradation and humiliation in the earlier poem, in the new poem exhibits merely low cunning.

Satan has learned of the birth of Jesus and heard him called the son of God. He summons another infernal council and warns the demons that they must find out what this means. Is Jesus merely human, or is he divine? To find out, the Devil must determine whether he will yield to temptation. God, observing this new plot from heaven, permits the Evil One to tempt Christ in order that the Son may demonstrate that the new Adam has the strength to restore the damage done by the first Adam. The Father will use the temptation providentially. It begins the Passion, the suffering that God uses to break Satan's power over the earth. As God turns the Passion into the salvation of humankind, so he first turns Satan's test of Jesus into the confirmation of Christ's divinity.

When Jesus goes out into the desert to pray, the Devil approaches him disguised as an old man in country clothing. Still evading responsibility, Satan whines that he is an unfortunate victim whom misery, not sin, has brought low. The Son of God is not taken in: "Deservedly thou griev'st, / composed of lies / From the beginning, and in lies wilt end." No joy can make you happy, for you have chosen unhappiness, and you are most miserable when in the presence of joy, "never more in Hell than when in Heaven."

Satan takes advice from his demons' parliament, and the sensuous Belial suggests that they tempt Jesus with women, but Satan prefers "manlier objects," honor, glory, and popular praise. He returns to the desert in sophisticated clothing and urbanely offers Jesus food, riches, glory, and the kingdoms of the earth. The temptations fail because Christ discerns that Satan can never offer anything but illusions. The Devil is not yet convinced and still wonders "in what degree or meaning thou art call'd / The Son of God, which bears no single sense." I too am a son of God, he muses, or at least I used to be, and all men are sons of God.

> Therefore to know what more thou art than man,
> Worth naming Son of God by voice from Heavn'n,
> Another method I must now begin.

Setting Jesus upon the pinnacle of the Temple, Satan urges him to prove his divine power by hurling himself down and allowing the angels to catch his fall. Jesus replies: "Tempt not the Lord your God," both an affirmation of his own faith in the Father and a reproach to Satan for tempting the Son. His reply sends Satan staggering back into darkness.

Satan is surprised at the failure of his temptations. Because all he understands is power, he cannot grasp that Christ's motive in coming to earth is love. Christ warns him that he cannot hope much longer to

> Rule in the clouds; like an Autumnal Star
> Or lightning thou shalt fall from Heav'n trod down. . . .
> Yet not thy last and deadliest wound
> By this repulse received.

Milton's is the last and greatest full-length portrait of the traditional lord of evil. The concept would in the eighteenth century be worn down by rationalists and distorted by Romantics, who, ironically, regarded Milton's Satan as the most important symbol of the rebelliousness that they considered the greatest good.

13   *The Disintegration of Hell*

DURING the eighteenth century the traditional Christian world view weakened, and old questions that Christianity had considered settled surfaced anew. Once again people questioned divine providence: did the universe look like one ruled by a just and intelligent mind, or did it look like one ruled by chance or mere mechanics? As the assumptions of educated society became more secular, Christians themselves slowly conformed to the new concern with this world. Both Catholics and Protestants turned their attention to the external and tangential aspects of religion such as social action and other good works. This development was both a sign and a cause of the secularization of Christianity, the gradual extrusion of God from the center of life out to an increasingly distant periphery from which he could slowly drift out of human consciousness. As for the thinkers of the eighteenth-century "Enlightenment," they opposed the churches, though sometimes advocating a Christianity drawn to their own specifications: a religion of social betterment, free of miracles, independent of tradition, and obedient to the sedate philosophers in their temple of reason.

The worldliness, moral laxity, and intellectual flabbiness of the eighteenth-century church reduced its resistance to the Enlightenment and to the Revolution of 1789, which was fiercely hostile to Christianity. Conservative Christians clung to the old ways, but the old symbols were losing their effectiveness. On the other hand, liberal Christians retreated, apologized, and adapted to materialism until Christianity all but lost its meaning. Abandoning the independent epistemological bases of Christianity in experience, revelation, and tradition, they tried to fit

Christianity within the empirical, scientific framework, an effort that proved futile and ultimately self-destructive.

This error derived from an earlier one. Traditional Christianity had arrogated to itself the task, unnecessary to religion, of explaining natural phenomena, and it now paid the price as the advance of scientific knowledge painted supernatural explanations of nature into a shrinking corner. In 1700 nature was believed to show forth the splendors of God. Later in the century, God faded, and Nature was itself personified as the active power shaping the universe. Finally, by 1800, interest shifted from personifying *Nature* to describing nature in terms of physical phenomena. The power that shaped these phenomena—whether God or Nature—was increasingly ignored.

Eighteenth-century skeptics pointed to the Devil as an example of the absurdity of Christian beliefs, while liberal Christians regarded diabology as an encumbrance to a Christianity that best traveled without much theological baggage. Conservatives tried to hold the line. One mode of defense was fideism, which, like medieval nominalism, accepted that Christianity could not be rationally proved. Fideism declared that God's truths lay forever beyond the limits of human reason. Neither reason nor science can reach these truths, but our internal experience teaches us that the cosmos is inscrutable, mysterious, and divine. This democratic mysticism avoided the untenable claim that Christianity rested on the same basis as science, and the skeptic Voltaire recognized it as the most effective Christian riposte to deism. Fideism had divergent effects. In its rejection of theological certainty it led to a broad, undoctrinaire view that eventually merged with liberalism; on the other hand, it reinforced conservatism by returning to Scripture as the basis for Christian belief.

Fideist reliance on Scripture typified the pietism and Methodism dominant in many Protestant churches by the end of the century. Pietism, like fideism, rejected intricate doctrinal statements and was skeptical of tradition. Fearing that rational philosophy would lead to atheism, the pietists emphasized feelings, emotions, and sentiment. Salvation did not lie in assenting to a creed, but rather in radical personal change characterized by abandonment of sinful alienation and total yielding to God's grace and love. The evangelical movement, springing from pietism, repudiated secularism energetically and was little touched by the revolutionary intellectual changes of the eighteenth and nineteenth centuries. Of all the movements of the eighteenth century, only pietism strongly upheld belief in Satan as attested by the Bible—although the pietists did not realize how much they were also relying on traditional interpretations of the Bible. They waged solitary battle against the Evil One and carried the war to the Enemy by going into the streets and across the seas to preach the gospel.

On the other hand, most of the educated leaders of the older churches rushed to accommodate secularism. Many adopted the broad, only vaguely Christian optimism associated with Gottfried Leibniz (1646–1716), who argued that this was the best of all possible universes, and with Alexander Pope (1688–1744), who maintained that "whatever is, is RIGHT." Rejecting the traditional view of a humanity corrupted by original sin, the optimists believed that an enlightened mind could discern the rational pattern of the cosmos rationally and abide by it. Such optimism was assaulted from opposite sides. The traditional Christian Samuel Johnson flayed it in his novel *Rasselas* (1759), and the deist Voltaire devastated it in his "Poem on the Lisbon Disaster" (1755), observing that a world in which thousands of people are destroyed in an earthquake can hardly be the best world possible. In his novel *Candide* (1759), Voltaire dismissed optimism as the fad of maintaining that everything is all right when in fact everything is all wrong.

Voltaire and the other French philosophes (the term indicates that they were not so much philosophers as advocates of the new faith in reason, materialism, and empiricism) argued that although the existence of God as the rational force that designed the universe was obvious, we can know absolutely nothing about him. True religion, said Voltaire, must therefore ignore dogma and rest upon a purely natural morality. Christianity was false because it tried to make doctrinal statements about the unknowable; it was socially destructive because its fanaticism and superstition made it the cause of most of society's evils. Voltaire was tempted to say that since we know nothing about the existence of God, we also know nothing about absolute good and evil. But he saw that this view would lead to complacency and moral relativism. Moreover, he was never a cool, indifferent observer; he was outraged by the evils in the world. In the Lisbon earthquake Voltaire saw disproof not only of optimistic philosophy but also of benevolent providence.

Wherever evil came from, Voltaire was sure it did not come from the Devil, whom he regarded as a grotesque superstition and a "disgusting fantasy." Since few educated Christians could be found to argue for his existence, the philosophes considered him a straw figure not worth their time and dismissed him with contempt.

The most sophisticated skeptic of the period was the philosopher

David Hume (1711–1776), who provided the rational basis for religious skepticism. He argued that human reason has no power to obtain certainty about anything at all—not even matter, and certainly not God. In order to get along in everyday life, we postulate the existence of a world outside ourselves, but we have no certain knowledge of it. Still, the sense impressions we receive follow certain regular patterns, and from these we may construct "laws" of nature. Although these laws are descriptive rather than prescriptive and cannot in any way bind nature, Hume still believed it necessary to assume their regularity and predictability. If y has followed x a million times, it will follow x the million and first time. Hume's followers went further and made his system practically prescriptive, insisting that observed regularities are immutable, so that y *must* follow x the next time. They failed to grasp that the assumption that observed regularities are immutable is itself an act of faith for which there can be no empirical evidence.

Hume's attack on religion followed five main lines. The first was that we can know absolutely nothing about the transcendent, since the only valid knowledge is empirical knowledge. The second is psychological: the origin of all religion is the projection of human hopes and fears upon external objects. The third is historical: religion is a human invention that has developed, like other intellectual constructs, in a purely natural, historical fashion.

The fourth line of attack—a rather effective one—was against the idea that spiritual intervention could occur in the universe. Hume correctly reasoned that if he could disprove the possibility of miracles he would thereby destroy the viability of a religion based upon such miracles as the resurrection. He urged that "a miracle is a violation of the laws of nature; and as firm and unalterable experience has established these laws, the proof against a miracle, in the very nature of the fact, is as entire as any argument from experience can possibly be imagined." However strong the evidence for a miracle—or for the existence of any "supernatural" figure such as either God or Devil—it cannot be as strong as the evidence against. If all the historians of England reported that Elizabeth I had risen from the grave to govern her realm for three years after her demise, the likelihood of all historians being mad or engaged in a plot is (however small) greater than the likelihood of the queen's actual resurrection. The philosophe Diderot later expanded Hume's example. If one honest man reported to Diderot that the king had won a battle at Passy, Diderot would be inclined to believe him, but if all Paris declared that a man had risen from the dead at Passy, Diderot would not believe it, even (Peter

Gay added) if it were certified by a committee headed by his fellow philosophes.

The weakness in Hume's argument is his assumption that the "laws" of nature are unchangeable and that all knowledge must be empirical. Hume was in the odd position of being a dedicated empiricist denying the possibility of empirical observation of unique events on the basis of an unempirical act of faith in the regularity of "laws of nature." The weakness becomes clear if we conceive of two different models of the universe in which we live. In model A, supermaterial entities such as God or the Devil may be active; in model B they are not. Most educated people today would assume that there is a presumption in favor of model B. In fact neither model is essentially more likely than the other. Additionally, no empirical evidence can be summoned to refute Model A. Science is by definition limited to the study of the physical qualities of space/time and its inhabitants; it cannot by definition deal with super-material entities. History by definition deals with the action of human beings; it cannot by definition deal with the activities of alleged super-natural entities. The roles of science and history are equally stringent whether model A or model B represents the truth. Historical and scientific evidence point to neither one model nor the other. Model A is as likely as model B, and it cannot be assumed that unique events or "miracles" that violate natural "laws" cannot occur. Actually, much in human experience points toward model A, though this sort of experience cannot serve as scientific or historical "evidence" because history and science by definition do not discuss such things. To insist categorically that something beyond the limits of history and science cannot exist is a peculiar modern arrogance like that ascribed to the great classicist Benjamin Jowett: "Good afternoon, my name is Jowett; what there is to know I know it. I am the Master of this college; what I don't know is not knowledge."

Hume's fifth and most coherent argument against monotheistic religions was based on the existence of evil. Christians cannot reconcile the existence of God with the existence of evil, he said, without modifying their assumptions about one or the other. Either God is not omnipotent, or else God's goodness is totally different from human goodness, in which case it is meaningless to call him good. If God's moral nature is absolutely incomprehensible to us, he is no longer the Christian God. Further, since we observe that the universe contains vast and intense evils, we cannot legitimately infer the existence of God from the universe that we experience. On the contrary, it is more logical to infer that God does not exist. This argument was devastating to deism as well as to Christianity because it undermined the ancient assumption that one can argue to the existence of God from observation of the cosmos.

Hume's argument forced religion's defenders to abandon traditional proofs and rely on the experiential grounds for belief. If one experiences God and begins with the premise that he exists, then one can avoid Hume's conclusions and reconcile God's existence with that of evil. But if one begins without that premise, then the existence of evil points away from that of God.

Hume did not deign to mention the Devil, for if the existence of God and miracles is removed, the Devil simply evaporates. By the late twentieth century Hume's news had spread so widely as to have attained almost the status of common sense among the educated. Hume's assumptions are neither necessary nor compelling, but so long as they are dominant, it is natural that society should consider both God and Devil to be illusions.

For the many who carried Hume's conclusions as far as atheism, good and evil were human constructs, practical aspects of human relationships, not absolutes. The atheists' denial of objective meaning to good and evil left them with three alternatives. They could find a totally different basis for ethics, such as consensus or legal and constitutional traditions. They could argue that although standards are purely arbitrary, it is socially necessary to have some. Or they could declare that we are truly free of all values, all morality. From this last alternative most of the eighteenth-century atheist philosophes shrank in horror. At least one, however, was undeterred.

Donatien Alphonse François, Marquis de Sade (1740–1814), who lent his name to sadism, took the principles of atheistic relativism to their logical conclusion. Sade treated Devil, God, and the principle of Nature with equal contempt. Nature, far from being purposive, orderly, or kindly, is absolutely indifferent to the struggles of humanity. It smiles upon the success of the wicked at least as frequently as upon the efforts of the good—more, because the wicked are smart enough to seize whatever they can. "The author of the universe" wrote Sade, "is the most wicked, ferocious, frightening of all beings." Or would be, if it existed. In fact, there was no God, no Nature, no absolute standards of right and wrong, no intrinsic values.

In an intrinsically relative, valueless world, Sade argued, the only sensible thing to do is to seek personal pleasures. Whatever you feel like doing is good for you. If you enjoy torture, well and good. If others do not enjoy torturing, they need not do it, but they have no business imposing their views on you. Violations of so-called moral laws are actually laudable, because they demonstrate the artificiality of restraints impeding the only demonstrable good: personal pleasure. Virtue and law are fantasies; mercy, love, and kindness are perversions.

Because sexual pleasures are usually the most intense, they should be pursued without restraint. Crime can be even more exciting than sex under some circumstances, and a sex crime is best of all. The greatest pleasure derives from torture, especially of children, and if one humiliates and degrades the victim the delight is enhanced. Murder is an excellent stimulus, especially when preceded by torture and sexual abuse. Some will enjoy adding to the intensity of the experience by feasting upon the flesh of the victim. Sade may have belabored his point in the interests of argument, but he was right to do so. If there are no moral boundaries, then there are no moral boundaries. Sade's fellow philosophes viewed him with disgust and horror, not least because he revealed the logical implications of their own beliefs. If God and Nature do not exist, if there is no ruling reason in the cosmos, then absolute standards do not exist and we are free to create our own. Why should a child molester not be free to rape and torture his victims? The response that one should not impose his desires upon another, Sade pointed out, is itself quite an unnecessary assumption. It might be objected that Sade's pleasures would disrupt other pleasures: if we did nothing but rape and torture there would be no specialty restaurants or theaters, let alone physicians to tune our bodies to their highest sensual pitch. But to this Sade would reply that if you prefer dining to raping he would by no means deny you the choice. The very core of his doctrine is that he pays no attention to others' choices at all, including that of his victim.

Sade defined the dilemma. Either there is real evil, or not. Either there are grounds of ultimate concern by which to judge actions, or not. Either the cosmos has meaning, or not. If not, Sade's arguments are right; they are the legitimate outcome of pure atheism, the denial of any ultimate ground of being. Like Satan, Sade dwelt wistfully on the pleasure one might feel in destroying the entire cosmos, "to halt the course of the stars, to throw down the globes that float in space."

Eighteenth-century history and science followed philosophy in attacking the theological system that underlay diabology. Traditional theology had assumed a static view of nature, but in the course of the eighteenth century the enormous reaches of geological, astronomical, and cosmological time began to be discovered, and a new view began to emerge, that of a dynamic cosmos in constant change. Biblical chronology had placed the origins of the universe only about six thousand years ago, but in 1755 Immanuel Kant's *General History and Theory of the Heavens* claimed that the cosmos, including the earth, had gradually evolved over a period of millions of years. During the century from 1750 to 1850 a mutual interaction of geology, history, and astronomy gradually established an evolutionary view of the cosmos, the physical earth, and human society. The discovery of the immense age of the universe (presently calculated at about fifteen billion years) undermined Christian cosmology and supported the arguments for atheism.

History had further effects. Although educated Christians had always interpreted the Bible symbolically, they had assumed that it was historically reliable as well. But if the world were much older than the Bible indicated, then that reliability was gone for at least part of the Old Testament, and if part, why not all, and if the Old Testament, why not the New? Such questions undermined the epistemological bases of Christianity.

The idea of historical development also affected doctrine. If the earth and the cosmos were evolving, then why not ideas, including Christian doctrines? The old idea that Christian theology was essentially unchanging came into question. Historical theorists argued that what we know certainly are human ideas of things, not things in themselves. We are incapable of discovering what the Devil is in itself, but we can establish with complete certainty what the Devil is as a human concept. Because human ideas are in constant change, constant evolution, the best way to analyze concepts is historically. We cannot investigate how closely a concept does (or does not) correspond to absolute reality. We must define the Devil in historical terms.

The historical criticism of the Bible that arose in the eighteenth century even began to weaken trust in the ultimate criterion of Christian truth, the words of Jesus. The new critics argued that Jesus must be seen as a man of his own time, an ignorant peasant in an obscure province of an ancient empire. His views were unadvanced, his ideas primitive. When he spoke of the Devil or demons, he merely reflected the superstitions of his day. Because his life and ideas were reported by his equally ignorant followers, the New Testament was riddled with superstition and confusion.

Such a view was natural to atheists, but it was a sign of the enormous confusion of Christian thought at the time that liberal Christians unthinkingly embraced it as well, taking the curious stance that biblical

Engraving from a nineteenth-century catechism contrasting the death of the sinner (below) with that of the just man (above). The sinner's guardian angel departs, while demons pull him down toward hell. Courtesy Photo Jean-Loup Charmet, Paris.

views were valid only insofar as they conformed to whatever historical theories were current. Liberal Christianity retreated rapidly before the advance of science and history, regrouping every so often to fight another losing skirmish before giving up more ground. Already by the end of the eighteenth century the most advanced liberal Christians had abandoned the core of Christian beliefs. As for Satan, he was a painful embarrassment, an outmoded idea that Jesus had not really believed or believed only because of the limitations of his time. When the liberals also abandoned original sin—and therefore the redemption—they were left defenseless against the atheist argument from evil.

Friedrich Schleiermacher (1768–1824), a leader in liberal theology, hoped to eliminate the idea of the Devil. His most direct line of attack lay through the Bible itself. In order to discredit the doctrine of the Devil, he tried to show that Christ had never intended it. Neither Christ nor the apostles ever referred to the Devil with the intention of teaching anything distinctive; they were merely thoughtlessly reflecting the assumptions of their benighted age. Christ referred to the Devil only offhandedly or in quoting proverbs, or in symbolic reference to evil humans. The story of the temptation of Christ is a didactic tale without historical foundation. Schleiermacher's conclusion attempted to cover both bases: Christ and the apostles did not believe in the Devil, and if they did, they were merely drawing upon the superstitions of their own time. In order to square his conviction that the idea of Satan was unfashionable and embarrassing with his conviction that Christianity was somehow valid and the Bible somehow inspired, Schleiermacher had to construct complex arguments to explain away the fact that the New Testament teaches the existence and power of the Devil.

Another deep shift in thought in the late eighteenth century was the transition from Enlightenment to Romanticism, prefigured by Jean-Jacques Rousseau (1712–1778). Intensely emotional and erratic, Rousseau alienated the philosophes by professing Christianity and Christians by espousing an emotional, aesthetic religiosity while denying the Incarnation, redemption, and other essentials of Christianity. Contemptuous of "organized religion," he rejected the church and the communal nature of Christianity in favor of individual sentiment.

For Rousseau, evil was social rather than metaphysical: "Man, look no farther for the author of evil: you are he." It was the precursor of Pogo's "We have met the enemy, and he is us." Still, Rousseau sentimentally insisted that human nature is basically good; it is society that has corrupted it. By removing the smothering, warping influences of society we can restore ourselves to natural goodness and to a natural social order characterized by liberty and equality. By education, social reform, even revolution, we can erase our repressive institutions and enter a new era of happiness. These ideas helped provoke the Revolution of 1789, and by the end of the eighteenth century literature had begun to reflect them brightly.

After the age of witchcraft, the Devil made few literary appearances until the end of the eighteenth century, and when he revived he appeared in a new form. When aestheticism superseded theology, Satan's metaphysical existence was dismissed, and he became a symbol that could float free of its traditional meanings. Having ceased to be a person, he became a personality, a literary character that could play a variety of roles. Among these roles the most novel was that of a positive symbol of rebellion against unjust authority. In part because of Rousseau's influence, this role gradually shaded into the figure of the sympathetic Romantic Devil, a sad, rebellious power evoking both yearning and pain.

In the latter part of the century, literary interest in Satan was rekindled by the revival of the Faust legend. Like the Devil himself, Faust became a symbol both of rebellion and of the search for personal perfection and power. In *Faust: A Tragedy*, Johann Wolfgang von Goethe (1748–1832) created a new and enormously influential Mephistopheles. Taking an ironical, Enlightenment view of Christianity, Goethe drew upon Christian symbolism while despising the church. *Faust*, spanning sixty years of creative effort from Goethe's twenties to his eighties, has no single meaning or even set of meanings. Goethe intended it to express the complexities and incongruencies of his own mind, of his culture, and of Western civilization as a whole.

The character of Mephistopheles is as varied as the poem. Mephisto is too complex, diverse, and ambiguous to be equated with the Christian Devil. Goethe gladly used and developed the traditional myth while denying the Devil's real existence. Mephisto is amorphous, lacking moral definition, a nature spirit representing the undifferentiated world as it presents itself to the human experience. *Faust's* influence meant that most of the literary Devils of the following two centuries took the suave, ironic, and ambiguous shape of Goethe's Mephistopheles. There are exceptions, but writers wishing their Devils to be taken seriously as traditional personifications of evil have had, since *Faust*, to overcome powerful resistance.

Mephistopheles possesses a slick intelligence and superficial charm that permit him to manipulate people, but on a deeper level he is a fool, for he fails to grasp that the essential reality of the cosmos is the power of love. Blind to reality, he tries to negate and destroy it. He hates beauty, freedom, and life itself; he ruins individuals and promotes social policies that destroy multitudes. Like the traditional Devil, Mephisto is a liar and cheater, a master of illusion who repeatedly shifts his shape, sowing doubt and distrust, disrupting justice, delighting in cruelty and suffering, promoting coarseness and brutal sexuality. He regrets his past but refuses to repent.

After a prelude, the poem opens with the "Prologue in Heaven," where the Lord is surrounded by heavenly courtiers led by Raphael, Gabriel, Michael, and Mephistopheles. The setting recalls the Book of Job, with Mephistopheles playing the part of Satan. The angels praise God for the beauty of the cosmos, but Mephisto shifts the focus to the condition of humanity, arguing that in spite of the alleged harmonies of the cosmos, humanity is wretched, brutish, and unhappy. God reproaches him for this negativism, but Mephisto persists: "I feel such compassion for their wretched lives that I hesitate to afflict them any more myself." The Devil's role in the court is ironic, almost that of a heavenly jester or fool cleverly suggesting the failings of his master. His disagreement with God over humanity hints at Romantic rebellion against a tyrant and Promethean sympathy for humans against the gods.

As God once called Job to Satan's attention as an example of a just and incorruptible man, he now draws Mephisto's attention to Faust as representative both of individual genius and of humanity as a whole. The Lord observes that Faust is a faithful seeker after truth who would never turn away from his goal, but Mephisto challenges this: You say that Faust is steadfast? Then give me permission to tempt him; what can you lose? What do you bet that he will resist me? God accepts the wager.

The scene shifts to Faust's study, with the great scholar sunk in despair because incessant intellectual effort has failed to penetrate the secrets of the universe for him. He decides to try to compel spirits to reveal their occult knowledge, unaware that what he needs is not knowledge but love. The next scene takes Faust into streets populated by taverners, students, wenches, and soldiers; here the scholar and his assistant Wagner drink and debate. Faust argues the beauty of nature and Wagner the glory of scholarship, both failing to enter into the real life going on around them. Faust complains that he feels two spirits within him, one drawing him toward worldly pleasure and the other toward infinite wisdom. Neither is rooted in love. As they talk, Faust points out a black dog sniffing nearby. Wagner takes it for a poodle, but Faust senses that it is something more, for it trails a streak of fire. Mephistopheles has appeared, and in one of the traditional Devil's favorite forms, a black dog. He comes unbidden by Faust's conscious will but attracted by Faust's despair.

Later, back in the study, the poodle appears again, assumes a variety of disturbing shapes, and finally settles on the form of a wandering scholar. Faust, guessing the truth, demands that he declare his true identity. Mephisto responds that he is "a part of that power that ever seeks evil and ever does good." He exerts himself to destroy all that has been created but is compelled by divine providence to do good. Mephisto—and evil—are a part of that dark material out of which God brought light, and Faust understands him: "Thou art Chaos' wondrous son."

Faust suggests a pact to Mephistopheles in order to gain access to his occult powers; Mephisto's own plan is to lull the scholar into mindless sensuality and thereby win his bet with God. He offers to be Faust's servant in this world if Faust will be his in the next, and the pact transposes into a second wager recapitulating the one made in heaven. Mephisto urges Faust to abandon academic abstractions for "life's golden tree," treacherously omitting the middle ground between pedantry and sensuality: the ground of generosity and love.

As he comes to believe that Faust is in his power, Mephistopheles shows himself increasingly coarse and brutal. In a scene in the Witch's Kitchen this coarseness becomes overt, though Mephisto still maintains his ironic distance, calmly recounting his own historical decline and noting that modern cultural fashion obliges him to be genteel and remove his horns, tail, and claws. The modern world is uncomfortable with symbols of evil and prefers the Devil comfortably disguised as a suave gentleman with only the hint of a hidden deformity—the cloven hoof easily diguised by heavy shoes. For the same reason, Mephisto no longer uses the name Satan, because everyone now considers the Devil a superstition—not that this disbelief makes people any less vicious, he observes.

Mephistopheles lures Faust deeper into sensuality by playing upon his desire for the young Gretchen. By sharpening the scholar's lust and at the same time making him responsible for the girl's ruin, Mephisto hopes to score a double blow against his soul. After Gretchen gives birth to an illegitimate child, she goes mad, drowns the infant, and is executed for her crime. Mephistopheles savors his victory, but his success is hollow, for Faust's lust has become real love for Gretchen: the Devil's evil has once again caused a good he did not intend. The sensuality he has instilled in Faust breaks down the scholar's cold pedantry and opens his heart to tenderness and compassion, and when he takes Faust to a witches' revel where they see Gretchen's lost and wandering soul, Faust feels the first pang of the loving remorse that will eventually save him.

Mephistopheles is less evident in the more abstract second part of the tragedy; when he does appear it is as a shadowy sorcerer urging disastrous social policies. Only in the final scene does the focus return to the struggle for Faust's soul. The dying scholar has a vision of a better world created by human progress, while Mephisto sneers that Faust's life, and that of humanity as a whole, is an idle dream. Mephisto claims the scholar's soul, but Faust has won the bet, for he has never ceased to strive for truth, never wholly abandoned himself to sensuality. The contract is void because Faust—humanity—struggling for meaning and finding love, is saved. The Blessed Virgin welcomes Gretchen into heaven as choirs of angels bear Faust's soul aloft. Mephistopheles, his perceptions so distorted by evil that his response to the sight of the boyish angels is to fantasize about sodomizing them, has lost the bet, the soul, and the point of existence. He is left in the prison house of darkness he has created for himself.

The symbolism of this final scene is aesthetic, not theological. Goethe's Faust is saved, not from sin in the Christian sense, but from sensuality and intellectualism. His ascension into heaven is not the beatification of an individual but rather a program for the human race: we, like Faust, are called to abandon selfishness and to seek a society based upon regard for others. Mephistopheles is the most important literary Devil since Milton's, but the difference between Milton's Satan and Goethe's Mephisto is the difference between a basically Christian and a basically secular world view.

14　*From Romance to Nihilism*

THE shift from Enlightenment to Romanticism increased the variety of views on the Devil. Curiously, early-nineteenth attitudes toward the Evil One were correlated with views on the French Revolution. Monarchists and traditional Catholics regarded the revolution as the work of the Devil and the restoration of the monarchy in 1815 as the triumph of Christ the King over Satan. Republicans and revolutionaries, on the other hand, attacked Christianity as part of the old, repressive order: since kings are evil, Christ, the greatest king, is the greatest evil. For the revolutionaries, Satan symbolized resistance to the tyranny of the Old Regime. The bourgeois were also prepared for a shift in symbols, perceiving in Satan a metaphor of individualism and aggressive competition. The rural population tended to hold to the traditional views, but the urban proletariat, uprooted from rural community life, was quickly losing religion.

Satan continued to fade among professed Christians. The Catholic revival after 1815 reaffirmed traditional teachings but did little to convince society at large of Satan's existence. Protestantism, which had less regard for tradition, found the Bible undermined by increasing acceptance of historical criticism by Protestant theologians. With the weakening of the twin pillars of Christianity—Scripture and tradition—first theologians, then preachers, and finally the laity came to question nearly every aspect of Christian belief: heaven, the soul, sin, the Incarnation, and certainly hell and the Devil. By the end of the century, the English statesman and churchman William Ewart Gladstone could speak of hell as a shadowy thing relegated to the dusty corners of the Christian mind.

Unmoored from its epistemological anchor, liberal Protestantism joined secularism in rejecting the Devil as old-fashioned and outdated. Against this view a counterforce gradually asserted itself among those who continued loyal to the Reformation faith in Scripture. These "conservative" Christians rejected compromise with secularism and joined Catholics and Eastern Orthodox in continuing to affirm the reality of the Evil One.

The story of the Devil in the nineteenth century developed in literature more than in theology, especially in Romanticism, a vaguely defined movement emphasizing the aesthetic and the emotional as against the rational and the intellectual. Whether an idea was powerfully affecting was more important than whether it was true in the sense of being well buttressed in logic; the emotions were a surer guide to life than the intellect. This attitude encouraged psychological introspection and exalted the virtues of love, pity, and mercy against rational and scientific calculation. On the other hand, the tendency to dismiss reason also led to wishful thinking and a self-satisfied, elitist contempt for those considered less fine, noble, or sensitive. Further, the quest for the emotionally stimulating encouraged a taste for the miraculous, the supernatural, the weird, and the grotesque.

Intensely concerned with the conflict of good and evil within the human heart, the Romantics used Christian symbols without regard for their theological content, detaching them from their basic meanings. In a world view that eschewed logic in favor of emotion were bound to be many contradictions. Many Romantics of the revolutionary sort argued that if the greatest enemy of traditional Christianity was Satan, then Satan must be a heroic rebel against unjust authority and one greatly to be praised. They did not intend such a statement as a theological proposition, but rather as a symbolic challenge and a political program.

The Romantic idea of the hero is an individual alone against the world, assertive, ambitious, and powerful, a rebel seeking to liberate humanity from a society that blocks progress toward liberty, beauty, and love. This Romantic admiration for Satan was not Satanic worship of evil, for the Romantic Devil was not "the Evil One" but good. But since the Romantics' view of what was good was not radically different from the Christian, this transposition of symbols was confusing and unhelpful. Reversing terms and calling "God" evil and "the Devil" good did not enhance anyone's understanding of the nature of evil. Some Romantics, aware of the difficulties in shifting symbols so radically, chose a classical figure such as Prometheus to represent their rebellious hero rather than

William Blake's *Christ Tempted by Satan to Turn the Stones into Bread* depicts the Devil as a wise old man. In a statement of moral ambiguity, Blake portrays Christ and Satan almost as doublets locked in a dance. Watercolor with india ink and grey wash, 1816–1818. Courtesy Fitzwilliam Museum, Cambridge.

Satan. The Romantic Devil could be a hero, but he could also symbolize isolation, unhappiness, hardness of heart, lovelessness, insensitivity, ugliness, sarcasm, and all that impedes the progress of the human spirit.

One of the aspects of the Romantic treatment of evil was the Gothic novel or *roman noir*. The Gothic novel used—or degraded—the sublime in order to produce thrills, shudders, sensations. Its favorite theme was the decay underlying the veneer of the apparently good, rational, and familiar. It dwelt upon the fanciful, grotesque, and decadent, including physical and moral deformity, sadism, sexual frenzy, crags and castles, distant lands, the Middle Ages, and the macabre side of the supernatural with its witches, ghosts, phantoms, vampires, and demons. When the Devil himself made an appearance, it was less as a serious symbol of evil than as one among many evil monsters designed to entertain and thrill the reader.

Matthew Lewis's Gothic novel *The Monk* (1796) had enormous influence on both English and continental literature. Written when Lewis was nineteen, it entertains the reader with ghosts, incest, poison, rape, and drugs. Ambrosio, to outward appearance an ascetic monk, is secretly seething with sexuality. An arrogant cleric of that notoriously degenerate body the Catholic church, Ambrosio is easily corrupted by Satan. He plunges into ever deeper and more grotesque vices, finally ravishing the virgin Antonia in a dark vault upon the moldering bones of long deceased monks. For Antonia, "to linger out a life of misery in a narrow loathsome cell, known to exist by no human Being save her Ravisher, surrounded by mouldering Corpses, breathing the pestilential air of corruption, never more to behold the light, or drink the pure gale of heaven, the idea was more terrible than She could support." She need not have worried, for Ambrosio proceeds to murder her. English readers could savor the sense of being instructed about the evils of the Catholic church while being titillated by Lewis's purple prose. But Ambrosio's evil is limited to the narrow boundaries of Lewis's adolescent lechery; it fails to plumb the depths, as Sade had done. Further, such literary excesses were grist to the mills of satirists, who produced parodies of the Gothic tale that only trivialized radical evil even further. Along with the specters and ghouls with which the Gothic writers associated him, Satan became an absurd figure.

The most original artist of the period, William Blake (1757–1827), produced a Devil symbolizing the extremes of both good and evil. For Blake, Satan's self-righteousness is evil, his rebellion against the divine tyrant good. In Blake's *Marriage of Heaven and Hell* (1790), Satan is the symbol of creativity, activity, and energy struggling to be free. Milton's Satan, rebelling against repressive authority, represented to Blake the human desire for freedom. "The reason Milton wrote in fetters when he wrote of Angels and God, and at liberty when of Devils and Hell, is because he was a true Poet, and of the Devil's party without knowing it." Satan was good, and Jesus himself was Satanic (in the good sense), for he acted from impulse rather than from rules and cheerfully "broke all the commandments." Blake contrasted this loving, free Jesus to Milton's judgemental God the Father and took it as a cruel irony that the followers of Jesus had remade him into a version of his tyrant Father: "Thinking as I do that the Creator of this World is a very Cruel Being, and being a worshipper of Christ, I cannot help saying: 'The Son, O how unlike the Father!'"

For Blake, no goods or evils are absolute. "All deities reside in the Human breast," and no element of the psyche is wholly good or evil. True evil arises from the lack of integration of psychic elements; true good from the balance, union, and integration of the opposites. For the title page of *The Marriage*, Blake drew an angel and a demon embracing. Reason and energy, love and hatred, passive and active, apparent good and evil, must all merge in a transcendent, integrated whole of which creativity will be the leading spirit. The true god is poetic creativity—that spirit, poet, and maker who makes not only art but the entire cosmos.

Blake's empathetic understanding of evil was most poignantly expressed in "The Sick Rose:"

> O Rose, thou art sick!
> The invisible worm
> That flies in the night,
> In the howling storm,
> Hath found out thy bed
> Of crimson joy:
> And his dark secret love
> Does thy life destroy.

Blake and the Romantics opened the doors of the unconscious to a degree unprecedented except by the mystics. Despite their idiosyncratic and incoherent use of symbols, their deepening of psychological understanding of evil constitutes an enduring contribution to the concept of the Devil.

The quintessential Romantic, George Gordon, Lord Byron (1788–1824), opposed traditional Christian views of evil throughout his life. Still, like Blake, he was deeply troubled by the problem. The degree of evil in the world convinced Byron that the Creator could not be good. In his poetic drama *Cain: A Mystery* (1821), Cain is puzzled when his father Adam tells him that God is omnipotent. "Then why is evil, he being good?" Later, Lucifer asks Cain, "What does thy God love?" And Cain can only reply, "All things, my father says, but I confess / I see it not in their allotment here." When Lucifer claims to be eternal himself, Cain quickly counters, asking whether he can do humanity any good and, if so, why he has not done it already. Lucifer's riposte is just as quick: Why hasn't God (Jehovah)? Byron was torn between the Romantic optimism that human liberty would eventually triumph and a pessimism derived from his observation of reality.

Byron composed the character of Cain from the original figure in Genesis, Promethean elements of benevolence toward humanity, and Satanic (Miltonic) elements of the sublime. The character Lucifer is ambivalent, good in his support of Cain's rebellion against tyranny yet evil in his ironic distance from human suffering. His essential flaw is that he lacks empathy and love.

Early in the poem Lucifer instructs Cain that God rules the world with rigid, unjust laws. Cain's wife/sister Adah expresses the traditional view that God is both good and omnipotent, but for Byron Jehovah is a pathetic symbol of human striving, creating world after world in an effort to alleviate his loneliness and isolation, finding each defective, and one after another destroying them. Lucifer announces that Jehovah is both good and evil, both maker and destroyer, and that the cosmos he has created is both beautiful and cruel. In this Lucifer speaks for Byron: any understanding of the world that sees only the beauty or only the cruelty is false. The conflict in the cosmos is less between good and evil than between various ambivalences, which we must attempt to integrate.

Lucifer sneeringly asks Cain who is the real Evil One: Lucifer, who wanted Adam and Eve to have knowledge and prompted the serpent to tell them the truth about the tree, or Jehovah, who drove them out of the garden into exile and death? But though Jehovah is law-bound, insensitive, and sometimes cruel, the rebellious Lucifer is even worse, for Jehovah at least feels the pull of creative love; Lucifer, although he promotes intellectual freedom and progress, is deliberately blind, self-absorbed, and loveless. Though Jehovah both creates and destroys, Lucifer, although he praises creativity, ultimately creates nothing. Worst of all,

Lucifer blocks the only road to a perfect cosmos, the integration of himself with Jehovah, instead blaming everything on God and demanding that humans replace serving Jehovah with serving himself. His vindictiveness and hatred of God's cosmos is limitless:

> All, all will I dispute. And world by world
> And star by star and universe by universe
> Shall tremble in the balance, till the great
> Conflict shall cease, if ever it shall cease,
> Which it ne'er shall, till he or I be quenched.

Percy Bysshe Shelley (1782–1822) used the demonic for its aesthetic effects of terror and sublimity. Expelled from Oxford in 1811 for his pamphlet "The Necessity of Atheism," he always rejected "organized religion." Jesus, he argued, had taught the gospel of love in rebellion against organized religion. Shelley's religion was evolutionary and progressive: the spirit of love is moving toward a better, freer, more loving future. Evil is what blocks this benign progress, and Satan symbolizes the destructive and regressive tendencies within humanity.

On the Devil and Devils (1820–1821) reveals Shelley's preoccupation with the problem of evil. The ancient Manichean view that two spirits exist, of balanced power and opposite dispositions, represented, Shelley believed, an insight into the divided state of the human soul. The Christian view of the Devil as a creature subject to the divine will missed the divided nature of psychic reality. Still, Shelley was as ambivalent about the quality of Satan as Blake or Byron. On the one hand, he insisted that a truly Satanic figure was needed to express the terrible might of human evil; on the other, he took Satan as the symbol of progressive rebellion against repression. Like Blake, he admired Milton's Satan as the sublime rebel pledging his very essence to the struggle against tyranny; as he said in his *Defence of Poetry*:

Nothing can exceed the energy and magnificence of the character of Satan as expressed in "Paradise Lost." It is a mistake to suppose that he could ever have been intended for the popular personification of evil. . . . Milton's Devil as a novel being is as far superior to his God as One who perseveres in some purpose which he has conceived to be excellent in spite of adversity and torture, is to One who in the cold severity of his undoubted triumph inflicts the most horrible revenge upon his enemy. . . . Milton . . . alleged no superiority of moral virtue of his God over his Devil. And this bold neglect of a direct moral purpose is the most decisive proof of the supremacy of Milton's genius.

Chagrined as Milton would have been at this interpretation, it epito-
mized the Romantic reading of the poem, and Milton's Satan became the
archetype of the Romantic hero.

Still, Shelley saw the difficulties in making Satan a hero. Satan might
be majestic and courageous, but he was also ambitious, envious, aggressive, and vengeful. Shelley selected Prometheus as a better symbol, for
his rebellion, defeat, and bondage were the result not of his faults, but of
his love for humanity. For Shelley, Prometheus symbolized Christ, who
sacrifices himself for the good of his people; humanity, which struggles
toward freedom under the guidance of the spirit of love; and the poet,
whose love and creative word are weapons against the darkness. The
symbolic cluster around Prometheus is Christ, humanity, the poet,
Shelley, and Satan (in his good aspects). Prometheus' antagonist is Jupiter, an evil tyrant; the symbolic cluster around Jupiter is Jehovah and
Satan (in his evil aspects). If we can integrate and transcend the opposition of Prometheus and Jupiter within ourselves, Shelley suggested, we
shall be ready to proceed on the road that winds upward in peace through
the green, high country of understanding, freedom, and love. Shelley,
like Blake, prefigured the integrationist depth psychology associated
with Carl G. Jung a century later.

Shelley's wife Mary (1797–1851) held a darker view. Her *Frankenstein,
or the Modern Prometheus* (1818) has enjoyed enduring popularity, though
the author's philosophical intentions have usually been ignored. Mary
Shelley drew upon the Gothic love of horrors, and *Frankenstein* was a
bridge between the Gothic and the modern horror story. It is also one of
the original sources of science fiction, for she made some important
changes in the Gothic plot. The creator of the monster, Dr. Frankenstein, is no sorcerer, magician, or monk, but a scientist, and the monster
is no demon or specter, but a material being of flesh and blood manufac-
tured in a laboratory. *Frankenstein* replaced old, supernatural horror with
modern, positivst horror.

The author did not mean this break to be a clean one. In fact, Frankenstein and other human characters in the novel repeatedly call the
monster a daemon, fiend, or devil. But Mary Shelley intended irony, for
the evil does not lie in the monster's nature; the monster becomes evil
only when he is taught evil by the humans he encounters. Here is another
shift of symbols, for humanity here represents the creator, whose pride
and selfishness produced a spoiled creation, yet the monster also represents the innocent, open aspect of humanity that is corrupted by its
experience of evil. The individual human is born innocent; he is de-

A nineteenth-century sculpture in bronze and ivory. The Devil as Mephistopheles, with scholar's cap, forked beard, and sinister smirk. Courtesy Sylvie Mercier, photographe "La Licornière," Paris.

stroyed by the viciousness of the world around him. The monster grieves, "I was benevolent and good; misery made me a fiend. Make me happy, and I shall again be virtuous." But the people whom the monster encounters shun, fear, and despise him, deforming his character until he becomes the murdering fiend that they assume him to be.

The monster's last hope of reform lies in Frankenstein's promise to construct him a female companion, but in the midst of the new experiment the scientist is shaken by revulsion and destroys the half-formed woman along with the scientific equipment. The disappointed monster pursues the scientist with unremitting vengeance, while the latter in turn seeks the monster in order to destroy him. As each seeks the other, it becomes clear that Frankenstein and his monster represent two warring aspects of one human character. If only we could transcend the conflict within us, Mary Shelley agreed with her husband, we could enter a world of peace, but the novel's conclusion was closer to Byron's pessimism. After a weird, extended chase through the limitless arctic night, Frankenstein and the monster finally meet, but the doctor dies of the exhaustion of his long pursuit, and the monster, feeling for his creator both frustrated revenge and frustrated love, vanishes forever in the icy darkness. No reconciliation or integration: both aspects of humanity perish.

The French Romantics, like the English, varied their treatment of Satan, some treating him ironically, others as comic, some linking witchcraft and Satanism to social protest. A few, such as Chateaubriand (1786–1848), used him in more or less his traditional sense. The greatest Romantic Satan was the sad, isolated angel created by Victor Hugo (1802–1885). A true Romantic, Hugo based his views less on intellectual than on emotional and aesthetic grounds. Insisting upon a God of pity and mercy, he hated the traditional doctrines of original sin, salvation through crucifixion, and hell. Humanity was intrinsically good, and God was intrinsically benevolent. Christianity was false, but Jesus himself was a noble teacher, a model for the pursuit of real truth, which is love.

This alleged tension between Jesus and Christianity, assumed by so many Enlightenment and Romantic thinkers, entailed the belief that they were the true Christians as against the false Christianity of the church. Hugo and the Romantics *felt* that they had got to the real Jesus behind Christianity. The claim is rationally indefensible, but reason was much less important to Hugo than feelings. Kind and generous, he repudiated a God who was able to prevent evil yet chose not to do so. Rejecting the traditional Devil, he remained acutely concerned with the problem of evil. The progress of humanity toward love and liberty was being blocked by cruelty and selfishness.

Hugo's Devil was as diverse as the author's own ever-changing views: he was a fantastic Gothic fiend or monster used to excite terror and thrills; he was a prop in dramas about the Middle Ages, used along with witches and hunchbacks to convey a sense of weird medieval darkness. He was also the symbol of revolution. In Hugo's conservative early days, this made Satan a symbol of evil; later, when Hugo turned progressive, Satan came to represent both oppressive governments and rebellion against oppression. Hugo felt that alienation, defeat, sadness, and regret are as inherent in evil as cruelty and selfishness, and he painted a dimension of evil that had been neglected: the poignant sadness and isolation of the sinner. Satan became a metaphor of the longing of humanity to be reintegrated into that loving spirit of life from which we have exiled ourselves by our own foolishness and selfishness. Hugo believed that reintegration would occur; the spirit of light, infinite in its mercy, would eventually restore all creatures to the embrace of the union of love. Until that happy moment, evil remains a stark reality.

Hugo could see the Devil as Mephistopheles—mocking, ironic, supercilious, and worldweary in the mode favored by the French. His poem "Rosa's Good Intentions" describes him:

> The fellow had troubled eyes,
> And on his furrowed forehead
> The distortion of two horns
> Was quite visible.
> His forked foot was bursting his stockings.
> Enjoying his leave from hell, he breathed the fresh air;
> Though his teeth were not false
> His glances were not true.
> He came to earth poised for prey.
> In the iron talons of his hands
> He clutched a hunting permit
> Signed by God and countersigned by Lucifer.
> He was that worthy Devil Beelzebub.

Hugo's deepest vision appeared in *La fin de Satan*, "Satan's End," where the Devil is a vivid, convincing personality. He has truly sinned, truly distorted himself and the world through his own blindness and selfishness, yet the pain and suffering he feels from his alienation render him sympathetic. He represents the lack of equilibrium, peace, and balance in the cosmos and the alienation of humanity from its proper repose in love and liberty. Like Satan, we are each so wrapped up in our interior world that we cannot see the reality around us, and we isolate ourselves from it, though it speaks to us in every tree, bird, and human voice. Isolated and miserable though we are, the spirit of love draws us to itself and in the end all will be saved, for none can forever resist infinite love and mercy. All the opposites will be reconciled, and the cosmos will be reintegrated in liberty and love.

The poem begins with the fall of Satan. As he falls, his angelic nature is transformed: "Suddenly he sees himself growing bat wings; he sees himself becoming a monster; as the angel in him died, the rebel felt a pang of regret." His prideful envy of God turns into the more bitter envy born of yearning for what he has lost: "God shall have the blue heavens, but I a dark and empty sky." A terrible voice retorts, "Accursed one, around you the stars shall fade away." Satan falls, year after year, for millennia, and as he falls the stars gradually disappear, leaving the sky darker, emptier, more silent, until only three faint points of light remain. Then only one is left. Toward this last, dimming star he concentrates all the efforts of his depleted being.

> Toward the star trembling pale on the horizon
> He pressed, leaping from one dark foothold to another. . . .
> He ran, he flew, he cried out: Golden star!
> Brother! Wait for me! I am coming! Do not die yet!
> Do not leave me alone. . . .
> The star was now only a spark. . . .
> The spark
> Was now only a point of red in the depths of the dark gulf. . . .
> Hoping to make the star glow brighter,
> He blew upon it as one would on coals,
> And anguish flared his fierce nostrils.
> He flew toward it ten thousand years. Ten thousand years,
> Stretching out his pale neck and his mad fingers,
> He flew without finding a single place of rest.
> From time to time the star seemed to darken and die,
> And the horror of the tomb made the dark angel tremble.
> As he approached the star,
> Satan, like a swimmer making a final effort,
> Stretched his bald and taloned wings forward; a wan specter,
> Gasping, broken, exhausted, smoking with sweat,
> He collapsed at the steep brink of darkness. . . .
> The star was almost gone. The dark angel was so weary

That no voice, no breath was left to him.
And the star was dying beneath his anguished gaze . . .
And the star went out.

But a feather falls from the wing of the ruined spirit, and that feather takes the form of a beautiful angel, whose name is Liberty. Thus Satan's prideful rebellion entails the seed of the return to liberty and love. Liberty goes to the earth and encourages humanity to rebel against the prison, symbolized by the Bastille, that keeps us from our freedom. The revolution fulfills the mission of the angel Liberty under the permission of both God and Devil.

Meanwhile Satan suffers the pain of knowing that the cosmos rejects him:

Throughout the universe I hear the word: Begone!
Even the pig sneers to the dungheap, "I despise Satan."
I feel the night thinking that I dishonor her. . . .
Once that pure white light of dawn
Was I. I! I was the splendid-browed archangel. . . .
But I was envious. That was
My crime. The word was spoken; the divine mouth
Pronounced me evil. And God spat me out into the pit.
Ah! I love him! That is the horror, that is the burning flame!
What will become of me, abyss? I love God!
Hell is his eternal absence,
Hell is to love, to cry, "Alas, where is my light,
Where is my life and my illumination?"
[When first I fell, I boasted:]
This God, world's heart, this bright Father
Whom angel, star, man, and beast bear within,
This shepherd round whom his flock of creatures nestles,
This being, the source of life, alone true, alone necessary—
I can do without him, I the punished giant. . . .
Yet I love him! . . .
I know the truth! God is no spirit, but a heart.
God, the loving center of the world, connects with his divine fibers
The filaments and roots of all living things.
[God loves every creature]
Except Satan, forever rejected, sad, condemned.
God leaves me out; he terminates at me; I am his boundary.
God would be infinite if I did not exist. . . .
A hundred hundred times I repeat my vow:

I love! God tortures me, yet my only blasphemy,
My only frenzy, my only cry, is that I love!
My love is enough to make the sky tremble. But in vain!

In his agony, Satan cries, "Love hates me!" But God replies:

No, I do not hate you! . . .
O Satan, you need only say, I shall live!
Come, your prison will be pulled down and hell abolished!
Come, the angel Liberty is your daughter and mine:
This sublime parentage unites us.
The archangel is born and the demon dies;
I erase the baleful darkness so that none remains.
Satan is dead; be born again, heavenly Lucifer!
Come, rise up from the shadow with dawn on your brow.

This poignant portrait of the Devil expresses a poetic moral view: Our stupidity and selfishness alienate us from the cosmos, but love waits patiently till we understand that selfishness, anger, and pride are nothing but a blind refusal to see, nothing but a negation of reality. We have been shamefully staring down into our own dark isolation, but when we open our eyes even a chink, love floods in and fills our darkness to bursting, until nothing is left but light.

The Romantic reversal of symbols sometimes led to extremes. The abbé Alphonse Louis Constant (1810–1875) began by attempting to integrate God and Satan but eventually came to believe that Satan suffered under the unjust condemnation of an arbitrary God. Sinking into the occult, Constant changed his name to Eliphas Lévi and wrote a number of books portraying the Devil as a positive spiritual force. After Lévi came to admire Napoleon III, his Satan became the hieratic supporter of law and order. This occult, positive interpretation of Satan laid the foundation for *fin-de-siècle* Satanism.

Apart from the solemnity of Hugo and the pomposity of Lévi, irony, parody, and whimsy were the dominant modes in nineteenth-century treatments of Satan. One of the ironic masters was Théophile Gautier (1811–1872), whose short story "Onuphrius" (1832) is a parody in which Onuphrius, a young dandy poet and painter obsessed by medievalism and the marvelous begins to see the Devil's hand in everything until Satan really does appear, smearing his painting and poems, ruining his stragegy at checkers, and spoiling his love affair. At a literary soirée where Onuphrius is to read his verse, the Devil sits behind him transforming all his words into pompous and ridiculous phrases. Gautier's Devil is the perfect ironic Mephisto. He is young and handsome, with regular features, a red imperial and moustache, green eyes, thin, pale, ironic lips, and a knowing look. The complete dandy, he wears a black coat, red waistcoat, white gloves, and golden spectacles; on his long, delicate fingers he sports a large ruby. Gautier thus linked himself and his fellow dandies—aesthetic and elegant, disdainful of convention, dressing and speaking so as to draw attention to themselves and shock the bourgeois, spurning morality, arrogant, self-absorbed, witty, and charming rather than truthful—with the Devil, whose real existence Gautier in fact regarded as absurd. The story is a glittering mockery of God, Devil, humanity, art, society, and even the artist himself.

By midcentury, Romanticism was beginning to shade off in two directions: naturalism, which spurned the supernatural and the internal in favor of realistic descriptions of everyday life, and decadence, which combined elements of dandyism with exploration of the depths of human corruption, especially sexual depravity. In 1846 a circle of young French poets collaborated in a session celebrating the seven cardinal sins and dedicated their work to Satan in words best left unuttered:

> To thee, Satan, fair fallen angel,
> To whom fell the perilous honor
> Of struggling against an unjust rule,
> I offer myself wholly and forever,
> My mind, my senses, my heart, my love,
> And my dark verses in their corrupted beauty.

A theatrical prop for the dandies, Satan was a political symbol for the anarchist Pierre Joseph Proudhon (1809–1865). "Come, Satan," he prayed, "you who have been defamed by priests and kings, that I may kiss you and hold you against my breast." The fashionableness of such rhetoric may give an exaggerated view of the importance of Satan in the late nineteenth century. A few real Satanists certainly existed, but the term is properly limited to the tiny number who believed in, and worshiped, Satan as a personal principle of true evil and selfishness.

Charles Baudelaire (1821–1867), an important figure in the transition from Romanticism to naturalism and decadence, has sometimes been considered—quite mistakenly—a Satanist. Baudelaire was skeptical of scientism as well as of religion, and he regarded the facile materialist progressivism of his day as absurd. Atheism seemed to him incapable of dealing with alienation and evil, the deepest realities of human existence. Raised a Catholic, he eventually returned to the church. His honest personal grappling with evil led him to acknowledge that evil is attractive as well as destructive and that we are each torn between the opposing demands of God and Satan. "In each person two tendencies exist at every moment, one toward God and the other toward Satan," he wrote in his journal. "Spirituality, the call to God, is a desire to mount higher; animality, the call to Satan, takes joy in falling lower." Evil destroys by drawing us down into selfishness and isolation. This darkness holds deep attractions that everyone feels and only hypocrites deny. Baudelaire was pitiless in his determination to strip the blinder of hypocrisy from his own eyes and those of others.

"I have always been obsessed," he said in a letter, "by the impossibility of accounting for certain sudden human actions or thoughts without the hypothesis of an external evil force." The sudden irruption into the mind of intensely destructive thoughts or feelings can be explained only by reference to a power beyond human consciousness. Baudelaire was skeptical of the skeptics. "My dear brothers," he cautioned, "never forget, when you hear the progress of the Enlightenment praised, that the Devil's cleverest ploy is to persuade you that he doesn't exist."

Baudelaire's masterpiece was his collection of poems called *Les fleurs du mal* ("The Flowers of Evil"). Though his intent has sometimes been mistaken as Satanic, his true purpose was to call us to face evil down by recognizing the hold that it has on us:

> It is the Devil who pulls the strings that move us:
> We find charm in the most disgusting things;
> Each day we take another step down into hell,
> Deadened to horror, through stinking shadows. . . .
> Reader, you recognize this delicate monster,
> Hypocrite reader, my likeness, my brother.

Likewise, the poet's "Litanies to Satan" are not to be taken literally:

> Prince of the exile, you have been wronged;
> Defeated, you rise up ever stronger. . . .
> You who even to lepers and accursed outcasts
> Teach through love a longing for Paradise. . . .
> Glory and praise to you, Lord Satan, in the highest,
> Where once you reigned, and in the depths

> Of hell, where you lie defeated and dreaming.
> Let my soul one day, in the shadow of the tree of knowledge,
> Rest next to you.

This praiseworthy Satan is on one level Jesus, on another the ambivalence of the human heart, and on yet another the artist himself with his terrible double-edged sword of creative ambiguity.

The irony combined with longing for truth that characterized Baudelaire was lost on some of his followers, who imitated his Satanic symbolism without being concerned about true evil. The true Satanist among the decadents was Isidore Ducasse (1846–1870), who wrote under the name of Lautréamont. Lautréamont agreed with Baudelaire that we must face evil in its most intense and shocking forms, but he went on to make the transition from facing evil to embracing it. Impressed by Sade, Lautréamont regarded creative cruelty as a mark of genius and honesty, and he used the attack on hypocrisy as an excuse to explore the most loathsome recesses of his own soul. Maldoror, the persona of his ugly masterpiece *The Chants of Maldoror*, is a combination of Sade, Satan, and Ducasse himself. Maldoror contemplates or commits an endless series of perverted outrages. It is unclear whether Lautréamont was mad; he clearly did not practice everything his character did; yet it is insane to hope that one can summon up such dark forces and not become their slave.

Maldoror sees a child sitting on a park bench and immediately imagines a hog gnawing away her genitals and burrowing through her body. He dreams of torturing young boys and drinking their blood and tears. When he kisses a baby, he fantasizes about slashing its cheeks with a razor. Vampirism, necrophilia, blasphemy, bestiality, incest, bondage, pederasty, mutilation, murder, and cannibalism obsess him. "Maldoror was born evil. He admitted the truth that he was cruel." Reacting against the bland assumption of the Enlightenment and the Romantics that human nature is essentially good, Lautréamont plunged to the opposite extreme. Just as the belief in natural human goodness leaves the presence of evil unexplained, the assumption that humans are evil leaves unexplained the presence of good.

In the last years of the century Satanism sank from the level of literature to that of crude practice. The most infamous diabolism of the period was exposed by the novelist J.-K. Huysmans (1848–1907). Huysmans did research in both historical and contemporary Satanism, met the leading Satanists of his day, and wrote a fictional account of his experiences. The protagonist of the novel *Là-bas* ("Down There") is Durtal, who in the course of his research attends black masses in Paris. He describes one presided over by the repulsive Canon Docre. Docre and his congregation meet secretly in a darkened room decorated luridly with black, flickering candles. The canon, who wears the cross tattooed on the soles of his feet so as to tread upon the Savior with every step, feeds consecrated hosts to mice and mixes excrement with the sacrament. While incense smoulders, drugs are handed round, the Devil is invoked, and a hymn to Satan is intoned. A long litany of blasphemies and insults to Christ is read out, with choirboys saying the responses. The drugged congregation howls and rolls on the floor. The priest sexually abuses the host at the altar, and women come forward to eat of it while men violate the choirboys. Although *Là-bas* became popular—indeed, notorious—Huysmans himself, repelled by what he had seen, left the decadent movement and returned to Catholicism.

Even more than Europeans, American writers tended to detach serious studies of evil from the Devil, relegating him to tales of whimsy or horror stories. The horror story, an American adaptation from the Gothic, found its first great exponent in Edgar Allan Poe (1809–1849). When Poe wrote of real evil, as in "The Pit and the Pendulum," "The Cask of Amontillado," or "The Facts in the Case of Monsieur Valdemar," the Evil One played no role. He is a presence only in Poe's comic tales, such as "The Devil in the Belfry," in which the Devil causes the bells of a church to ring thirteen, and "Never Bet the Devil Your Head," in which a reprobate named Toby incautiously enters into a wager with Satan, and "a little lame gentlemen of venerable aspect" supernaturally causes an accident in which Toby loses his head; eventually Toby notices the loss and dies. This sort of whimsy, loosely derived from folklore, is typical of American Devil stories. The favorite theme of both American and English writers has been the bargain with the Devil, which affords opportunity for everything from broad humor through satire and permits virtuosity in devising ways for the protagonist to outwit the Devil or to be outwitted by him. In Washington Irving's "The Devil and Tom Walker" (1824), Tom cuts a deal with the "black man" for money, but in the end the "black man" carries him off while "all his bonds and mortgages are reduced to ashes."

Far from whimsical, *The Mysterious Stranger*, by Mark Twain (1835–1910), is a bleak American expression of nihilism. The book, which Twain began in 1897, appeared in three different versions. Twain's original idea was to write the story of an unfallen angel who bore the

Cover of a book by Jehan Sylvius, published in 1929 in Paris. The naked woman on the altar, the horned Devil, and the Satanic pentagram illustrate the title *Black Masses* and the late-nineteenth-century love of such thrills as seen in the work of J.-K. Huysmans.

Devil's name, a numinous, powerful Young Satan who would sardonically reject conventional religion and ethics and at the same time represent a positive rebellion of clarity, reason, and humanity against the evils of convention. Young Satan would first appear to readers as evil but eventually would be revealed through Twain's irony as good. The categories were confused and shifting, and Twain struggled with the idea through a number of versions.

In the early version, a stranger suddenly appears in a medieval Austrian village. He offers his name as Philip Traum ("Dream"), but the reader soon learns that he is really Young Satan, the nephew of the Dark Lord. Young Satan's magical tricks make fools of the villagers; he ridicules customs, unmasks frauds and hypocrites, and teaches the young boys a catechism that mocks Christianity. He seems a charming though irresponsible trickster, but on occasion an appalling cruelty flashes to the surface, as when to amuse the boys he creates a village of tiny living people and then crushes them under his thumb. Twain intended this episode as a reproach to God: Satan's cruelty to the tiny village represents God's cruelty to the world of real people.

In the last version, the stranger is no longer Young Satan but a mysterious "Number 44," whose moral ambivalence was easier for Twain to bring off. Number 44 leaves his young Austrian friend at the end of the story with a devastating statement of emptiness, words of pure pessimistic negation that seem the core of the Devil's message to the dawning twentieth century.

Nothing exists; all is a dream. God—man—the world—the sun, the moon, the wilderness of stars; a dream, all a dream; they have no existence. *Nothing exists save empty space—and you!* . . . And you are not you—you have no body, no blood, no bones, you are but a *thought*. I myself have no existence, I am but a dream—your dream. . . . Strange! that you should not have suspected, years ago, centuries, ages, aeons ago! for you have existed, companionless through all the eternities. Strange, indeed, that you should not have suspected that your universe and its contents were only dreams, visions, fictions! Strange, because they are so frankly and hysterically insane—like all dreams: a God who could make good children as easily as bad, yet preferred to make bad ones; who could have made every one of them happy, yet never made a single happy one; who made them prize their bitter life, yet stingily cut it short; . . . who mouths justice, and invented hell—mouths mercy, and invented hell—mouths Golden Rules, and forgiveness multiplied seventy times seven, and invented hell; who mouths morals to other people and has none himself; who frowns upon crimes, yet commits them all; . . . and finally, with altogether divine obtuseness, invites this poor abused slave to worship him! . . . It is true, that which I have revealed to you: there is no God, no universe, no human race, no earthly life, no heaven, no hell. It is all a dream, a grotesque and foolish dream.

These words, which the traditional Satan might eagerly have uttered himself, are Twain's last literary statement. They have crossed the bridge between Romantic Satanism and nihilism and started along the road to the despairing meaninglessness of the twentieth century. The narrator's response, and the last words of the book are: "He vanished, and left me appalled, for I knew, and realized, that all that he had said was true."

The inconsistencies and vagaries of literary uses of the symbol of the Devil in the nineteenth century tended to dissipate and blur the symbolic meaning. Combined with the decline of the authority of traditional Christianity and the gradual rise of positivism, this confusion helped undermine belief in the Devil throughout society. Traditional and conservative Christians continued to believe, but secularism and materialism were gradually replacing Christianity as the dominant world view of Western society.

15   *The Integration of Evil*

DURING the late nineteenth and early twentieth centuries materialist assumptions almost overwhelmed religious traditions, including serious belief in radical evil. In their various ways the ideas of Charles Darwin (1809–1882), Karl Marx (1818–1883), Friedrich Nietzsche (1844–1900), and Sigmund Freud (1856–1939) all contributed to the growing intellectual consensus that both God and Devil were illusions. Yet countercurrents were beginning to form, and the depth psychology Freud founded began to point (often against the intentions of the Freudians themselves) toward a greater understanding of evil—even as Christianity, weakened by secularist attacks, seemed increasingly unwilling to face the problem.

Catholic thought remained determinedly traditional. The Roman ritual continued to include the rite of exorcism and specified standard tests of the validity of alleged cases of possession. Priests were enjoined to take great care to avoid being duped, but if the allegedly possessed person could understand a real language completely unknown to him or demonstrated knowledge of distant or future events or manifested physical strength far beyond his or her natural capacities, then the priest might consider the possibility of demonic activity. Leo XIII in 1879 affirmed the timeless validity of Thomistic theology, which firmly included the existence of the Devil in its world view. The Catholic Church thus remained in accord with the Eastern Orthodox and conservative Protestants in defending the reality of the Devil's personal existence.

Mainstream, liberal Protestant theology on the other hand tended to deny or at least ignore the Devil. Many argued that the concept, if it were to be kept at all, should be retained merely as a metaphor for human evil, and the view that Satan exists only as realized in human sin gradually

242 The Prince of Darkness

became a liberal dogma. The doctrine of Satan was dismissed as traditional rather than biblical, and Jesus was assumed to have been speaking merely metaphorically when referring to the Devil or demons. Such views arose less from dispassionate historical and biblical scholarship than from simple embarrassment surrounding belief in spiritual entities in the midst of an increasingly materialist society.

The philosopher and psychologist William James (1842–1910) was less embarrassed by religious beliefs. James, who understood that "the world is all the richer for having a devil in it, so long as we keep our foot upon his neck," described some examples of direct intuitive experience of the Evil One and courageously faced the radical nature of evil: "It may be that there are forms of evil so extreme as to enter into no good system whatsoever . . . the evil facts are as genuine parts of nature as the good ones."

James was an unusual psychologist in his sympathy with religion. Freud and his followers were intensely hostile, and the general effect of depth psychology was further to undermine traditional beliefs. The first three pillars of Christian belief—Scripture, tradition, and reason—had been shaken by philosophy, history, and biblical criticism. Now the fourth—personal experience—was questioned by psychoanalysis, which compared religious experience with neurotic experience, rejected religion as illusion, and found the roots of moral behavior in the unconscious rather than in conscious choice of the will. Most modern psychologists avoid the term "evil," preferring "aggression." For most, God and Devil are only projections of the psyche, expressions of elements of the unconscious.

Sigmund Freud took religion as a mere psychological phenomenon whose origins and nature can be not only explained but explained away. Yet although Freud did not believe in metaphysical evil, he became interested in the Devil and demons as a result of his work on alleged cases of possession with Jean-Martin Charcot at the Salpêtrière hospital in the 1880s. Charcot argued that possession was a real disease having psychological rather than spiritual causes, and Freud continued to be fascinated with the Devil as a symbol of the dark, repressed depths of the unconscious. When a librarian called his attention to a manuscript containing the story of a seventeenth-century Austrian who had made a pact with the Devil, Freud was fascinated and wrote a book on the case.

In this and other works, Freud developed a diabology whose central point was that "the Devil is clearly nothing other than the personification of repressed, unconscious drives." Because the Evil One traditionally took on many shapes and forms, Freud was able to identify him with an equally diverse number of mental disorders. Most generally, the Devil repesented the counter-will created by unconscious repression. For example, a woman wishes to nurse her baby but develops an illness preventing her from doing so; the woman has unconsciously repressed her disgust with the process; the repression creates a counter-will that expresses itself in her incapacity. Thus the unconscious works against the conscious will, just as the traditional Devil was always supposed to do. Noting the frequent association of the Devil with anal imagery (in Luther for example), Freud considered him especially the symbol of repressed anal eroticism.

Most important, the Devil was a substitute for the seductive father, a view that Freud emphasized in the earlier part of his career. A father's sexual abuse of a child or the child's own fantasies of paternal seduction create a powerful force in the child's unconscious that is personified as the Devil. As Freud moved away from his emphasis on the seductive father, he came to regard the Devil as a more general symbol of a parent hated for any reason, or of the child's own repressed desire for the hated parent's death. Still later he came to see the Devil as a symbol of repressed fear of death or of death itself. The Devil always represented whatever element of the unconscious Freud saw as most in opposition to the conscious will.

Ernest Jones, one of Freud's leading disciples, developed a full psychoanalytic theory of the Devil, beginning with the idea that religious beliefs are fantasies arising from the repression of impulses condemned by society. The force of the repressed libido expresses itself in images of incubi, witches, demons, and the Devil. In a sense Christians are right in seeing the Devil as their chief opponent, said Jones, for he represents the libidinous energies that the Christian religion has always tried to eradicate. Using now discredited anthropological theories, Jones described diabolism as a primitive religion that Christianity had over the centuries failed to suppress. The Devil, witches, fearsome goddesses, and other evil figures represent fierce and irrational forces of authority and repression. Jones took the Devil seriously as a powerful symbol of threatening, unbiddable unconscious forces whose destructiveness is infinite unless they are brought up into the light of unconsciousnes where they can be controlled.

It is an important tenet of depth psychology that when we are unaware of the hostility that we have unconsciously repressed, we ascribe it to others in a process known as negative projection. If I cannot be cruel, the

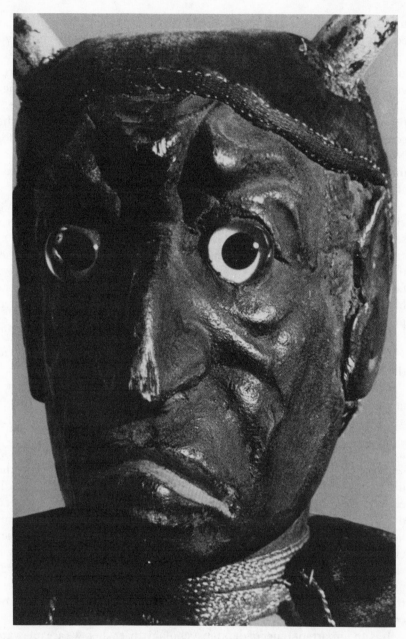

Marionette from the theater of the Jardin des Tuileries c. 1880–1908. This poor Devil's face reflects irony and malice turned to defeat. Courtesy Musée National des Arts et Traditions Populaires, Paris.

source of the cruel feelings that I sense within me must be X, whom I dislike. Having defined X as cruel, I can justify my hostility to X. The more powerful my own expressed cruelty, the more cruel I imagine X to be. If the feelings are powerful enough, I may self righteously attack X, even claim that he must be destroyed, on the grounds of the cruelty that I have myself projected upon him. Negative projection is the most important cause of the dehumanization of individuals and groups. For depth psychology, it was the most important source of the Devil: the Devil is the projection onto a metaphysical being of the whole hostility of Christian society.

Freud's discipline Melanie Klein perceived the relationship between negative projection and a process she called "splitting." Splitting arises from the desire to preserve the absolute goodness of a beloved object by denying that there is any imperfection in it. Any evil or imperfection must be transferred from the beloved object to something else. This behavior is normal among young children, who split people and objects into good and bad. As the normal person develops, he or she gradually accepts ambivalence and progressively restricts the spheres of absolute goodness and absolute evil. Klein viewed the tendency to divide the cosmos between God and Devil as a fixation of the immature tendency to split rather than to recognize ambivalence.

Carl G. Jung (1875–1961), disagreeing with the Freudians, saw religion as a necessary and psychologically valid part of the psyche and civilization. For Jung, God and the Devil are not inventions of the repressed unconscious but omnipresent psychological realities. The center of Jung's system is the process of integrating the power of the unconscious with that of the conscious. Psychological wholeness and health depend upon recognizing unconscious elements, facing them squarely, and integrating them into the consciousness in the light of reason. Jung distinguished between suppression and repression. Suppression is a healthy process in which we consciously recognize negative feelings and choose not to act on them. Repression is an unhealthy process in which we unconsciously deny feelings and refuse to deal with them. Repressions create forces in the unconscious that may burst out in destructive behavior.

Jung insisted that unconscious elements are not exclusively the product of repression; some are part of a collective unconscious transcending the individual and embracing all of humanity. The physical structure of the brain is the product of genetic evolution and is similar in all humans. The similarity of brain structure among people produces mental similarities including similar unconscious structures. Jung called these universal unconscious structures archetypes. The archetypes in turn produce structurally similar myths or images. We must come to terms both with the personal and with the collective aspects of our individual unconscious. For Jung, the Devil is much more than Freud's expression of individual repressions; he is a reflection of the autonomous, timeless, and universal collective unconscious. Still, Jung took demonic possession as a psychological rather than a spiritual fact. It is a neurotic or psychotic state occuring when unconscious shadow elements control the personality. Jung associated the Devil with particular archetypes, especially what he called "the Shadow."

The tendency of modern society to dismiss the Devil, Jung argued, shows its unwillingness to face the reality of evil. For the church to shirk reality in this way is particularly absurd; it becomes merely a society for "positive thinking" unable to deal with the intensity of human cruelty or the terrifying hand of God in natural disasters. Jung also argued that the traditional theory of evil as privation diverted us from identifying and dealing with the real darkness of the human personality.

For Jung, evil is as real as good; it is a necessary part of the cosmos and indeed of God. Jung's model for the cosmos and for the psyche was Nicholas of Cusa's "coincidence of opposites." God is completely beyond any of our categories; when we say that God is good, or God is powerful, we are only projecting human categories upon him. Only the totality of God is absolute. He is a coincidence of all opposites: great and small, just and merciful, old and young, transcendent and immanent. Unlike Nicholas, Jung went on to take the final step: God is both good and evil. Jung approved the Christian doctrine of the Trinity, which symbolizes the dynamic fullness of God. But the Christian Trinity seemed to him not to go far enough, for it included neither the principle of evil nor the feminine principle. Jung suggested that a Quaternity was a better idea, but this solution was always fuzzy, for sometimes he constructed his Quaternity by adding the feminine principle and sometimes by incorporating the Devil.

The good Lord and the Devil, Jung argued, are two sides to the fullness of a single reality: "The shadow belongs to the light as the evil belongs to the good, and *vice versa*." Light needs darkness to define it; otherwise it could not appear as good. Evil is ontologically real; the Devil is morally and psychologically real. Lucifer's challenge to God produces a higher, deeper wisdom in creation and so is part of God's ultimate plan.

The demonic energy is part of the natural order of the cosmos, but when it is repressed it manifests itself in overt evil. If the enormously powerful cosmic energy represented by the Devil is denied and repressed, it will burst forth with a destructiveness proportional to the degree of its repression. But if it is integrated, its energy can be turned toward the greater good. Repression leads to mental illness in individuals and to fanatical irrationality in society; integration leads to health, wholeness, and creativity. The demonic energy is never neutral; if it is not channeled toward the constructive, it will sweep with equal power into the destructive.

The modern refusal to accept the reality of the Devil, Jung argued, is a cause as well as a symptom of our impending ruin. Still, by "Devil" Jung meant a mythical, psychological symbol, not a metaphysical entity in the Christian sense. He sometimes thought of the Devil as "the Shadow," but the Jungian Shadow is not really congruent with the traditional Devil. The Shadow is a morally uncontrolled force of the unconscious, consisting of elements that have been repressed. Brooding in the darkness, these repressed elements take on force and cohesion. Since each individual represses different things, the Shadow varies with the individual. Therefore the individual Shadow does not necessarily correspond with social or metaphysical views of evil. For example, the Shadow of a criminal personality may contain elements that society considers good. Later Jungian analysts, notably John Sanford, suggest that a distorted ego may be the primary source of evil, rather than the Shadow. The distorted ego may crush healthy elements into the unconscious; if these elements are brought to the surface they can be integrated in a creative manner, but if left repressed they may fester and sap away strength. Because the Shadow consists of unintegrated elements, it is always dangerous. But, Sanford suggests, it may be the result, more than the cause, of evil.

Jung suggested that a collective Shadow, the Shadow of a group, society, or nation, might exist, manifesting itself in mass phenomena such as racism, violent revolution, or veneration of cruel leaders such as Hitler or Stalin. Beyond both individual and collective Shadows, he also thought that an archetypal Shadow might conceivably exist. Since it would tend to consist of the collective repressions of all humanity, the archetypal Shadow would be close to absolute evil, close to the traditional Devil. The more the Shadow is isolated and repressed, the more violent and destructive it becomes. The most destructive forces of the collective and perhaps archetypal Shadows are released in modern war. The enemy is dehumanized into demons, monsters, or subhumans on whom we project our Shadow and so justify destroying them.

Most other psychologists, whether humanistically or scientifically inclined, dismiss the notion of evil and prefer to use the social concept of violence or the psychological concept of aggression. Yet some thoughtful ones among them have perceived that the human psyche seems to have a positive need for transcendent values, whether their ultimate source lies within us or outside us. In this sense Viktor Frankl, Erich Fromm, Rollo May, and others have taken evil seriously. In the 1980s, Rex Beaber, a professor of medicine at UCLA, was led by his long practice with violent criminals to ask whether there is "an extra force, a dark force, that works through humans and perpetrates terror." The psychiatrist M. Scott Peck has argued that psychiatry must recognize that evil is an identifiable psychological state that can be dealt with only by recognizing it and naming it for what it is. Similar views were put forward by Samuel Yochelson and Stanton Samenow after their long experience in psychiatric practice with criminals in the New York State prisons.

The most intense psychological penetration of evil was achieved not by psychologists, however, but by Feodor Mikhailovich Dostoevsky (1821–1881). As a youth, Dostoevsky was attracted to nihilism, anarchism, atheism, and revolution. After imprisonment, exile, and a last-minute reprieve from execution, he abandoned radicalism in favor of Christianity. Rejecting Western politics and religion, he turned eventually to the Russian Orthodox spiritual tradition. His ideal was *sobornost*, the ancient Russian principle of a communion of believers centered on the love of Christ and mutual responsibility and charity. He worked fiercely to purge his character and his ideas of the slightest touch of facile optimism. The community of love can be realized, he believed, only by facing the human condition squarely with an intense sense of compassion, sin, and suffering.

For Dostoevsky the Devil was a transcendent spiritual power, though one best observed in his effect on human behavior. The Devil's home is not hell, but the human soul. He is a shadow whose form and substance is filled out by the cruelty of sinners and the suffering of the weak and the poor. Dostoevsky grasped the reality of the Devil intensely and intuitively. He insisted that in order to master evil we must name it for what it is and counter it with love, for evil is not the last word in the cosmos; the last word is God who is love.

Each normal human being experiences an internal struggle between good and evil, a struggle that Dostoevsky frequently portrayed in doublets—two characters each displaying one side of a whole personality. The evil element in the doublets represents the evil side of the personality, which must be integrated and transformed if it is not to be destroyed. An evil human incarnates the Devil as an intellectual seeking knowledge without love; a liar distorting human relationships; a doubter and a cynic; an individualist reveling in his own isolation, despising people and lacking a sense of community. The hell these wretched people inhabit is alienation from love, from community, and from God.

In *The Possessed* (or *The Devils*), Dostoevsky focused his exploration of the demonic on Nikolai Vsevolodovich Stavrogin, the spiritual rebel. Stavrogin is torn between evil and guilt, but at every crucial moment when a choice is to be made he chooses evil. He is capable of great charm; he talks well, is convivial, and appears bluff and friendly; yet he excels in deceiving both himself and others. Under his façade, Stavrogin is composed, cold, and careful, lacking tenderness, compassion, empathy, and enthusiasm. When he eventually commits suicide, the act expresses the meaningless selfishness of his entire life.

Stavrogin's spiritual state appears plainly in the episode of Matryosha, a twelve-year-old girl, the daughter of Stavrogin's landlady. Stavrogin works patiently at seducing the child and finally has his way with her. Worse, he accomplishes the seduction totally without love and joy, feeling only a monstrous combination of lust and despair. Aware of his own corruption, he chooses not to resist it and succumbs to a fatalistic indifference as to whether he is discovered and punished. The child, obsessed by shame and guilt, hangs herself. Stavrogin will eventually do the same, but his immediate response to the girl's suicide is to enter into a grotesque marriage with an idiot. His motives here are even more lifelessly diabolical than in the seduction of the child. He marries the idiot to mock her, to punish himself for Matryosha, to make light of marriage, to flout every value, even the value of personal success and status, and to pursue a directionless curiosity to see "what would come of it." Underlying all his behavior is the conviction that life is an empty, meaningless absurdity.

Later Stavrogin decides to confess to the holy priest Tihon. He presents himself to the priest with that combination of diffidence and frankness that constitutes charm and that in evil people such as Stavrogin can be a façade for a dark, complex, and chaotic personality. Tihon asks Stavrogin whether he has really seen the Devil, and Stavrogin replies in an ironic tone: "Of course I see him. I see him just as plainly as I see you. . . . And sometimes I do not know who is real, he or I." But the presence of a saint such as Tihon always compels the Devil to utter the truth, and though Stavrogin protects himself with ironic mockery, he finds himself revealing his true self to the priest. Tihon, sensing the chaos in Stavrogin, retains his distance. Stavrogin jeers at him that of all people a priest should least doubt the Devil's presence in Stavrogin's soul, but Tihon cautions, "It's more likely a disease." Certainly the Devil exists, the priest admits, and certainly he can possess people, but it is prudent to be cautious about affirming his presence. Again the Devil is forced to bear witness to the truth: Stavrogin bursts out in reply, "I do believe in the Devil, I believe canonically, in a personal Devil, not in an allegory, and I don't need confirmation from anybody." Stavrogin intends to mock what he takes as Tihon's simplicity, but of course the truth is that he needs no confirmation because he experiences the Devil in his soul directly.

Stavrogin continues to suppose that he is playing with Tihon. "Is it possible to believe in the Devil without believing in God?" he inquires with a smile, and Tihon replies, "That is quite possible. It's done right and left." The confession proceeds on the knife edge between salvation and damnation. Stavrogin is free, even this late, to open his heart, and at one point that possibility becomes poignantly acute. "I love you," he suddenly bursts out to Tihon, and to the Christ who speaks in Tihon. The saving grace rises in his heart, but his life has been so long lost in lies that he loses the moment; he is so used to self-deception that he does not realize when at last he sees the truth. But God is patient, and even this last opportunity is not yet passed. Stavrogin boasts that he feels no repentance for his crime, yet a moment later, caught unaware by pity, he declares that he would gladly die to make it not have happened. He has had a full confession of his guilt printed up and plans to distribute it. This is no shameless boast of sin; neither lust nor pride dominates his mind, but despair. The planned publication is a deliberate act of self-degradation, a recognition of total and irredeemable corruption. Stavrogin knows that even though God has compelled him to tell Tihon the truth despite himself, his confession has not been made with honesty or love. "I know for a certainty that I am doomed," he says, and his absentminded breaking of a small crucifix between his fingers as he speaks is a sign of his rejection of salvation.

Even after the confession Stavrogin may have had a chance. The meaning of his suicide note is eternally ambiguous. "No one is to blame. I did it myself." Are the words a final act of mocking pride, a boast that is autonomous to the end, independent, isolated, refusing to be obligated to the community even for his own death? Or are they a burst of true self-recognition? If so, they are immediately negated by the suicide itself, which for Orthodoxy is an unforgivable sin. Stavrogin perfectly represents the person who has given himself fully and truly to the Devil, who quickly snuffs out every flash of redeeming grace that springs up in his soul, who condemns himself to the lightlessness of joyless sin and despair, who incarnates the essential sadness of sin.

Satan is very close in *The Possessed*; in *The Brothers Karamazov* he appears face to face. The Karamazov family consists of several different personalities together forming a supercharacter, a coincidence of opposites. The father is an irrepressible sensualist whose personality is reflected in the eldest of the three legitimate sons, Dmitri. The second son, Ivan, is an intellectual motivated by a prideful and cynical desire for knowledge; the youngest son, Alyosha, is of all Dostoevsky's characters closest to the author's own ideal, a spiritual, thoughtful, friendly, cheerful young man. Drawn to God through love of community, Alyosha knows that if one loves fully one's love spreads to others. In the end it is Alyosha's life that is the only effective answer to his family's corruption. The illegitimate son, Smerdyakov, is motivated by hatred and envy owing to his inferior origin and position. The most important character outside the family is Father Zossima, Alyosha's confessor. Zossima is Alyosha at a mature age, a man of deep spirituality whose life is lived according to the principle of sobornost, the belief that people can be truly free only when they learn to act freely in loving cooperation. The selfless love that sobornost entails conforms a person to Christ; individualism, with the selfishness and envy it brings with it, conforms a person to Satan.

Smerdyakov falls under the influence of Ivan's atheistic, individualistic ideas, which provide him an intellectual rationalization for his own hatred and envy. Ivan argues that since the definition of God is an unlimited being to whom all is permitted, and since God does not exist, it is the human individual to whom all is permitted. God does not exist, and "there's no devil either," Ivan tells his father, but he forgets that if an individual can take God's place he can also take the Devil's. Ivan is too selfishly clever to follow his own moral relativism to its logical ends, but the stupid Smerdyakov translates his brother's theories into action and murders their father. Circumstantial evidence, however, points to the eldest brother Dmitri, and he is arrested, tried, and convicted.

The heart of the book is the section in which Ivan and Alyosha discuss the existence of God. Ivan's argument in favor of atheism has never been surpassed in intensity. Its heart is the existence of evil. Human beings are infinitely worse than beasts because they are deliberately cruel, and the idea that God would tolerate, much less create, such beings is evidence that he cannot exist. Ivan's examples of evil, all taken from the daily newspapers of 1876, are stark: the nobleman who orders his hounds to tear the peasant boy to pieces in front of his mother; the man who whips his struggling horse "on its gentle eyes;" the parents who lock their small daughter all night in the freezing privy while she knocks on the walls pleading for mercy; the soldier who entertains a baby with a shiny pistol before he blows its brains out. Ivan knows that such horrors occur daily and can be multiplied without end. "I took the case of children," Ivan explains, "to make my case clearer. Of the other tears with which the earth is soaked from its crust to its center, I will say nothing. . . . If the Devil doesn't exist, but man has created him, he has created him in his own image and likeness." To the theory that all these horrors somehow fit into a divine harmony beyond our poor powers to conceive, Ivan replies with contempt. "If all must suffer for the eternal harmony," he inquires, "what have children to do with it, tell me, please." He concludes, "I can't accept that harmony. . . . I renounce the higher harmony altogether. It's not worth the tears of one tortured child. . . . Imagine that you are creating a fabric of human destiny with the object of making them happy in the end, giving them peace and rest at last, but that it was essential and inevitable to torture to death only one tiny creature. . . . Would you consent to be the architect on those conditions?" Ivan permits himself no evasion. He is struggling with the deepness of evil and sees no way through it. He awaits Alyosha's rebuttal, half hoping to be convinced.

Alyosha has little to say. He has argued that "suffering will be healed and made up for . . . that in the world's finale, at the moment of eternal harmony, something so precious will come to pass that it will suffice . . . for the atonement of all the crimes of humanity." But he is not confident. "My brothers are destroying themselves . . . my father too. It's the 'primitive force of the Karamazovs.' . . . Does the spirit of God move above that force? Even that I don't know. . . . Perhaps I don't even believe in God." When Ivan poses the crucial question, "Would you consent to be the architect on those conditions," Alyosha quietly replies, "No, I wouldn't consent." Yet Alyosha's final word is that God's forgiveness for us far surpasses our forgiveness for God. The only possible answer to Ivan is Alyosha's life, Father Zossima's life, Christ's life.

Alyosha stands as silent before Ivan as Christ stood before Pilate. There is no argument that can overcome Ivan's objections; there is only love.

Ivan presses Alyosha further with the shocking parable of the Grand Inquisitor. Ivan sets his tale in sixteenth-century Seville, where Christ comes a second time to earth. Christ raises a little girl from the dead and performs other miracles; the people recognize and love him; but the Grand Inquisitor, the chief ecclesiastical authority of Seville, orders his arrest. When Jesus appears before him, the Inquisitor tells him that he has no right to come back and add to his revelation, since the church now has everything under control. By returning, Christ is only interfering with the authority he has given the church. The Grand Inquisitor regards the Devil as "the wise and mighty spirit in the wilderness" and informs Christ that "we are not working with Thee—but with *him*. It's long . . . since we have been on *his* side."

Dostoevsky made his villain a Catholic prelate because of his dislike of Western ideas and because he shared the ancient Eastern Orthodox distrust of Rome. His deeper intent was to condemn the whole Christian church and indeed all human institutions. The Grand Inquisitor is a symbol of everyman, for we each prefer our own comforts and our own prejudices to the shattering, transforming truth thrust upon us by Christ. In his argument with Alyosha, Ivan has condemned God; in his parable, he condemns humanity as well. The Inquisitor's reaction to Jesus is ours: he condemns him, sentences him to death, and then commutes the sentence to banishment with the terrible words, "Go and come no more. . . . Come not at all, never, never!" To the Inquisitor Jesus has no response, as Alyosha has none to Ivan. None would be effective: those who choose to blind themselves go blind, and those who refuse healing remain blind.

As Alyosha's life answers Ivan's argument, Father Zossima's life answers Ivan's parable, for soon after the Grand Inquisitor passage, Dostoevsky introduces the biography of the priest, who lives for the community. "Brothers," Zossima says,

Have no fear of men's sin. Love a man even for his sin, for that is the semblance of Divine love and is the highest love on earth. Love all God's creation, the whole and every grain of sand in it. Love every leaf, every ray of God's light. Love the animals, love the plants, love everything. If you love everything, you will perceive the divine mystery in things. Once you perceive it, you will begin to comprehend it better every day. And you will come at last to love the whole world in an all-embracing love. . . . My brother asked the birds to forgive him;

that sounds senseless, but it is right; for all is like an ocean, all is flowing and blending; a touch in one place sets up movement at the other end of the earth.

Understand evil, Zossima entreats, but understand too that joy and love triumph over evil. Hell is "the suffering of being unable to love." As for atheism such as Ivan's, it is the product of Faustian Western society, coldly pursuing knowledge without love.

Ivan's denial of the Devil's existence is a denial of the demonic in himself, but both burst back upon him in the form of a vision or nightmare. Ivan first sees the Devil as a handsome, charming gentleman a bit down on his luck, but, true to his nature as a trickster and shapeshifter, Satan keeps changing his appearance before Ivan's eyes. His expression is "accommodating and ready to assume any amiable expression as occasion might arise. . . . " People say I am a fallen angel, he adds disarmingly, but really I am just an old gentleman, "and I live as I can, trying to make myself agreeable." The old shapeshifter soon reveals himself, though. "I am Satan," he explains, "and I consider nothing human alien to me." Satan's version of the original tag from Horace ("I am *human* and consider nothing human alien to me") states his identity as both Devil and man. More particularly, the Devil is Ivan himself. Ivan realizes this, though he also senses that the demonic has less power over him than it claims. "You are the incarnation of myself," he explains to the apparition, "but of only one side of me."

Satan obligingly agrees with Ivan: "I am only your nightmare, nothing more." The Devil's eager admission that he is a figment of Ivan's unconscious warns the reader that Dostoevsky intends us to suspect that he is in fact real. Ivan is equally eager to deny the reality. When he catches Satan telling him an anecdote that Ivan had made up himself, Ivan pounces on this as proof of the vision's unreality, and the Devil replies urbanely, "I told you that anecdote you'd forgotten, on purpose, so as to destroy your faith in me completely." For Dostoevsky as for Baudelaire, Satan's cleverest ploy is to convince us that he does not exist. When Ivan angrily flings his wineglass at the Devil, Satan ironically approves: "He remembers Luther's inkstand," and obligingly vanishes. His disappearance is followed immediately by Alyosha's entering the room bearing another proof of the Devil's real action in the world, the news that Smerdyakov has hanged himself.

The struggle of unbelief against belief in Ivan's dialogue with Alyosha and in Ivan's dialogue with Satan is a struggle in the mind of the supercharacter that all the Karamazovs represent and who, ultimately, is

Dostoevsky himself. Dostoevsky's faith in God and his belief in the Devil were built upon a mature experience of evil and the grace that overcomes evil, of intellectual doubt and the love that overcomes doubt. The last word of the Karamazov brothers is Alyosha's affirmation of the resurrection to a loving community of friends, along with his attention (like Jesus) to the simple pleasures of life:

"Certainly we shall all rise again, certainly we shall see each other and shall tell each other with joy and gladness all that has happened!," Alyosha answered, half laughing, half enthusiastic. "Well, now we will finish talking and go to the funeral dinner. Don't be put out at our eating pancakes—it's a very old custom and there's something to that!" laughed Alyosha. "Well, let us go! And now we go hand in hand."

Dostoevsky's vision was steeped in intense understanding of evil yet nurtured by the conviction that the greatness of evil is outweighed by one greater than evil, that the reality of emptiness is filled by the greater reality of divine love. His pessimism about human nature was combined with his hope in saving grace, his sense of evil integrated with his intuition of good in a profound, and profoundly practical, affirmation of meaning and truth. It was a vision whose unflinching grasp on darkness could survive the horrors of the twentieth century symbolized by Auschwitz and Hiroshima.

16   *Auschwitz and Hiroshima*

Sɪɴᴄᴇ 1914 the suffering of humanity has reached a new level of intensity with the world wars, the Holocaust, the Cambodian genocide, unprecedented famine, and the threat of nuclear extinction. By the 1980s the use of only a small proportion of the nuclear arsenal could kill every living vertebrate on earth. The Devil is defined as the spirit that seeks to the limit of his ability to destroy the cosmos. May the force urging us to deploy weapons of annihilation be the same force that has always striven to negate life itself?

Under the shadow of such collective evils as Auschwitz and Hiroshima, modern societies with their bureaucratization of responsibility have produced what Hannah Arendt named the banality of evil. Forms are filled out so that Jews may be herded more efficiently into ovens; maps with anonymous coordinates are issued so that bomber crews may attack schools and hospitals without troubling their consciences. Abstractions—democracy, socialism, religion, communism—disguise, hide, and nourish the demonic forces of hatred. Only when the abstractions are put aside can we see the face of the Devil gloating over suffering. The modern experience of evil is the reek of burning children. Every honest view of reality must confront the immediate, personal, physical reality of the burning child.

The horrors of the twentieth century produced both a sharpened sense of evil and a cynical dullness, relativism, and cultural despair. The tension between the two dominated postwar existentialism. Albert Camus (1912–1960) courageously faced the enigma of evil in a world without transcendent values in novels such as *The Plague* (1947), which describes the effects of a terrible epidemic on the life of a French Algerian city and the efforts of its inhabitants to make sense of the disaster. The honest, faithful priest Paneloux fails to explain the plague as part of God's mysterious plan for the world; the secularist Dr. Rieux knows that one must simply continue to do one's best in a world where such horrors have no meaning except in the resistance we offer them. Camus' deep and compassionate work accurately represented the state of mind prevailing in post-Christian Western society, but in a world with no absolute values, the courage and honesty of a Rieux is intrinsically no better than selfishness, cowardice, or cruelty.

The optimistic progressivism characterizing theology before 1914 could not survive the shocks of the twentieth century, and many theologians turned back to serious consideration of evil. Leszek Kolakowski insisted that we experience evil directly and intuitively. When we observe an act of cruelty, we do not engage in a complicated process of subjecting data to value analysis or the criteria of an abstract ethical system. We react with certain intuitive knowledge that the act is evil. It is abstractions that distract us from that immediate reality and reduce evil to a statistic.

Surprisingly, other theologians evaded this intuition by continuing to ignore or deny radical evil, as if they were just catching up with the dominant thought of seventy years ago. In liberal Protestantism the tendency to "demythologize" Christianity continued to dominate despite the neo-orthodox revival brought about by Karl Barth and his followers and the insights of Jung and Mircea Eliade on the value of myth. Relatively unified before the 1960s, Catholicism has since tended, like Protestantism, to divide into vaguely defined liberal and conservative groups. Whereas the debate between traditional and skeptical views of the Devil had been fought out in Protestantism in the previous century, the argument in the twentieth century was most intense, and therefore most instructive, in Catholicism.

Skeptical Catholic theologians attacked the existence of the Devil on grounds ranging from doctrine to social practice. Their strongest argument was that the Devil does nothing ultimately to explain the problem of evil. Because shifting the original blame from humans to angels does not explain the introduction of evil into the world, the Devil is an unnecessary hypothesis, and it would be better to deal with the question of good and evil in the context of the human mind, which produced the question to begin with. The cosmic struggle between transcendent good and evil is a projection of the human experience of particular goods and evils, and all the evil in the world can be explained in terms of human sin.

Further, in the skeptics' view, it is meaningless to call the Devil a person or personality, since the only kind of "person" that we know is a human being, and the Devil obviously cannot be a person in the human sense. Thus the Devil is no more than a projection of human categories upon a figure that we have invented.

The skeptics bolstered their position with historical and biblical arguments. They submitted that the concept of the Devil has pagan, Mazdaist, and gnostic roots extraneous to biblical revelation and that the postexilic Hebrews invented him in an effort to shift the responsibility for evil from the Lord onto another being. There is no clear picture of the Devil in the Old Testament, they argue, and the New Testament references to the Devil show no coherent pattern. The terms "sin" and "evil" can effectively replace every New Testament reference to the Devil. Against indications in the New Testament that Jesus took the Devil seriously, the skeptics object that the authors of the Gospels merely put such words into his mouth. Or, Jesus and the apostles did refer to the Devil, but only because they needed to communicate with first-century people in terms familiar to them. Or, Jesus and the apostles really did believe in the Devil, but this belief, like the beliefs that demons cause disease or the sun revolves around the earth, was part of an outdated world view relevant only as a historical curiosity.

The skeptics also argued that belief in the Devil is socially destructive, encouraging negative projection and demonization of outsiders, and weakening human responsibility for evil by attempting to shift it onto another being.

Conservatives mounted a vigorous counterattack against the skeptics in the 1970s. A homily of Pope Paul VI on June 29, 1972, was followed by a formal allocution by the pope on November 15, 1972. The pope ordered a formal study of the issue by the Sacred Congregation of the Faith, which published a long article in the *Osservatore Romano* on June 26, 1975, supporting his position. Both Paul VI and John Paul II, supported by a variety of theologians, including Cardinal Joseph Ratzinger, defended diabology on both biblical and traditional grounds.

The arguments against the skeptics range, like those of the skeptics themselves, from biblical criticism to questions of immediate practicality. In the first place, biblical criticism hardly presents a unified voice: critics and exegetes differ, sometimes sharply, on the meaning and importance of passages. Further, biblical criticism often intrudes contemporary assumptions into our understanding of the past. This blurs efforts to get at a *literal* understanding of Scripture, for the best definition of

"Une fête aux enfers" (a party in hell). The poster announces a café-concert c. 1880; the Devil has been reduced to a joke.

"literal" is the original intent of the author. To get at that original intent means scraping away not only encrustations of tradition but also encrustations of current historical assumptions. As James Kallas observed, "Every facet of Jesus' life was dominated by his belief in the reality of demonic forces. Whether or not it makes sense or is embarrassing to contemporary thought is entirely beside the point."

The suggestion that Jesus' belief in the Devil was merely part of a primitive world view poses serious difficulties. The notion that the first century was a benighted age compared with the twentieth is mere chronocentrism—ethnocentrism shifted to time. The fallacy of chronocentrism affects everyone, but it is peculiarly odd for Christians to maintain that the biblical world view is inferior to that of modern historians; that Jesus and the apostles were not as enlightened as we are. Since belief in the Devil permeates the New Testament, it follows that if belief in the Devil is rejected on the grounds that it does not fit modern assumptions, belief in the Incarnation and resurrection is equally vulnerable, and some theologians have not hesitated to follow these implications.

The skeptics argued that no creed or council ever required belief in the Devil and that conciliar statements referring to the Devil's existence need not be taken as binding. It is true that the only ecumenical councils paying the Devil significant attention were the Fourth Lateran and Trent. But both affirmed his existence. The Fourth Lateran mentions his nature and activity prominently in its first and most important theological canon. The section in which the Devil appears is the most important statement issued by the council; further, the sentences constitute a significant part of that statement both quantitatively and logically. The language clearly implies that the existence of the Devil is an already settled question needing no definition. Finally, the council was aiming the statement against the exaggeration of Satan's powers by the heretic Cathars, and this context afforded a supreme opportunity to question Satan's existence had there been any inclination to do so. In the end, the skeptics had to fall back on the argument that the council had a mistaken, primitive world view based upon "bad tradition," a position that undermines apostolic succession and the whole basis of traditional Christianity.

The argument that the Devil cannot be a "person" is also dubious. Certainly the Devil is not a person in the same way that a human being is a person, but in fact we do not limit the term "person" to human beings. We would call an extraterrestrial or an angel or any creature a "person" if it possessed such attributes as consciousness, intelligence, and will, however different from our own. Although the uses of the term "person" for human "person," "Person of the Trinity," extraterrestrial "person," and angelic "person" are clearly distinct in some ways, consciousness, intelligence, and will are common to all.

The argument that demonic possession as described in the New Testament can be explained away in terms of modern psychiatry is irrelevant to the Devil, for it improperly conflates demons and Devil, physical distress and moral evil, into one category. Medicine may understand physical symptoms better than demonology does, but the Devil primarily represents moral evil, and science and medicine by definition cannot treat questions of morality. The concept of radical evil embodied in the Devil cannot be outmoded or superseded by any developments of modern science.

The argument that belief in the Devil is socially undesirable neglects that fact that the dehumanization of enemies has always gone on effectively in ideologies denying the Devil's existence. Nor does belief in the Devil impair moral responsibility any more than the modern belief that behavior is determined by environment. Moreover, Christianity always insisted on individual responsibility for evil and firmly maintained that the Devil could not compel anyone to sin.

In society as a whole, beyond theological circles, belief in the existence of both God and Devil has drastically declined since the eighteenth century, less because of theological arguments than because of the growing predominance of materialism. Although decline of belief in radical evil has not been accompanied by any noticeable decline in the action of radical evil, by the 1980s belief in the Devil remained strong only among conservative Christians and Muslims—and a few occultists.

The revival of the occult after 1965, part of the counterculture movement of those years, included a component of diabology. The popularity of such films as *Rosemary's Baby* (1968) and *The Exorcist* (1973) encouraged interest in the Devil. But although the media exploited the subject, the deepest cause of renewed attention to the Devil was the need for pseudoreligions to fill the void created by the disappearance of traditional religions. The modern materialist denial of the transcendent leads to a repression of transcendence in the modern psyche. Repressed transcendence then reasserts itself in bizarre forms.

The Satanist groups of the 1970s were on the whole frivolous, an odd form of chic. Anton Szandor LaVey founded his Church of Satan in 1966; in 1974 a splinter group formed the Temple of Set. Their *Satanic Bible* is a melange of hedonistic maxims and incoherent occultism. Most

262 *The Prince of Darkness*

occult groups spuriously claim origins in antiquity, and LaVey's claimed to stretch back to the god Seth in ancient Egypt. For "Sethians," the Devil is a hidden force of nature, a good, creative power associated with sex, success, and freedom from restraints. The proposition that the Devil is good rather than evil is literal nonsense, a proposition without meaning, for it contradicts the basic definition of the word.

The overt, organized Satanism of the 1970s faded, but elements of cultural Satanism continued in the 1980s with "heavy metal" rock music, which involved little serious Satanism but occasional invocation of the Devil's name along with some drug abuse and apparent respect for the Satanic values of cruelty, ugliness, insensitivity, depression, violence, coarseness, self-indulgence, and joylessness. Rooted in adolescent resentment of authority, "heavy metal" groups used the trappings of the occult as part of cultural rebellion.

Modern literature, like philosophy and theology, had to come to grips with the horrors of the twentieth century. One reaction was cynical disgust with the world. In 1925 André Gide wrote: "Have you noticed that in this world God always keeps silent? It's only the Devil who speaks. . . . His noise drowns out the voice of God. . . . The Devil and God are one and the same; they work together. . . . God plays with us like a cat tormenting a mouse. . . . And then afterward he wants us to be grateful to him as well. . . . Cruelty! That's the primordial attitude of God." Gide of course denied real existence to both God and Devil; they were merely symbols of a meaningless cosmos.

By the middle of the century cynicism and skepticism had made it difficult to portray the traditional Devil effectively without disguising him either mythologically or in a horror tale. J. R. R. Tolkien (1892–1973) cast the struggle between transcendent good and evil in the fantasy world of Middle Earth, with Sauron, the dark lord of Mordor, representing Satan. Twentieth-century mythology and science fiction tended to transfer demonic or angelic qualities from "supernatural" entities to supposedly "scientific" extraterrestrials. The films *2001* and *2010* (1968 and 1985) present angels in the form of disembodied space aliens, and the 1978 remake of *The Invasion of the Body Snatchers* featured extraterrestrials whose hissing, darting tongues, cruelty, and ability to replicate human appearance reproduced traditional demonic characteristics.

The mythical statement truest to the tradition appeared in the work of C. S. Lewis (1898–1963). Lewis's most original contribution was the idea that demons are motivated by both fear and hunger. Cut off from God, the source of real nourishment, they roam the world seeking human souls to consume. If thwarted, they turn and devour one another. No amount of feeding can mitigate their infinite emptiness, for they refuse the bread of life, which alone can satisfy. Lewis set forth this idea in *The Screwtape Letters* (1942), which he feigned were written by a senior demon Screwtape to offer his nephew Wormwood practical advice on the corruption of humanity.

In *Perelandra* (1943) and its companion "deep space" novels, Lewis imagined that each planet is ruled by an "oyarsa," an angel. Mars is inhabited by older civilizations that have successfully withstood temptation and live in harmony with Maleldil the creator. Because of the original sin of humanity, Earth has fallen under the power of a "bent oyarsa," an evil archon, and Maleldil has quarantined it for the benefit of the other planets. Perelandra—Venus—is a paradise into which temptation has not yet intruded. Its inhabitants are beautiful plants and animals, and one intelligent couple, the Lord and Lady, the Adam and Eve of this fresh new world. The bent archon sends a vicious scientist named Weston from Earth to introduce sin into Perelandra by corrupting the Lord and Lady. Maleldil responds by sending Ransom, an Oxford don, to counter him. Weston and Ransom must persuade the Lord and Lady of their views, for the first Perelandrans, like Adam and Eve, have complete freedom of will. The Devil cannot, and God will not, compel them. Weston represents not only the Devil but also Western materialism with its efforts to bend the world to its own desires. Weston's blind devotion to Faustian knowledge and power opens his soul to the dark angel, and by the time he arrives on Venus he has permitted his own personality to be submerged in Satan's.

Maleldil has given the Lord and Lady the freedom of the planet, restricting them only from passing the night on the one dry, fixed island. Their trust must be in Maleldil, who guides the floating islands for their good, rather than in the illusion that they can hold and hoard God's gifts on the unchanging land. The evil archon's purpose is to use Weston's smooth tongue to persuade the Lady to trust her own will and persuade her husband to do the same. Weston uses every cunning rhetorical trick, including ostensibly reasonable arguments concealing the empty gulf beneath. When not whispering lies to the Lady, he engages Ransom in endless clever debates. Weston's ingenuity in these debates is astounding, and Ransom realizes that reason cannot defeat a being who cares nothing for the truth.

Whenever Weston suspends his busy intent for a moment, he lapses into the idiot emptiness of evil. Among the creatures of the floating islands are small, froglike animals. To his horror, Ransom discovers that Weston has been mindlessly slitting the frogs open with his fingernails and leaving them to die in agony. This cruelty for cruelty's sake compels Ransom to confront evil, not in its fancy dress of philosophical argument but in its naked simplicity as an "intolerable obscenity which afflicted him with shame. It would have been better, or so he thought at that moment, for the whole universe never to have existed than for this one thing to have happened."

Realizing that verbal struggle with the Devil would be endless, the Oxford don comes to see, with shock and repulsion, that God calls him to fight crudely and physically, to pit his body against the body that the Devil is using. Sick with fear and revulsion, he hesitates, but a voice from Maleldil reminds him, "My name also is Ransom." The hideous battle begins, hand to hand and nail to nail. The war between good and evil, Lewis intended—writing during the Allied war effort against Hitler—is more often particular and crude than abstract.

For Georges Bernanos (1888–1948), the leading novelist of the French Catholic revival, evil is essentially incomprehensible because it has no essence; its heart is the coldness of the void; it squats in the deepest part of the mind, seething hatred of God and desire for death. At times in the 1940s Bernanos nearly allowed this darkness to drive him to despair. "To hell with this world," he exclaimed, "crouched over its nuclear arsenal, yellow with hatred, and its heart absolutely empty of love." Satan is the negative personality at the heart of evil just as Christ is the positive personality at the heart of good. Bernanos did not doubt the existence of either. Without belief in Satan, he argued, one cannot fully believe in God. The scale of evil in the world far transcends what humans could cause by themselves or collectively, and all efforts to improve the world without understanding this are doomed to failure.

Bernanos began his first novel, *Under Satan's Sun*, in the dark days of World War I and published it in 1926. The title's metaphor is the dark light and intolerable coldness of Satan's sun, the anti-sun, the empty hole in the sky that is the sign of the Devil's power over us. The main part of the novel concerns the abbé Donissan, vicar of the village of Campagne and later curé of Lumbres. Donissan is fully and intensely devoted to God. As a result, he has no close friends; isolated and vulnerable, he is subject to fits of despair. His soul is open to deep intuitions of good and evil. At one point, lost on a country road at night and unable to find his way to Campagne, he encounters a jovial little man who offers to help him. Friendly, helpful, sympathetic, and full of insight, the man gains

Donissan's confidence, guides him, gives him his cloak, and even rocks him to sleep. The good fellow drops hints as to his real identity: he lives "nowhere," he is "married to misery," and he has a sharp, whinnying laugh. But because Donissan is lonely and needs a friend, the priest permits himself to be duped. "I will be your true friend," the man assures him, "I will love you tenderly."

Gradually Donissan senses who his new friend really is, and at last the little man identifies himself: "I am Lucifer, the lightbearer, but the essence of my light is an intolerable coldness." "Stop mumbling your prayers," he sneers, "your exorcisms aren't worth a pin." He picks up a stone from the road, holds it up, and jeeringly offers the words of Eucharistic consecration. When Donissan looks into his companion's eyes, he is almost overcome with fear. But, to Satan's surprise and Donissan's own, the core of resistance in the priest's soul is unyielding. He finds the courage to tell the Evil One that he knows that Satan is forever crushed under the weight of his own misery to the point of nothingness. Momentarily overcome by the truth, the Devil hurls himself down into the mud, racked by terrible spasms. When he recovers, he offers a last, hideous temptation: he becomes the priest's double, a double whose eyes are a mirror in which Donissan reads all his own fears and doubts. He is terrified that there is no difference between him and his double, that resistance is impossible.

The priest nonetheless pulls himself together and bids the Devil go. But just on the verge of winning, he is undermined by curiosity and vanity. Impressed by his own ability to resist and curious how far he can push his adversary, he takes the offensive, demanding that the Devil surrender all his influence over the people of his parish. Satan immediately revives, sensing the return of opportunity, and offers the priest a tempting bait. Today, he tells him, God has granted you a special grace. Donissan, curious, demands to know what it is. "You'll see," Satan replies. Overcome with pride, the priest vows, "I'll get your secret; I'll wrest it from you if I have to follow you where you live to do it. I don't fear you." Donissan immediately realizes that he has forgotten that God's grace, rather than his own merit, has enabled him to resist, and he trembles in shame while the Devil replies with an assured, mocking laugh. Satan leaves him with the confident threat that he will return.

Years later, when Donissan has become curé of Lumbres, the Evil One makes good his threat. The priest is summoned to the bedside of a child dying of meningitis. The call comes when he is in deep depression. When he reaches the child only to find him dead, a cold despair grips him so completely that his heart seems to fail and the world seems to crumble beneath him and spiral down into the void. His sins and weaknesses surge over him. He is filled with fear that the horrors of the world are too great for God to overcome; with anger at God for the child's death; with anger at himself for failing to help; with doubt in God's redeeming love; with idle curiosity to see what God can really do; with pride in his own spiritual gifts. The combination is deadly. Swept away, he asks God to raise the child from the dead. It is less a request than a demand, made not out of love but out of anger, and it fails, "for God yields only to love." So when the child's eyes open for an instant, it is not the child who looks up at him, but one he had met years before on the dark road to Campagne. He recoils in horror, the eyes close, and the child mercifully returns to death. The effects of Donissan's sin persist, for the child's mother, whose hopes that he might live have been raised for a moment, now suffers renewed anguish. Still, the priest's life for all its failings is testimony to the desire for God. The greatest saints are subject to the greatest temptations; if the personality as a whole is oriented toward God, grace will break through, sometimes incomprehensibly and violently.

Doktor Faustus (1947), by the German exile novelist Thomas Mann (1875–1955) is a reworking of the Faust motif in modern, secular terms. Adrian Leverkühn is a composer who sells his capacity for love to Mephistopheles in return for twenty-four years of intense creativity as a musician. Satan appears to Leverkühn in a scene deliberately reminiscent of Satan's visit to Ivan Karamazov. The Devil changes his shape and his conversation to fit Adrian's moods. He appears as a short, frail man with reddish hair, a pale face, a crooked nose, and bloodshot eyes. His clothes are not quite right: he wears a cap and a checkered jacket over a striped shirt, yellow shoes, and suggestively tight trousers.

In the course of their conversation, Satan shifts from confidence man to theologian, physician, procurer, businessman, criminal—whatever fits Adrian's own mind, for he speaks entirely out of Adrian's memories and knows only what Adrian knows. When he offers Adrian the pact, Adrian eagerly accepts, for the Devil and the pact he offers arise from Adrian's own ambition, selfishness, and syphilitic mental disorders. The Devil himself declares, "You see me, so I am here for you. Is it worth asking whether I am real? Isn't what is real what really works; isn't reality experience and feeling?" The dark power intent on destroying Adrian Leverkühn was that which was using Nazism to destroy Mann's native Germany and threatening to bring down civilization as a whole.

After twenty-four years of success, Leverkühn is ravaged by both spiritual and physical afflictions; he has lost the ability to love, and his body is riddled with syphilis. At this last concert, to whom he has invited distinguished friends and colleagues, he falls from the piano bench and is taken away to a mental hospital. Nonetheless, the last note of his doomed oratorio, "The Lament of Dr. Faustus," is a sustained high G on the cello, a tone of mourning that is transformed as it is uttered into a light in the darkness.

To penetrate comfortable illusions was the purpose of Flannery O'Connor (1925–1964), who described her subject as "the action of grace in territory held largely by the Devil." The Evil One has helped us to construct around our souls a thick rind that can be pierced only by the action of grace. O'Connor combined a tragic view of the human condition with an optimism rooted in God's power to redeem. To show that every word and action of daily life reflect the struggle between sin and grace, she set her stories squarely in the everyday comedy of human behavior and in the stark immediacy of the Southern landscape. In O'Connor's characters we recognize the absurdity of our own complacency and self-satisfaction. In the twentieth century, when people are not only unbelievers but praise unbelief as a virtue, the rind of complacency is so thick that grace needs violence to break through.

The heads of O'Connor's twentieth-century characters are so hard that nothing but violence can penetrate them. Some are so complacent that they must receive enormous and repeated shocks before their shell is shattered; others hide insecurity, fear, and anxiety beneath their apparent smugness. In a world as dulled to reality as ours, O'Connor wrote in a letter, "I don't know if anybody can be convinced without seeing themselves in a kind of blasting annihilating light, a blast that will last a lifetime."

O'Connor drew some of her most powerful characters from Southern Protestant fundamentalism, because fundamentalism, like O'Connor's own Catholicism, takes the Bible, God, and the Devil seriously. She intended her fundamentalist characters to seem comic and grotesque in order to increase the shock when the reader realizes that she also intends that every word they utter is true. She was determined that good and evil appear without ambiguity. "Literature, like virtue, does not thrive in an atmosphere where the Devil is not recognized as existing both in himself and as a dramatic necessity for the writer."

The modern materialist "puts little stock either in grace or the Devil" and "fails to recognize the Devil when he sees him," so O'Connor took pains to make it clear that she believed in the Devil as an external, personal entity. "Our salvation is played out with the Devil," she said in a lecture, "a Devil who is not simply generalized evil, but an evil intelligence determined on its own supremacy. . . . I want to be certain that the Devil gets identified as the Devil and not simply taken for this or that psychological tendency."

Despite Satan's ability to produce real suffering, he is also comically absurd, for God turns his every effort into an occasion of good so that he is "always accomplishing ends other than his own. . . . More than in the Devil," O'Connor wrote in a letter, "I am interested in the indication of Grace." Whenever the Evil One assaults a character for his own ends, God uses the breach opened in the character's defenses to pour in his own grace and love. "The Devil teaches most of the lessons that lead to self-knowledge," she said in another letter. Demonic assault is always an occasion for grace.

The Devil's influence on the characters of O'Connor's stories is pronounced. In "The Lame Shall Enter First," the child Norton is in a state of dull depression because of the recent death of his mother. His father, Sheppard, is a dry intellectual who thinks that hard work and determination can set the world right. Angry at Norton for brooding about his mother, Sheppard decides to teach the boy how to care for others by bringing a juvenile delinquent, Rufus Johnson, home to live with them. Rufus' club foot is a sign of his demonic nature, which he takes no trouble to hide. Johnson's clear understanding that he is on the Devil's business contrasts with Sheppard's liberal illusions about human goodness and his own ability to cope with criminals. "Maybe I can explain your Devil to you," he offers Rufus patronizingly. But Rufus knows better. "I already know why I do what I do. . . . Satan has me in his power. . . . Not only me. You too." Sheppard's self-satisfied smugness is more demonically destructive than Johnson's outright criminality.

The bad shepherd neglects his own son to prove his own nobility. Sheppard is oblivious to the fact that Johnson's personality and fundamentalist ideas have begun to dominate Norton. Rufus is demonic, but he is also the vehicle for God's truth against Sheppard's insensitive liberal dogmatism. Sheppard tells the boy that his mother lives on only in their memory, but Johnson informs him that she is alive in the heavens with the stars, and Norton believes the delinquent—who tells more of the truth as O'Connor sees it than Sheppard does. At last, after Rufus has repeatedly betrayed him, Sheppard finally grasps that he has himself betrayed Norton. Love for his son belatedly wells up and strips the scales of self-delusion from his eyes. He understands that he has "stuffed his

Félix Labisse, *Asmodée, Balaam, and Astaroth planning the possession of Sister Jeanne of the Angels,* 1975. Oil on canvas. Courtesy Galerie Isy Brachot, Brussels and Paris.

own emptiness with good works like a glutton. [He has] ignored his own child to feed this vision of himself. He saw the clear-eyed Devil, the sounder of hearts, leering at him from the eyes of Johnson." But it is too late. In the attic room where Sheppard has installed a telescope to teach Rufus astronomy, Norton hangs dead from the beam from which he has launched himself to find his mother among the stars.

The struggle between the Devil and grace dominates O'Connor's last novel, *The Violent Bear It Away*. The evil characters are more than demonic; they are epiphanies of Satan himself. O'Connor was impatient with critics who failed to understand who these voices were. "If the modern reader is so far de-Christianized that he doesn't recognize the Devil when he sees him, I fear for the reception of the book," she exclaimed ruefully. The protagonist is Young Tarwater, an adolescent boy who has been brought up on a remote farm by his greatuncle, a prophetic old evangelical who cuts a grotesque figure to the modern eye but whose every word is O'Connor's truth. Old Tarwater has brought up the boy to believe that he too is called to be a prophet. The heart of the novel is the struggle within the boy's soul between the secular world and the prophetic calling.

Soon after Old Tarwater's death, the boy hears in his mind a Stranger's voice that uses every wile to persuade him to abandon his prophetic vocation. The voice is Tarwater's Shadow, everything within him that resists the painful life of sacrifice to which the old man assures him he has been called. It is also the voice of Satan himself. So Young Tarwater gradually conforms himself to Satan. The Stranger's voice becomes more and more familiar, until "only now and then it sounded like a stranger's voice to him; he began to feel that he was only just now meeting himself." Eventually the Stranger becomes so familiar that he is now "his friend— no longer a stranger."

Just as every word that Old Tarwater speaks, no matter how implausible, is true, so every word the Stranger speaks, no matter how reasonable it sounds, is a lie. The Stranger's voice says that the old man is crazy; it denies grace, resurrection, and hell; it ridicules the Old Testament prophets and Jesus. Tarwater's Satan, like Ivan's and Leverkühn's, denies his own existence: "There ain't no such thing as a Devil. I can tell you that from my own self-experience. I know that for a fact." The irony is multiple. Since the Devil is a liar, everything he intends is a falsehood, and his statement that he does not exist is a lie. But the Devil is always ultimately compelled to tell the truth, and he betrays himself with a slip of the tongue when he says that he knows that the Devil doesn't exist—

not from *experience* but from *self-experience*, experience of himself. And when he says, "There ain't no such thing," he unintentionally reveals the truth that evil is ultimately only nothingness, a negation of reality.

The Devil's efforts to corrupt Tarwater focus on persuading the boy to drown his idiot cousin Bishop in the lake at which they are vacationing. As Tarwater looks out over the lake, Satan insinuates the idea of drowning the child by observing that "water is made for more than one thing." Tarwater assents, accepting the erstwhile "Stranger" as his "Friend." But when Satan becomes a Friend, a new "Stranger" emerges in the boy's soul, a Stranger that turns the act of violence into an occasion of grace. Again the Devil outwits himself, for water is indeed made for more than one thing, and at the moment of drowning Bishop, Tarwater baptizes him.

Still, Tarwater continues to opt for his Friend even as the force of grace rises within him; grace needs further violence to complete its victory. Seeing Tarwater beginning to slip out of his grasp, Satan takes the form of a man who offers Tarwater a ride in a lavender car. When the man gives him drugged liquor, he accepts it with a cry: "It is better than the Bread of Life." The driver takes the drugged youth to a clearing in the woods and rapes him. When Tarwater awakens and sees what has happened, he purges the polluted earth with fire. He is shattered and transformed. "His scorched eyes no longer looked hollow or as if they were meant only to guide him forward. They looked as if, touched with coal like the eyes of the prophet, they would never be used for ordinary sights again." The Devil's aim was to use the violation to snatch Tarwater back from the brink of salvation, but God uses it to seize him from the lips of hell.

Dazed by the rape, Tarwater still mounts a last rearguard action against God. He wanders down the road toward his uncle's farm where he had been raised, and when he arrives the Devil is still clinging around him, "a warm, sweet body of air encircling him, a violet shadow hanging around his shoulders," but now he "shook himself free." At the beginning of the novel, Young Tarwater had tried to burn down the farm with Old Tarwater's body in it in order to destroy the spirit of prophecy, but he failed. Now he tries again, but this time with the purpose of consigning Satan, not the old man, to the flames. This time he succeeds. "His spirits rose as he saw that his adversary would soon be consumed in a roaring blaze." The Evil One, who has moved in Tarwater's mind from Stranger to friend to Adversary, now vanishes forever. His eyes burnt clean, the boy receives his prophetic call: "Go WARN THE CHILDREN OF

GOD OF THE TERRIBLE SPEED OF MERCY." The old prophet had been called to the city many years before; now the young prophet turns his own "singed eyes, black in their deep sockets" in that direction and "moves steadily on, his face set toward the dark city, where the children of God lay sleeping."

Flannery O'Connor urged the Devil's existence in the midst of a society increasingly dominated by materialism and relativism. In this society, resolutely determined to deny the reality of radical evil, evil has seldom been more manifest.

17 *The Meaning of Evil*

GLOBALLY radical evil expresses itself in genocide, terrorism, and preparations for nuclear war. Individually it appears in actions of callousness and cruelty. On August 24, 1987, *Time* magazine described the state of mind of Michael Hagan, a twenty-three-year-old who methodically shot a young girl whom he had never met six times in the back, killing her "just for kicks. . . . He does not care about Kellie Mosier or her family or her dreams of being a model or the fact that she never belonged to any gang. 'I done did something, and I'm known,' he boasts, smiling broadly as he lounges behind the bars of the Los Angeles County jail." This is the state of mind of a person who has given himself wholly to radical evil and who takes pride and delight in having done so. It is the true face of Satan; unlike the Romantic visions of the noble warrior, it is hideous, coarse, and idiotic. It defies redemption.

The story of Michael Hagan is not merely the story of one ruined soul; it is also a symptom of contemporary human society, pouring its wealth into arms while refusing to face its moral and social problems. Radical evil has always existed; it now threatens to overwhelm us entirely.

What may a truly evil person be? There is a difference between the motion of the will in particulars and the general, overall direction of a person's will. Everyone commits some evil in life, but a person whose will is generally turned outward toward the light is not an evil person. On the other side, there are persons whose whole character is pointed down into darkness, who have given up their wills and personalities and lives to evil. Often these people are outwardly charming, even charismatic, and sometimes they seem to be doing good. But the effect of their characters upon those around them is immensely destructive; when a

Hitler or Stalin attains a position of great power, he can shake the foundations of the earth.

The flat, materialistic assumptions of contemporary Western society have effectively censored concern with radical evil by expressions of contempt or condescension for transcendent views. Secular efforts to define and deal with evil in purely "scientific" terms concern themselves with genetics or environment. By definition they exclude the concept of radical evil. Radical evil is a force transcending the human consciousness and is therefore not subject to rational analysis or control—unless it is recognized for what it is. It is a force that operates on a number of levels. It may operate as a free choice of the conscious will, though it more often operates in the unconscious, influencing our behavior in ways we do not realize. It may operate transpersonally, affecting whole groups, even nations; it may even be a cosmic force transcending humanity as a whole.

The existence of radical evil is immediately plain to the direct moral intuition. It is a matter of deep personal and societal concern that we learn to recognize it for what it is. If we do not, we shall have no way of controlling it.

But if the existence of radical evil is clear, that of a personality controlling it is not. Does such a personality exist, under the name of the Devil or any other? The first step in approaching the question is to define the Devil as a person or personality with consciousness, will, and intelligence, whose intent is entirely focused upon causing suffering and misery for their own sake.

Is this the definition of an imaginary being, or does such a being exist beyond the human mind? The question cannot be meaningfully approached by science, since science is by definition restricted to investigating the physical and can say nothing about the spiritual. For many people today, the statement that a question cannot be investigated by science is equivalent to saying that it cannot be investigated at all. They are confident that there is nothing that transcends the material universe and therefore nothing real that science cannot investigate. Such assumptions, still widely regarded as common sense, are now questioned by philosophers, scientists, and historians, who know the precariousness of any world view. Whether the Devil exists or not depends upon one's world view. In the materialist view that has dominated Western society for nearly three centuries he clearly cannot exist. But as this view fades, we are permitted to ask the question again.

What indications are there that the Devil—a transcendent personality devoted entirely to evil—really exists? The question has to be broken into two modes; First, what indications exist without reference to revelation or religion? And second, what indications exist within a religious context?

Natural reason offers certain indications that the Devil may exist. The first is that we do not experience a morally neutral world. Psychology confirms that we begin to experience things as good or evil at a very early age, though with maturity we learn the refinements of ambivalence. The experience of good and evil applies both to what is done to us and to what we do to others, and in normal people it remains inherent. We also experience good and evil beyond the human race. We regard cancer, meningitis, and other natural evils as a blot upon the cosmos. We also extrapolate evil to whatever other intelligent beings may exist in the cosmos, whether angels or extraterrestrials. Whenever we imagine extraterrestrials as real persons having intellect and will, we imagine them as capable of good and evil, of suffering and of inflicting suffering. There is no reason to assume that the active evil in the universe is limited to humanity.

There is also no reason to assume that the cause of human evil lies in human nature alone. We are preparing for a nuclear war that at the least would bring desperate suffering to thousands of millions of people. Many assume that this unlimited destructiveness is an extension of individual human destructiveness. It is true that there is evil in each of us, but adding together even large numbers of individual evils does not enable anyone to explain an Auschwitz, let alone the destruction of the planet. Evil on this scale seems to be qualitatively as well as quantitatively different. It is no longer a personal evil, but a transpersonal evil, arising perhaps from a collective unconscious. Or, possibly, it is truly transcendent, an entity beyond as well as within the human mind. Natural reason's indications of the existence of the Devil are suggestive but inconclusive.

Within the world view of Christianity (or Islam), however, the evidence is strong. Christian epistemology is based upon Scripture and tradition, and both clearly affirm the existence of the Devil. It is true that belief in the Devil is not part of the core of Christianity and that no major Christian tradition insists upon it as a matter of dogma. At the same time, it is intellectually incoherent to affirm Christianity while affirming a view contrary to Scripture and tradition.

Still, there is no way now to return, even if it were desirable, to a world view in which the Devil is simply accepted as a given. We are unable to return to a naive acceptance of earlier (or even current) ideas, because we can never get beyond our self-consciousness and ironic distance from them. We cannot (whether we want to or not) believe in the Devil as people did in the sixteenth century, because we know the arguments for and against the Devil's existence in a way that people in the sixteenth century did not. This does not mean that the Devil does not exist, or that we cannot believe in him—only that we are now aware of the precariousness of any belief or system of belief.

Whether we believe in the Devil or not, we ignore the radical evil that Satan symbolizes at our extreme peril. Radical evil must be dealt with both philosophically and pratically. Philosophically we must break out of the narrow limitations of materialistic reductionism and investigate radical evil as a real phenomenon; socially we must undertake policies aimed at minimizing the force of evil in the world; psychologically we must strive to integrate the evil within ourselves.

If the Devil does exist, what is he? If the concept has any meaning at all, he is the traditional Prince of Darkness, a mighty person with intelligence and will whose energies are bent on the destruction of the cosmos and the misery of its creatures. He is the personification of radical evil, and he can never be irrelevant because humans have always sought to understand and to confront that evil. That search, that need, is a sign that meaning is there, however obscurely it seems to be hidden from the intellect.

Perhaps love can do what the intellect cannot. Perhaps the cloud of unknowing can be pierced with the arrow of love. For if we do evil, we also love, and love is the remedy for evil. We are called to fight evil, but we are also called to know *how* to fight it. Evil is not effectively resisted with hatred and with guns. Evil cannot be defeated with evil, negation with negation, terror with terror, missile with missile. The process of negation must be reversed. Only affirmation can overcome negation; evil can be integrated only by good; hatred can be laid to rest only by love. The only response to evil that has ever worked is the response of Jesus, or of Alyosha Karamazov, and that is to lead a life of love. That means what it has always meant: visiting the sick, giving to the poor, helping those who need help. It also means seeking to understand how the work of love can be advanced in complex, modern societies where rootlessness and meaninglessness are widespread. Above all, it means fostering children, loving them, not harming them, so that future generations may be less twisted, so that Michael Hagans may not endlessly reappear. The prescription is the same as it has always been; it remains only to follow it, at last.

Everyone knows that this is no easy thing. It is easier to go the Devil's way with hatred and violence and indifference. But the Devil's way it not only morally wrong; it is stupid. It will never work; it has never worked. Violence always provokes violence; hatred everywhere provokes hatred. Daily we are reminded that we have not yet learned this. The Devil stands like a blind man in the sun, seeing only darkness where he stands among the brilliant green fields of God's creation. We have thought the Devil's way long enough. It is time for a new way of thinking.

Examples of Biblical Passages
Showing the Ambivalence of God

Gen. 12:17
Exod. 3:19; 4:21–25; 7–11; 12:23; 13:15; 14:4–8, 17; 32:14
Deut. 2:30; 32:41–42
Joshua
Jud. 9:22–23
1 Sam. 2:25; 6:6; 15:1–3; 16:14–23; 18:10–20; 19:9
2 Sam. 12:11; 17:14; 22:9; 24:1; 24:13–16
1 Kings 14:10; 21:21–29; 22:19–23
2 Kings 22:16–20
1 Chron. 18:22; 34:24–28
Job, esp. 41:10
Psalms 17/18:9–13
Isaiah 45:7
Jer. 11:11–23; 18:11; 19:15; 23:12; 25:29; 26:3; 32:42; 35:17; 36:31; 42:10–17;
    44:2–11; 45:5; 49:37; 51:64
Lam. 3:38
Ezech. 6:10; 14:22
Jon. 3:10
Zech. 8:14
Matt. 18:7
Rom. 3:5–8; 6:1–2; 6:15; 9:19–26

APPENDIX 2

The Devil in the New Testament

GENERAL REFERENCES

Matt. 4.1–11; 5.37; 6.13; 9.34; 10.25; 12.24–29; 12.43; 13.39; 25.41
Mark 1.12–13; 3.22–27; 4.15; 8.28–34; 12.22–45
Luke 4.1–13; 8.12; 10.18; 11.15–19; 13.16; 22.3; 22.31–32
John 8.44; 12.31; 13.2; 13.27–30; 14.30; 16.11
Acts 10.38; 13.10
Rom. 16.20
1 Cor. 5.5; 7.5
2 Cor. 2.11; 4.4; 11.14; 12.7
Gal. 5.7?
Eph. 2.2; 4.27; 6.10–16
Col. 1.13
1 Thess. 2.18; 3.5?
1 Tim. 1.20; 3.6–7; 5.15
2 Tim. 2.26
Heb. 2.14
James 4.7
1 Pet. 3.19?; 5.8
1 John 3.8
Jude 1.9
Rev. 9.1–2, 11?; 12.1–3.18; 19.17–20.15

NAMES OF THE DEVIL

Satan: Matt. 4.11; 12.26; Mark 1.13; 3.22–26; 4.15; 8.33; Luke 8.12; 10.18;
13.16; John 13.2; 13.27; Rom. 16.20; 1 Cor. 5.5; 7.5; 2 Cor. 2.11; 11.15;
12.7; 1 Thess. 2.18; 1 Tim. 1.20; 5.5; Rev. 12.8–9; 20.2–7

Devil: Matt. 4.11; Luke 4.1–13; John 8.44; Eph. 4.27; 6.11–12; 2 Tim. 2.26; Heb. 2.14; James 4.7; 1 Pet. 5–8; 1 John 3.8–10; Jude 1.9; Rev. 12.1–13.18; 20.10

Beelzebub: Matt. 10.25; 12.27; Mark 3.22–26; Luke 11.14–15

The Evil One: Matt. 6.13; Eph. 6.16

Prince (archon): Matt. 12.24; John 12.31; 14.30; 16.11; Eph. 2.2

Belial: 2 Cor. 6–15

Abaddon or Apollyon: Rev. 9.11

Also associated with archas, exousias, kosmokratores, and pneumatika: Eph. 6.12; Col. 1.13

Index